D1201232

Unrelenting Innovation

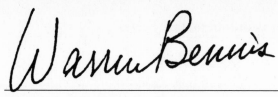

A WARREN BENNIS BOOK

This collection of books is devoted exclusively to new and exemplary contributions to management thought and practice. The books in this series are addressed to thoughtful leaders, executives, and managers of all organizations who are struggling with and committed to responsible change. My hope and goal is to spark new intellectual capital by sharing ideas positioned at an angle to conventional thought—in short, to publish books that disturb the present in the service of a better future.

Books in the Warren Bennis Signature Series

Unrelenting Innovation

How to Build a Culture for Market Dominance

Gerard J. Tellis

JOSSEY-BASS
A Wiley Imprint
www.josseybass.com

Cover image: Copyright © Thinkstock
Cover design: Adrian Morgan

Jossey-Bass books and products are available through most bookstores. To contact Jossey-Bass directly call our Customer Care Department within the U.S. at 800-956-7739, outside the U.S. at 317-572-3986, or fax 317-572-4002.

Wiley publishes in a variety of print and electronic formats and by print-on-demand. Some material included with standard print versions of this book may not be included in e-books or in print-on-demand. If this book refers to media such as a CD or DVD that is not included in the version you purchased, you may download this material at http://booksupport.wiley.com. For more information about Wiley products, visit www.wiley.com.

Library of Congress Cataloging-in-Publication Data

Tellis, Gerard J., 1950-
  Unrelenting innovation : how to create a culture for market dominance /
Gerard J. Tellis.—1st ed.
    p. cm.—(Warren Bennis series)
  Includes bibliographical references and index.
  ISBN 978-1-118-35240-3 (cloth); ISBN 978-1-118-42039-3 (ebk.); ISBN 978-1-118-41690-7 (ebk.); ISBN 9781118434161 (ebk.)
  1. New products. 2. Diffusion of innovations. 3. Creative ability in business. 4. Technological innovations. 5. Strategic planning. 6. Market share. I. Title.
  HF5415.153.T45 2013
  658.4'063—dc23

                                                                    2012033736

Printed in the United States of America
FIRST EDITION

HB Printing 10 9 8 7 6 5 4 3 2 1

CONTENTS

Contents

Contents

FIGURES AND TABLES

Figures

Tables

FOREWORD

Today innovation is critical for the success of firms and the wealth of nations. But what causes or hinders innovation? Researchers throughout the world are trying to ascertain the principal driver of innovation itself. Through decades of rigorous research, Professor Gerard Tellis posits a powerful thesis: that the internal culture of a firm is the primary driver of innovation. His explanation based on culture contrasts with many others that have been proposed, such as size, open innovation, country of origin, or investment in R&D. In contrast to these variables that can be easily measured, culture is a soft, ambiguous factor. Moreover, culture is hard to control. Tellis shows that it is crucial.

I like the central argument of the book: success breeds complacency, lethargy, or arrogance—in short, a culture that embraces the status quo instead of the future abhors risk and protects current successful products. Because this culture arises from the success of current incumbents, Tellis calls it the incumbent's curse. He proposes a compelling antidote for this culture: three traits and three practices that promise unrelenting innovation and market dominance. His thesis is brilliant, simply developed, and powerful.

The three traits he proposes for innovation are a focus on the future, an embrace of risk, and a willingness to cannibalize successful products. These traits are tough to enforce in a firm, especially in a short time. That is why successful turnarounds are so rare, as Tellis persuasively argues. However, senior managers control three practices that can inculcate the traits. These practices are incentives, internal competition, and empowerment. Incentives are unquestionably the linchpin. As Tellis argues, set the incentives for enterprise and you have a vibrant, innovating company. Set the incentives for seniority or loyalty and you get an aging, stultifying culture. Tellis puts the onus entirely on senior managers of the firm to control the practices and set the tone and agenda of the organization. Besides these rich insights, this book offers valuable tools to implement the practices that foster the culture of unrelenting innovation.

Tellis is one of the few who moves seamlessly between the world of academics and the world of practice. He has won many prestigious awards from academic organizations for his groundbreaking research. He has presented with eloquence and conviction to executives from major corporations. This book is deep in theory and rich in insight. The theory is plainly accessible to managers. More important, it integrates findings from clever research on strategy with those from social and organizational psychology. The book combines the rigors of sophisticated models with interesting idiosyncrasies of human nature and practical tactics for change.

Tellis has woven his thesis with many examples. He shows that his thesis accounts for classic fumblings of innovations at Xerox and Kodak, with recent stagnation or decline at firms such as Microsoft, Sony, HP, Yahoo!, Nokia, and Research in Motion. The latter firms have had a reputation for innovation but have stumbled, declined sharply, or gone into bankruptcy—all afflicted by the incumbent's curse. Tellis argues that culture best explains the failures of these giants with the rise of the new stars such as Facebook, Google, and Apple, and the turnarounds of other innovative giants such as IBM and Samsung.

The lessons apply for large firms and young promising entrants alike: the incumbent's curse shadows success. A culture of innovation promises long-term market dominance. And there are lessons for government agencies and nonprofits, such as universities, who are threatened by new entrants and technologies that threaten to render their current businesses obsolete.

With his thesis of culture, Tellis has opened a whole new domain of discussion, research, and applications. *Unrelenting Innovation* is timely education for CEOs riding the wave of success. It is insightful reading for CEOs struggling to understand why their companies are in decline. It is a must read for all managers of innovations.

Vijay Govindarajan
Earl C. Daum 1924 Professor
at Tuck School at Dartmouth
Author, *New York Times* and *Wall Street Journal* best-seller *Reverse Innovation*

Unrelenting
Innovation

CHAPTER 1

Why Incumbents Fail

Success is empowering. But success is also enthralling and embeds the seeds of failure.

INCUMBENT FIRMS that dominate their markets often fail to maintain that domination for long, despite all the advantages they enjoy of market leadership. For example, Sony created the market for mobile music with the introduction of the Walkman. Yet, Apple's iPod now dominates that market. Kodak dominated the market for film photography but declined and ultimately went bankrupt as digital photography took off. Barnes and Noble dominated the book market for decades, but Amazon is now the biggest force in book retailing. Intel dominated the market for PC chips, yet is a minor player in the fast-growing market for cell phone and tablet chips. Research in Motion dominated the market for smartphones with their once popular Blackberry. Yet Apple now dominates that market.

Indeed, market leadership frequently passes from firm to firm in many markets. In the market for Internet search engines, leadership passed from Wandex to AltaVista to Overture to Yahoo! to Google. In the microcomputer market, leadership passed from Altair, to Tandy, to Apple, to IBM, to Compaq, to Dell, to HP. Now tablets are threatening HP's leadership. In retailing, market dominance has passed from Sears to Wal-Mart and is now moving toward Amazon. A review of the evolution of markets shows that many firms often do not stay as market leaders for long (see Table 1.1). Moreover, recent research suggests that the duration of market leadership is dropping by as much as half a year, every year![1]

Sometimes, firms not only fall from leadership but completely fail and exit the market. For example, three one-time leaders of the microcomputer market, MITS (owner of Altair), Tandy, and IBM, have since quit the market.

Why do great incumbents stumble, decline, or fail? Professor Peter Golder of Dartmouth College and I studied the origin, growth, and evolution of sixty-six markets spanning up to 150 years.[2] Our research strongly suggests that the primary reason for firm failure is a failure to innovate unrelentingly. No barrier to competitive entry provides a permanent protection against the force of innovation. Innovation regularly breaks down barriers, be they in economies of scale, patents, business models, or relationships with buyers and sellers. As a result, there are no permanently dominant firms or permanent market leaders. Perennial success belongs to those firms that innovate unrelentingly.

Table 1.1. Examples of Multiple Changes in Market Leadership

Category	Sequential Leaders Separated by Commas
Mobile music	Sony, Apple
Internet search	Gray's Wandex, AltaVista, Overture, Yahoo!, Google
Video games	Magnavox, Atari, Nintendo, Sega, Sony, Microsoft, Nintendo
Microcomputers	Altair, Tandy, Apple, IBM, Compaq, Dell, HP
Browser	Mosaic, Netscape, Internet Explorer
Word processing	IBM, Wang, Easy Writer, WordStar, WordPerfect, Word
Light beer	Trommer's, Gablinger's, Brau, Miller, Bud

Source: Adapted from Tellis and Golder, *Will and Vision: How Latecomers Grow to Dominate Markets*, New York: McGraw Hill, 2001.

Then, why do incumbent firms, especially market leaders, fail to innovate unrelentingly?

Why Incumbents Fail to Innovate Unrelentingly

A firm requires a great deal of resources to stay unrelentingly innovative. Incumbent firms have at their disposal more resources, experience, expertise, talent, and cash for innovation than lesser rivals or new entrants. Thus, incumbents are in the best position to stay innovative and dominate their markets. So, a lack of resources is not the reason that incumbents fail. On the contrary, many incumbents fail to innovate even though they are blessed with abundant resources. Ironically, market incumbents fail to innovate unrelentingly even though many, if not all, rose to that position of market dominance by introducing a radical innovation.[3] Nonetheless, some incumbents do maintain their leadership for decades.

Why do so some incumbents maintain their dominance while others fail? Professor Rajesh Chandy of London Business School and I sought to address this issue with an in-depth study of ninety-three innovations together with interviews of executives and a survey of about two hundred firms.[4] Our research suggests that incumbents fail because they fall victim to the "incumbent's curse": a self-destructive culture that results from their prior success.

Paradox of the Incumbent's Curse

Many incumbents are at the top of their game because they market a superior product that emerged from a radical innovation. Because of their dominant position, they enjoy high prices, large market share, and strong cash flows. This position imbues them with market power and prestige.

Market dominance does not come easily. It is the fruit of innovation, clever strategies, and effective management over many years—if not decades. But market dominance, power, and success contain the seeds of self-destruction. They lead to three traits that hamper continued innovation and hinder continued leadership.

First, incumbents fear cannibalizing their current successful products. Cannibalizing means letting a new product replace a current product in sales to customers. Incumbents are reluctant to change the status quo and endanger their successful products. When innovations threaten their successful products, market incumbents' immediate reaction is to protect those products that have brought them strength and success. Even though they themselves develop some radical innovations, incumbents are reluctant to commercialize them for fear of jeopardizing their cash flows from successful products. This reluctance arises from some economic and psychological principles. Chapter 2 explains the economics and psychology of this trait.

Second, incumbents are risk averse. They tend to overweight their current successful products relative to risky, uncertain innovations for the future. Leaders measure all new innovations by the speed with which they can yield returns that match up with those from their hugely successful products. This weighting is not illogical. Innovations that create new markets involve huge investments, take a long time to bear fruit, and encounter many failures. Thus, innovations are risky. Incumbents are averse due to three biases in their perception of risks and dealing with failures: the reflection effect, the hot-stove effect, and the expectations effect. Chapter 3 explains these causes of risk aversion.

Third, incumbents focus too much on the present. They channel their efforts to carefully market their current successful products to satisfy current customers. Because of their involvement with the current problems and crises, the present looms large while the future

4

seems distant. Thus, incumbents develop a bias that focuses on the present at the cost of the future, even though the future belongs to innovations rather than to present successful products. The legacy of the past and present becomes a hindrance to embrace the innovations of the future. Chapter 4 explains the psychological biases that cause this emphasis of the present over the future.

Fear of cannibalizing successful products, risk aversion, and focus on the present constitute three roadblocks for commercializing innovations. The strength and success of incumbents, especially market leaders, engender these traits that hamper future innovation and success. Though incumbents ascended by embracing radical innovations, their success creates a self-defeating culture of inertia that hampers commercializing future innovations. We call this the incumbent's curse. It explains the epigram at the start of this chapter, "Success . . . embeds the seeds of failure."

Lou Gerstner, the former CEO of IBM who transformed the culture of IBM between 1994 and 2003 and prevented impending demise, comments on this problem: "This codification, this rigor mortis that sets in around values and behaviors, is a problem that is unique to—and often devastating for—successful enterprises . . . What I think hurt the most was their [successful enterprises'] inability to change highly structured, sophisticated cultures."[5]

The following particular examples illustrate this paradox.

Telling Examples

In the late 1970s, Sony created the mobile music market with the launch of the Walkman. Sony's CEO had to push the Walkman to market against intense internal opposition from Sony's engineers and managers (see Chapter 7). Once introduced, the Walkman took off quickly, exceeded the expectations of all its managers, and created a whole new category. Yet when MP3 technology came along, Sony failed to retain dominance of the mobile music market with an easy-to-use MP3 player. Instead, it ceded that market to Apple and its iPod. Ironically, Sony did have an MP3 player before the iPod. However, Sony's MP3 player was not user-friendly partly due to its anti-piracy software. Such software was included in deference to the music business that wanted to protect royalties (see Chapter 2).[6] Here again, fear of cannibalizing royalties, a focus on the present, and risk aversion crippled Sony's MP3 player. Sony's huge music library could have been an asset in marketing its MP3 player, but instead became a handicap.

A similar story occurred at Xerox, though on a much larger scale. In the mid-1970s, Xerox had developed in its PARC labs most of the innovations of the modern personal computer generation. These innovations include the Ethernet, the personal computer, the laser printer, PC networking, e-mail, the mouse, graphical user interface (GUI), word processing, the WYSIWYG editor, and object-oriented programming. Xerox was ahead of all competitors in these technologies and was ready to launch the "paperless office," as envisaged by its late CEO, Joseph Wilson. However, we do not see Xerox's name on any of these products today. The reason is that Xerox's senior managers were too focused on the copying business. They did not see the value in the paperless office and were afraid that these new technologies would cannibalize its copying business.

Though unwilling to put forth newer technologies, Xerox itself sprang up from a radical innovation that incumbents at the time ignored and belittled. In 1935, the lone researcher Chester Carlson developed xerography, or dry copying, in his garage after being dissatisfied with existing alternatives for copying. However, none of the giant firms, including 3M, Kodak, RCA, or IBM, were interested in investing in xerography. In 1944, a small firm called Haloid took up the challenge of developing a copying machine from Carlson's innovation. That quest involved extensive research and development, extreme hardships, great risks, and fifteen years. Haloid's CEO, Wilson, championed the technology and steered Haloid through those tough times. By the end of that road, Haloid had developed the Xerox 914. When commercialized in 1959, the Xerox 914 was a huge success and propelled tiny Haloid to leadership of the copying market, ahead of all the incumbents of its time. Haloid changed its name to Xerox. However, its great success in xerography rendered Xerox short-sighted, risk averse, and fearful of cannibalizing its then successful copying business. Thus, it did not embrace and aggressively commercialize the next frontier of radical innovations in the form of the paperless office, which its own labs developed.

The examples of Sony and Xerox are not isolated but typical examples of roadblocks facing successful companies. Some CEOs of successful companies realize that their own success and indeed their own companies are the greatest threat to future innovations and success. For example, when Google CEO Larry Page was asked what was the greatest threat to Google, he replied in one word, "Google."[7] He had realized the paradox of the incumbent's curse. Ex-CEO Eric Schmidt elaborated, "The problems of Google's scale are always internal. . . . Large companies are their own worst enemies because internally they know what they should do, but they don't do it."[8] Eric Schmidt's explanation is right on target except for one word. It is not the problem of *scale* per se, but the incumbent's curse. Success creates large scale but success also creates the incumbent's curse that hinders future innovation and success.

The Preeminence of Culture

How can a firm overcome the incumbent's curse? Our research over two decades strongly suggests that the *internal culture of a firm is the most important driver of a firm's innovation.*[9] The cause of failure and the impediment to success lies not in hard formulae, models, technologies, buildings, or dollars, but in a soft, mushy, difficult-to-grasp, and tough-to-master thing called culture. The importance of culture is tersely summarized again by Lou Gerstner, "I came to see, in my time at IBM, that culture isn't just one aspect of the game—it *is* the game."[10] The culture at many firms is not fully explicit or written down in rule books. But as Gerstner states, "Still, you can quickly figure out, sometimes within hours of being in a place, what the culture encourages and discourages."[11] In a global survey of the top one thousand firms on the metric of R&D spending, Booz and Company conclude that "Culture Is Key."[12] However, neither of these sources provides a deep understanding of culture.

What does culture mean? How does it relate to innovation? Over a period of four years, Rajesh Chandy, Jaideep Prabhu of Cambridge University, and I studied over 770 firms across seventeen countries.[13] Our research suggests that a firm's culture is its set of traits or values and practices or traditions that constitute the internal human working environment for employees. In particular, the culture for innovation consists of a parsimonious set of three traits and three practices. The traits are a willingness to cannibalize current (successful) products, embracing risk, and focusing on future markets. These three traits overcome the incumbent's curse. The three practices are empowering innovation champions, providing incentives for enterprise, and fostering internal markets. Figure 1.1 summarizes these cultural components and shows how they relate to each other.

Traits are difficult to change. But practices are more amenable to change and can engender the traits. Creating a culture for unrelenting innovation is very tough for large, successful firms because of the incumbent's curse. For example, during his tenure as CEO of Sony, Howard Stringer struggled to change the culture

8

Figure 1.1. Dynamics of Components of Culture of Innovation

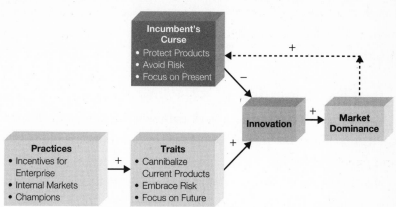

of the company to make it more nimble and innovative. In the end he failed because Sony's culture is highly resistant to change. Commenting on Sony's failure to change and innovate successfully in the 2000s, Howard quipped, "Love affairs with the status quo continue even after the quo has lost its status."[14]

In the world today, firms can get funds from their own reserves, angel investors, venture capitalists, banks, or investors at large. Due to relatively efficient financial markets, funds are not hard to get. Once they have these funds, firms can buy tools, land, building, and plants. They can invest in R&D to develop or buy intellectual property including patents. They can hire talent. In other words, given funds, firms can buy equipment, intellectual property, or talent. But they cannot buy culture. Culture is that uniquely human product that is complex, ambiguous, slow to develop, difficult to change, and hard to analyze. Money can't buy culture. And culture plays a critical role in innovation. Thus, carefully understanding what is the culture that helps or hinders innovation is critical to being innovative and dominating markets in the long term.

Chapters 2 to 4 explain in detail the three cultural traits that foster innovation; Chapters 5 to 7 explain the three practices that engender those traits. Here is a preview of each of these traits and practices.

Traits for Innovation

The examples above illustrate the incumbent's curse—success with current products provides a strong motive to sustain the status quo and resist innovation.

The first trait for innovation is a willingness to cannibalize one's own successful products. Incumbents have a high reluctance to cannibalize successful products; small rivals or new entrants have no such inhibitions. For example, the development of paid searched advertising made Google a huge and highly profitable firm in just ten years. However, few people know that Microsoft had a model for paid search advertising before Google. A few of Microsoft's own employees developed a search service with paid ads, called Keywords. However, Microsoft killed the service when it seemed it would cannibalize the banner ad business of MSN.[15] In this case, fear of cannibalizing existing products led Microsoft to forego one of the most profitable business opportunities in the last decade.

Chapter 2 explains with examples the importance of a willingness to cannibalize successful products. It explains the economic and psychological factors that cause incumbents to be reluctant to do so. It argues that for many organizations, the challenge is not only generating innovations but embracing them when they cannibalize successful products, even though these innovations arise from a firm's own employees. The chapter also explains the challenge of technological evolution and provides a framework to understand and manage it. Cannibalization is relatively easier when innovations occur in the same platform and market. Cannibalization is toughest when innovations occur in new platforms in new markets; it is greatly facilitated by a focus on the future and a willingness to embrace risk.

The second trait for innovation is embracing risk. The path to a successful innovation is strewn with failures, both before and after commercialization. Failure is endemic to innovation, with rates ranging from 50% to 90% at various stages of development and commercialization. Thus, innovation is a highly risky business. The risk looms especially large if a firm is currently dominant and has a steady stream of cash from a dominant market position. The risk appears lower for a new entrant that has no market to lose. As a result, incumbents prefer a modest but certain payoff over a huge uncertain payoff, even though the latter has a higher expected value. This psychological asymmetry in risk perception is called the reflection effect. Chapter 3 explains this effect and other effects that cause firms to be risk averse. It explains the essential tradeoff inherent in risk: balancing Type One errors (failed innovations) with Type Two errors (missed innovations). Four case histories illustrate these principles in action.

The third trait for innovation is a focus on the future. Success in the current generation of products leads to glorification of the past, preoccupation with the present, and neglect of the future. For example, in the case of mobile music, Sony failed to see the future market in MP3 players because of its involvement in the Walkman and its preoccupation with royalties from songs. Four biases underlie this misplaced focus on the present over the future: hot-hand bias, availability bias, paradigmatic bias, and commitment bias. Chapter 4 explains the psychology of these biases, which cause incumbents to value the present over the future. It describes four tools to foster a focus on the future: predicting underlying technological evolution, predicting takeoff of innovations, targeting future mass markets, and identifying emergent consumers. While none of these tools are infallible, their combined use encourages incumbents to take time off from the present and forces them to think about the future in constructive ways.

Thus, willingness to cannibalize current products, embracing risk, and focusing on the future are three traits that constitute a culture for innovation. However, the traits of an innovative culture do not develop spontaneously within a firm, nor can they be mandated by managerial fiat. On the contrary, they are deeply psychological characteristics that emerge slowly from a firm's practices. Understanding their psychology and economics is a first step toward their adoption. Certain practices foster these traits (Figure 1.1). Moreover, practices are more responsive to managerial dictates than are traits. Thus, although a firm may not be able to change its traits immediately in the short term, it can shape, cultivate, and foster them in the long term by adopting certain practices. What are these practices?

Practices for Innovation

Three practices promote the traits that engender innovation: providing incentives for enterprise, fostering internal markets, and empowering innovation champions. Here is a preview of these traits that are detailed in Chapters 5 through 7.

In successful, dominant firms, incentives are often set to current sales or satisfaction of current customers. What's worse, sometimes incentives may be set for seniority or longevity. Such incentives foster loyalty but not innovation. When incentives are linked to innovation, research shows that they do so in a perverse way: weak rewards for successful innovation but strong penalties for failure.[16] The problem of risk-averse employees can be attributed primarily to a perverse incentive structure of the organization. Such an incentive system suppresses innovation.

One critical practice for innovation is providing incentives for enterprise. Such incentives must be asymmetric in their reward structure: strong incentives for successful innovation but weak penalties for failure. An asymmetric incentive structure encourages employees to take on risky projects. Incentives are powerful, vitally important for innovations, and relatively easy to change by top management. Incentives can be monetary, social, and moral and must be carefully designed lest they backfire. Chapter 5 discusses the costs and benefits of setting asymmetric incentives for innovation. It describes five case histories that illustrate these principles in action.

For example, Google allows employees 20% of their time to focus on innovations. Google encourages *all* its employees to experiment. If they succeed they are rewarded. If they fail, they are asked to learn from their errors and move on. Thus, Google has strong incentives for success with little penalty for failure. Note, 20% time is risky (because most innovations fail) and costly (because it takes time away from current priorities). So, the firm absorbs the risk of innovation, but gives the employee rewards for success, motivating the employee to innovate.

The second practice for innovation is establishing internal markets. Most firms encourage cooperation among employees. Employees themselves much prefer a friendly, cooperative environment to a competitive one. In contrast, internal markets encourage teams, divisions, and business units within a firm to compete productively with each other to develop innovations. In so doing, the firm brings within the organization the competition that it faces in the external market. When a new group or division is entrusted with an innovation, the ensuing internal competition directly fosters a willingness to cannibalize current products, an essential trait for innovation.

For example, for over a decade, HP supported inkjet and laser technologies with competing laser printing and deskjet printing divisions within the company. Each division worked hard to promote its own technology. As a result, HP grew as both rival technologies flourished. An internal market is a powerful practice for innovation. However, it has tensions and costs and could easily degenerate in to self-destructive competition. Chapter 6 discusses with examples the characteristics and types of internal markets and means for implementing and managing them.

The third practice for innovation is empowering innovation champions. Many organizations today treat their talent as employees with set tasks, times, and routines. Employees tend to dislike change, prefer stability, and make decisions by consensus. An innovation champion is an individual within the firm who is entrusted with a mandate to explore and develop innovations for current or new markets. The champion is also provided with a team and resources to actualize this mandate. Because of the champion's special mandate, he or she is not encumbered with the firm's current successes, commitments, or products. Innovation champions exemplify the traits of an innovative culture. They are comfortable with change, embrace risk, and want to shape the future. The champion can then imbue the same spirit in the team. Champions are more than mere innovators. They not only invent innovations but also develop innovations, take them to market, and steer them into successful products. The history of innovation suggests that champions are sometimes not fully appreciated in the organization. The very traits that make them productive create conflict with the larger organization. The exodus of champions is one of the greatest losses an incumbent experiences in the field of innovation.

For example, one of the champions of the iPod was Tony Fadell. Fadell's vision to create a digital music player developed while he was a VP of Strategy and Ventures at Philips, where he was in charge of Philips's digital audio strategy. He left without being able to realize his vision. He tried to develop a digital music player as an entrepreneur, but failed on his own. However, Apple recruited him and entrusted him with the development of the iPod. In this case, Philips's inability to retain and empower a champion, and Apple's ability to attract and entrust the same individual as a champion, resulted in dramatically different fortunes for the two companies.

Chapter 7 discusses with four other case histories how firms must move from managing employees or supporting innovators to empowering champions. It discusses the tradeoffs involved with this move. One of the big myths in innovation is that innovators or champions are just lucky individuals. Chapter 7 dispels this myth with examples and scientific studies. The chapter also provides steps in empowering champions within the organization.

Figure 1.1 graphically depicts the dynamics of the components of establishing a culture for unrelenting innovation. It shows that three practices promote three traits that in turn drive innovation. This leads to market success and dominance. However, market dominance has a negative feedback loop, negatively affecting the prevalence of the traits—that is, the incumbent's curse. The practices have the potential to break the incumbent's curse and foster innovation.

This explanation of culture as a cause of failure differs substantially from other explanations offered in the literature on innovation.

Culture as a Primary Explanation

Various scholars have proposed numerous alternate explanations for why great incumbents fail. Some claim that incumbents fail because they fail to invest in research and development. Some claim that incumbents fail because they succumb to pressure from Wall Street (investors) for short-term profits. Others claim that incumbents fail because they do not invest in emergent technologies. Still others claim that incumbents fail because they lack patents. Although there is an element of truth in all these explanations, our research indicates that these explanations do not get to the root cause and do not fully gel with the evidence (see Chapter 8 for details). For example, Nokia had a color touch screen Phone more than seven years before Apple introduced the iPhone.[17] HP had an e-reader before the iPad. Microsoft had a search engine with paid ads before Google's search engine took off. Sony had an MP3 player before the iPod. Kodak had a digital camera before every other firm. Until recently it owned most of the patents in digital photography. Xerox had most of the innovations associated with the personal computer, well before every other firm. In all these cases, the incumbent had more resources, R&D, patents, and even prototypes of innovations than the firm that successfully commercialized the radical innovation. Yet the incumbent failed to do so.

Why then do these great incumbents fail? Simply, it's culture. Great firms fail because of the incumbent's curse—a culture that resists cannibalizing successful products, abhors risk, and focuses on the present. In so doing, the dominant firm overlooks radical innovations that often emerge deep in the bowels of the organization. In contrast, firms that succeed embrace a culture for unrelenting innovation embodied by the three traits and three practices summarized in this chapter.

Most rival explanations attribute failure of incumbents to external factors. My explanation is an internal one. Most rival explanations attribute failure to hard factors: resources, technology, patents, or country. My explanation is a soft one: culture. Most rival explanations attribute failure to a simple causal structure from one exogenous factor to innovation. Mine is a subtle one, involving a critical reverse pathway: success from innovation leads to the incumbent's curse which stifles further innovation. Culture is not only a driver of innovation. Culture is also endogenous to the system. Success corrodes culture through the phenomenon of the incumbent's curse. The enemy is within!

Firms differ in their grasp of the importance of culture. Some firms get it and have for the most part stayed at the cutting edge of innovation: for example, Facebook, Google, Gillette, 3M. Some firms stumbled but drastically changed culture to regain the lead in innovation, for example, IBM, Samsung, P&G, GM. Some firms struggled or struggle to grasp the causes of decline and the role culture plays, for example, Kodak, Sony, HP, Nokia, RIM. The thesis of this book is that culture distinguishes the first and third group of firms. A change in culture explains the change in the second group of firms.

Basis for the Book

This book is based on the collective wisdom of many research studies on innovation that my coauthors and I have conducted over the last two decades. Some of these studies have already been cited in this chapter. The data collection alone for each of these studies took two to four years. In addition, all the studies were published in top academic journals after going through double-blind peer review. The review process generally took another couple of years. There is an advantage in this self-inflicted pain: through such review, the methods are scrutinized, the reasoning carefully analyzed, and the hypotheses matched against data and models. After publication, a number of these studies won best paper awards from their respective journals and other groups.[18] A synopsis of some of the major studies that provide the basis for the conclusions of this book follows. Details are in Chapter 8.

1. One study tracked the evolution of sixty-six markets from inception to recent times. The goal of the study was to ascertain

the success of market pioneers and the persistence of market leaders.[19] For most markets we went back several decades; for twenty-five markets we went back over a hundred years.

2. Another study tracked the origins of ninety-three innovations in sixty-four markets of durable products.[20] Here again, our study covered several decades of archival records over a 150-year period. The purpose of this study was to assess the validity of the incumbent's curse. It also tried to statistically estimate the impact of size, incumbency, and calendar time on the introduction of radical innovations.

3. One study interviewed senior executives and surveyed about two hundred firms to better understand the culture of incumbents.[21] In particular, the study examined what role cannibalizing successful products played in innovation.

4. Another study analyzed the innovativeness of over 770 firms across seventeen countries. The purpose of this study was to identify the components of a culture for innovation.[22] The analysis covered a survey of a senior executive responsible for innovation at each of these firms. It also collected data about each firm on numerous variables. Overall, the data collection involved a mix of survey and hard market data on over two hundred variables. These rich data enabled a comparison of the effectiveness of culture versus other hard variables in driving innovation.

5. Still another study analyzed the patterns and effects of technological evolution.[23] We analyzed all the technologies that were ever commercialized in seven different markets. In all, the data collection covered thirty-six technologies on multiple dimensions of performance for each of the technologies.

6. A study related to that in item 5 built a hazard model to predict the timing of technological disruption based on causative factors.[24] These factors included size and incumbency of the

firm, price, performance, direction of attack, and order of entry of the technology.

7. Another study sought to ascertain how markets respond to the start, progress, and end of innovation projects. It analyzed 5,481 announcements made by sixty-nine firms in five markets between 1977 and 2006.[25]

8. A series of three studies collected information about the path of innovation after their commercializations.[26] The purpose of these studies was to ascertain which factor drove the takeoff of innovations and how one could predict it with a hazard model. Various studies in this sequence modeled takeoff in the United States, Western Europe, and various countries of the world. The total sample included over four hundred innovations in thirty-one countries.

Chapter 8 covers these studies in some detail and compares them with findings from other published work. In addition, I have made hundreds of presentations worldwide and talked about innovation with numerous executives from major multinational corporations and small start-ups. I also draw on research in other fields that has important lessons for the management of innovation.

These studies and extensive discussions provide the basis for the observations and conclusions of this book.

CONCLUSION

Technological evolution is constant and increasing. It shapes consumers' tastes and prompts them to demand ever-higher performance on ever-changing dimensions. Such change requires that firms innovate unrelentingly. Innovation requires great resources.

Dominant incumbents are in the best position to innovate and stay at the top of the game because of their deep pockets, vast experience, and great expertise.

Yet a review of the history of markets shows that many incumbents do not sustain their dominance for long. They fail primarily because they pass over the next wave of innovations that threaten to transform their markets, jeopardize their cash flows, or render their successful products obsolete. Ironically, many of these market leaders rose to their level of dominance by commercializing a radical innovation. The reason they fail is that their very success generates a culture that inhibits innovations. Such an unproductive culture involves three traits: a fear of cannibalizing current successful products, a focus on solving current problems, and an intolerance for risky, uncertain innovations. Because these self-destructive traits result from success, my coauthors and I call this phenomenon the incumbent's curse.

Fortunately, our research shows the incumbent's curse is not insurmountable. It can be broken by three traits that foster innovation: a willingness to cannibalize a firm's successful products, tolerance for risk, and focus on the future. However, such traits are deeply human characteristics that form slowly and do not respond to managerial fiat—that is, managers cannot simply enforce them. Our extensive research shows that firms can adopt three practices that foster these traits: providing incentives for enterprise, fostering internal markets, and empowering innovation champions. Figure 1.1 depicts the hypothesized model for breaking the incumbent's curse. The next six chapters discuss each of these six components of culture in depth. The chapters elaborate on the theory, explain the processes, and provide prototypical examples of each component of culture. The final chapter details evidence in support of this thesis and against other classic explanations of innovativeness. It describes precise metrics by which firms can measure each component of culture. It also describes a database of 770 global firms of varying sizes and in varying markets, against which firms can benchmark their own level of innovativeness.

The incumbent's curse involves a perennial paradox. Market dominance demands unrelenting innovation. Development of radical innovations has the potential for success and market dominance. But market dominance leads to confidence, complacency, and inertia resulting in a failure to innovate. The failure to innovate leads to loss of dominance and ultimately market failure. Thus, success carries the seeds of its own self-destruction. Innovation leads to market dominance, but market dominance corrodes the traits that foster innovation.

As a result, there are no permanently successful firms. Market dominance generates resources, experience, and expertise but no guarantee for continued success and market dominance. Long-term dominance belongs only to those firms that carefully nourish and sustain a culture for unrelenting innovation against the forces that destroy it.

CHAPTER 2

Willingness to Cannibalize Successful Products

Today's emerging giants face a paradox. Their
continued success requires turning away from what
made them successful.
—Tarun Khanna, Jaeyong Song, and Kyungmook Lee[1]

THE HISTORY OF INNOVATION is littered with firms that
pioneered and dominated markets but failed to capitalize on their
leadership. Often, the dominant firm failed to capture an emergent
market that splintered from the old market. Chapter 1 cites the
examples of Sony in digital music, Xerox in the electronic office,
Microsoft in search, Kodak in digital photography, Nokia in
smart phones, and HP in tablet computers. One important reason
for this failure was a reluctance to cannibalize the incumbent's
successful products. Ironically, in the cases mentioned, researchers
in the firms' own labs had developed the new technologies that
threatened their successful products.

Should a firm introduce an innovation that will cannibalize
its current successful products? This is a perennial problem facing dominant incumbents. For example, consider the following
dilemma, which HP faced in the mid-2000s.[2] Should it market a
tablet that makes it easy for consumers to create, distribute, and
read papers, newspapers, and magazines electronically? What if
potential sales and profits from the tablet are initially a fraction of

those from its leading products? What if margins from the tablet are lower than margins from printer cartridges? What if marketing the tablet runs the risk of cannibalizing sales of its printers, cartridges, PCs, and laptops? If one makes a strict cost-benefit analysis, then the answer to these questions, especially the last one, may well be no. Indeed, some economists have built sophisticated models to come to a similar conclusion.[3] This chapter will argue that being willing to cannibalize successful products is difficult but essential to commercializing radical innovations.

Why Incumbents Are Reluctant to Cannibalize Products

Our research suggests several economic and organizational factors that justify not cannibalizing the firms' own products with radical innovations.

Economic Factors

Many economic reasons weigh against cannibalizing successful products:

- **Costs and margins**. After taking into account the costs of capital, retooling, marketing, and smaller potential margins, returns from innovations may seem too low to allow the firm to cannibalize successful products. For example, the returns from Kodak's film business dwarfed expected profits from digital photography in its initial years. It does not seem to make sense to push an innovation that generates lower margins and costs more than current products.
- **Thresholds**. Some firms use thresholds to help with selection of innovations. Such thresholds can become daunting if the firm has high current sales. For example, at one time, P&G

used a threshold of 10% profit margin for introducing a new product. However, many new products do not turn profitable until after sales take off, which might not happen for two to six years. At one time, HP used a threshold for a radical innovation of 3% of corporate sales within three years. With over $100 billion in annual sales, this is a steep threshold for most new products.

- **Wait-and-see**. Firms can adopt a wait-and-see attitude. They may believe that they need not develop an innovation until a rival does so successfully.

- **Acquisition**. Firms may believe that there is always the option of acquisitions—that is, they can acquire successful innovators, especially if they are small.

These economic reasons can provide a strong rationale for not introducing an innovation that cannibalizes its own successful products.

Organizational Factors

Besides these economic reasons, several psychological factors also play a critical role.

- **Resistance from internal stakeholders**. To embrace an emerging innovation that threatens current products requires the support and involvement of all levels of the organization: junior employees, senior managers, and rival divisions. Sometimes senior managers agree to the change but middle or new managers do not. The latter, through delay or conscious effort, may sabotage plans for the emerging innovation. The case history of Kodak's digital photography described later in this chapter illustrates this challenge. At other times, junior managers spot the innovations, develop them, and bring them

25

to senior managers. But senior managers are not convinced. Senior managers may veto plans for change and even drive away the potential champions of the innovation. The latter go on to form new companies or join other competitors who market the radical innovations. The case history of Microsoft Keywords described later in this chapter illustrates this point. At still other times, innovations may be developed by one division, while current products are marketed by a rival decision. If the firm requires consensus building for launch, negatively affected divisions may never acquiesce into supporting a cannibalizing innovation. The case history of Sony's MP3 player described later in this chapter illustrates this point.

The internal stakeholders themselves may be motivated by one or more of the following psychological factors.

- **Bureaucratic committees and procedures**. To efficiently manage products, firms develop committees and procedures. However, success with current products can cause such committees and procedures to grow into bureaucratic obstacles to swift embrace of key innovations. For example, Nokia's delay in developing touch-screen smartphones was partly due to such internal bureaucracy. One analyst describes the environment like this, "A 'brand board' discussed branding. A 'capability board' looked at information technology investments. A 'sustainability and environment board' monitored Nokia's green credentials."[4] As a result, an employee complained that Chinese manufacturers were "cranking out a device much faster than . . . the time that it takes us to polish a PowerPoint presentation."[5]

- **Perceived invulnerability**. Firms with successful current products develop an aura of success, invincibility, and even arrogance. Such firms are suspicious of or belittle innovations, especially if they come from small entrants or appear inferior to current products, as innovations often do. Such firms may think they are almost invulnerable. For example, just prior to 2007, Research in Motion (RIM) was famous for its BlackBerry, which dominated the market for smartphones. The key features of the phone were secure email and hard QWERTY keyboard that appealed to business users who need to keep in constant touch with colleagues and customers. When Apple's iPhone first came out, the company's managers just could not believe it would present any challenge to the BlackBerry. Dartmouth Professor Ron Adner explains the attitude of senior managers thus, "They looked at the iPhone and dismissed it." By the time RIM introduced their touch keyboard, the iPhone was in its fourth generation and had grown to be a huge success. By 2012, RIM lost $60 billion, or 90% of its market value.

- **Biases**. In addition to these factors, biases can exaggerate the importance of the present moment and undermine the importance of the future. Chapter 4 discusses in depth how and why overweighting the present and underweighting the future sabotages the development and commercialization of innovations.

Thus, economic reasons provide a good rationale for not introducing innovations that might cannibalize a firm's own products. However, organizational factors lull firms into a false security or hamper change for innovations. The organization's reasons are particularly pernicious as some are difficult to spot and all are hard to change. The combination of organizational and economic reasons can cause a dominant firm to believe its position is safe, its stream of profits secure, and its promising innovations unnecessary. There is certainly no urgency to do the apparently irrational—to cannibalize its own successful products.

Why Willingness to Cannibalize Is Important

The organizational mind-set described above probably explains why so many firms that dominate markets fail to maintain that dominance when new technologies strike. These failures underscore the need for firms to be willing to cannibalize their successful products. Some strong reasons suggest why this policy should be a priority within the firm.

Finite Growth of Current Products

Success with current products is finite, because the growth that sustains them ultimately comes to an end; that is, growth is euphoric when it happens, but it cannot last forever. All growth markets eventually see maturity and, frequently, decline. Maturity sets in either because a new product has reached all potential consumers or because a better product enters the market.

Professor Deepa Chandrasekaran and I studied the introduction, growth, and decline of sales of over twenty radically new products across thirty countries (over four hundred life cycles in all).[6] One of our findings is in Figure 2.1, which shows the start, rise, and maturity of sales of some radically new products in a number of categories in the United States. The curves all show a slow start, rapid growth, and ultimate maturity. For older innovations, those introduced before 1980, the curves also show a sharp decline after maturity. Similar patterns exist for most countries. Firms need to be prepared with the next round of innovations well before the current products reach maturity.

Increasing Rate of Innovation

The speed of technological change is increasing over calendar time (see Figure 2.2, which depicts the rate of technological evolution).[7]

28

Figure 2.1. Life Cycle of Radically New Products in the United States

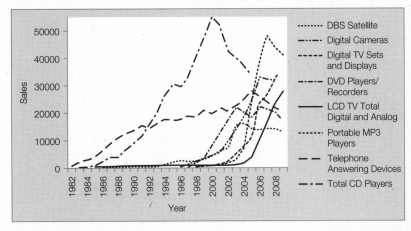

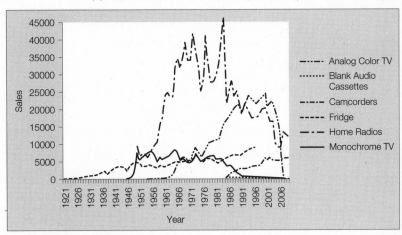

Source: Based on data collected by Prof. Deepa Chandrasakran.

We can see this pattern based on multiple dimensions. Figure 2.2A shows that the average time between introductions of entirely new technologies is steadily decreasing over time. Figure 2.2B shows that the average time between innovations within the same technology is also decreasing over time. Figure 2.2C shows the average annual rate

Figure 2.2. Rate of Technological Evolution

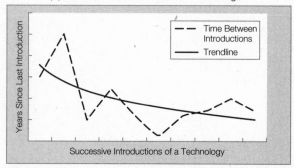

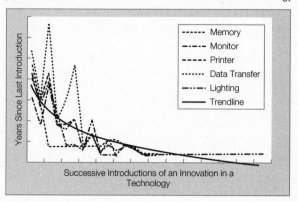

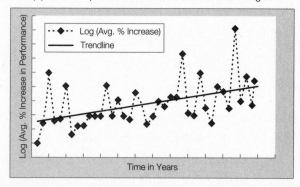

Source: Adapted from Sood, Ashish and Gerard J. Tellis, "Technological Evolution and Radical Innovations," *Journal of Marketing*, 69, no. 3 (July 2005): 152–168.

of improvement in performance of any technology is increasing exponentially over time. Thus technological change is not only occurring, but doing so at an increasingly rapid rate. So, firms have to be constantly vigilant.

For example, Samsung Electronics has grown to be one of the biggest technology firms in sales by regularly embracing new markets and new technologies. Its growth has been at least partly driven by the strong belief of its chairman, Lee Kun-Hee, that the firm has to constantly invent new businesses to survive and flourish. Under his stewardship, "Samsung thrives on a culture of impending doom"—a belief that "Samsung could disappear in an instant if it misjudges the next big trend."[8]

Limitations of Acquisitions

One can easily refute two of the defenses against cannibalization posited earlier: wait-and-see and acquisition. Wait-and-see implies that a firm should wait to see how an innovation fares and only market its own version when a rival's innovation appears to take off. In most cases, this strategy is not as simple as it appears because entering a new market with an innovation requires years of development that cannot be done overnight. Thus, wait-and-see generally means waiting till a rival's innovation has taken off in the market place and won acceptance if not become a standard. But at that point, it is late for a firm to start development of a rival product from scratch. Microsoft has still not found a competitor to Google's search despite striving to do so. Sony has still not found a rival to Apple's iPod though it's over a decade since the iPod's introduction. Google has still not found a rival to Facebook's social network despite many big attempts to do so.

What about acquiring the target with the hot new innovation? Acquisition is another common defense against cannibalizing current products; that is, a firm can acquire a target if and when its innovation is threatening a firm's own successful product. There are several risks with acquisition:

1. The innovation may come from a target that is too big to acquire. Sony was not in a position to acquire Apple for the latter's mobile movies and music.
2. By the time a target is successful enough to acquire, the price may be too high. Microsoft wanted to acquire Facebook when its membership took off. But it could only get 1.6% of the business for a steep $240 million in 2007.
3. The price paid might be too high for the potential benefits, which anyway might not accrue. eBay spent $2.6 billion to acquire Skype in 2005, but found the price too high and the benefits too low. A couple of years later, eBay took a $1.4 billion write-down for the loss of value in the Skype acquisition. Typically, multiple firms jump into the acquisition game at the same type, often bidding up the price of the target beyond its value.
4. Integrating the target's culture with that of the acquirer while retaining its talent is very tough. One or the other fails. There is also the danger that the bureaucracy of the acquirer can kill the innovation of the target.

Though acquisitions are common, and a few pay off handsomely, the risks are huge and the average net present value of acquisitions may well be negative. Our research shows quite clearly that making innovations internally leads to a consistently positive spike in the stock price of the innovating firm.[9] Acquiring firms for their innovations leads to a consistently negative spike in the stock price of the acquiring firm.[10] Thus, the market rewards internal organic innovation and punishes external acquisitions.

Challenge of Technological Change

Technology constantly changes due to basic research in academia, applied research in corporate labs, and numerous innovations by various companies. Success on one technological platform, however strong, does not guarantee permanent success. The history of technology evolution shows that new technologies constantly arise, providing new and better ways to solve old consumer needs. Understanding technological evolution may be critical to planning for the future and being willing to cannibalize existing products. The next section covers this issue in depth.

Understanding Technological Evolution

Threats to current products may come from a change in consumer tastes. However, in many if not most markets, threats to current products come primarily from technological evolution. Even for fashion goods that depend on passing consumer tastes, changes in technology frequently determine what new materials are available and what new fashions are possible. Thus, a deep understanding of the opportunity and threat of cannibalization depends on understanding the dynamics of technological evolution.

For this purpose, Professor Ashish Sood of Emory University and I conducted a study of the evolution of all technologies introduced in seven markets over broad time periods. Our findings show that technological evolution is rich, complex, but tractable. In particular, the analysis provides novel insights, which can be encapsulated into four managerial decisions: on which level to innovate, what are the patterns of evolution, on which dimension to focus, and which technology to choose.[11]

On Which Level to Innovate?

The received wisdom does not distinguish levels of technological change. In contrast, our deep study of technological evolution suggests three levels on which firms can innovate: platform, design, or component (see Table 2.1). A platform is the most basic level and relies on a unique scientific principle distinctly different from other principles. For example, in displays, four different technologies rely on four distinct scientific principles for forming an image on a screen: CRT, LCD, Plasma, and OLED. In this book, I use the terms *platform innovation* or *radical innovation* synonymously. On any platform, a variety of designs, which are layouts or linkages of parts, can achieve the same function. For example, a regular fluorescent bulb and a compact fluorescent bulb use different design, though both are based on the principle of fluorescence. A design innovation is a new layout or linkage of parts that is different from the prior one in use. On any platform or design, firms can use a variety of components, which are materials or parts to achieve some function. For example, a fuel cell could use hydrogen or methanol to generate electricity. A component innovation is a material or part that is different from the prior one in use.

Within any platform, innovation occurs almost constantly in design and components.[12] Routine innovation occurs at these two levels. Platform innovations are not frequent, but when they do

Table 2.1. Defining Levels of Technology Innovation

Level	Definition	Example in Displays
Platform	Unique scientific principle	CRT, LCD, Plasma, OLED
Design	Linkage or layout	5″, 25,″ 45″ size in LCDs
Component	Material or content	Glass, plastic in LCDs

Source: Adapted from Tellis, Gerard J. and Ashish Sood, "A New Framework to Help Firms Select Among Competing Technologies," *Visions*, PDMA, Vol. XXXIV, No. 3, 18–23, Oct 2010.

occur, they have the potential to disrupt markets and firms. The danger to firms is to be so focused on in design and component innovation as to miss platform innovations. For example, Sony's preoccupation with improving its CRT television sets with Trinitron technology led it to miss the oncoming revolution in flat-screen LCD TVs. Samsung innovated greatly in the latter technology so that Sony had to license technology from Samsung.

What Is the Pattern of Evolution?

The received wisdom is that a new technology always enters below an older technology and always follows a single S-shaped curve. In contrast, our analysis of these seven markets shows that technological evolution is rich, complex, but tractable (see Figure 2.3). In particular, we can identify several novel patterns of technological evolution.

1. Multiple technologies enter a market and compete with other technologies simultaneously. When new technologies enter a market, firms that are leaders in the old technology may stand to lose their position of dominance, unless they are willing to cannibalize the old technology.

2. A new technology enters the scene either above or below an earlier technology. For example in Figure 2.3D, laser enters the printer market above dot matrix while inkjet enters below dot matrix.

3. Once a new technology enters a market, its path of performance is neither linear nor S-shaped as many analysts believe. Rather, we find that it is frequently a step function (see Figure 2.3). Importantly, a technology may show a big spurt in performance after a long period of stagnation. Some analysts recommend abandoning a technology when it shows such a period of stagnation. Our analysis shows such abandonment may be

Figure 2.3. Technological Evolution in Six Markets

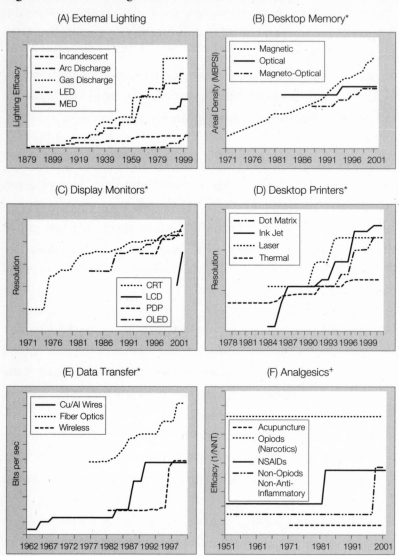

* Performance on Y axis in Log Scale.
+ Accurate performance records of efficacy of acupuncture not available prior to 1971.
Source: Adapted from Tellis, Gerard J. and Ashish Sood, "A New Framework for Choosing the Right Technology," *PDMA Visions* (October 2010):18–23.

premature. For example, in Figure 2.3A, gas discharge shows its biggest jump in performance and surpasses arc-discharge in 1983, after being flat in performance for about twenty-two years.

4. Most importantly, the paths of technological performance cross multiple times. This pattern suggests that superiority in technological performance is never permanent. Vigilance is important.

Take the case of technological competition in the desk top printer market in Figure 2.3D. In 1991 Laser technology surpassed ink jet technology in performance. That was not a sufficient reason to abandon the ink jet technology. Indeed in 1997, inject technology passed laser technology in performance. HP marketed printers with both technologies. It supported both these rival technologies simultaneously. This turned out to be a wise strategy because HP has dominated the printer market with superior products using both these technologies. The lesson for firms is that they need to support or at least monitor a portfolio of technologies so that firms are prepared for the sudden surge in performance of any single one technology.

On Which Dimension of Performance to Focus?

The current thinking in marketing and technology circles is that customer tastes determine which dimension of performance is important. Firms change their products to meet this changing demand. In other words, changes in tastes drive changes in technologies and products. In contrast, we find the reverse to be the case. That is, changes in technologies drive changes in tastes. In particular, in each market, each time a new technology enters the market it brings into play a one or more new dimensions of performance. Consumers then get excited about the new dimension

Table 2.2. Emergence of Dimensions by Market Across Time

Market	Emergence of Successive Dimensions Over Time
External Lighting	brightness → color rendition → life → compactness
Desktop Memory	density → reliability → portability
Display Monitor	resolution → compactness → screen size → convenience
Desktop Printers	resolution → graphics → speed → color rendition
Data Transfer	speed → bandwidth → connectivity
Analgesics	analgesia → reaction speed → targeted-action → reduced side effects

and begin to choose products based on their performance on that dimension. As a result, markets show a sequence of shifting focus on dimensions. Table 2.2 illustrates this point.

Consider the market for display monitors. When CRTs were the only technology, the dimension of interest was resolution. When LCDs entered the market, the dimension of performance shifted to compactness (thinness and lightness). When plasma entered the market, it brought the dimension of screen size into play. Now, as OLED becomes popular, it will bring into play the dimension of convenience. Thus, new technologies make possible new dimensions of performance that excite consumer interest. Technological change seems to drive or shape consumer tastes!

Technological change also makes possible new products for new or transformed markets. For example the development of LCD monitors made possible the market for laptops. The development of plasma transformed the market for large screen public displays. The development of LED made possible the market for compact high-definition TVs for home. Very thin OLED screen will revolutionize the markets for mobile displays and large screen TVs for the home.

So far, this chapter has discussed why cannibalization is difficult, why it is important, and how we can understand technological evolution. We now turn to five case histories. A close look at these cases illustrates how these various factors played out in real market situations and reemphasizes the importance of the principles discussed.

Blinded to an Opportunity: Microsoft Keywords?

From humble beginnings in the 1970s, Microsoft grew to become a giant company because of its innovative products (DOS, Windows, Office) in PC operating systems. However, in the 2000s, Google outshone Microsoft with explosive growth due to its innovation in search. Google grew from its origins in 1998 to a market capitalization of $234 billion at its peak in fall 2007. In this growth, Google surpassed and dwarfed Yahoo!, which had a search engine before Google. Google grew so fast that software giant Microsoft tried to catch up by developing a search engine of its own. When that effort was not successful, Microsoft tried to acquire Yahoo! in 2008, in order to build Yahoo!'s search engine. But Microsoft need not have gone so far. The company had a search service called Keywords, which it stymied and killed for fear it would cannibalize its older advertising business. The chain of events that led to the demise of Microsoft Keywords is instructive.[13]

At the start of the World Wide Web around 1995, a university of Illinois student, Scott Banister, thought of the idea of adding paid ads next to search results. To develop his idea, he quit college and moved to California in 1996. Two years later, he joined a company called LinkExchange, a popular Internet advertising cooperative. In November of that year, Microsoft bought LinkExchange for $265 million.

Microsoft's goal in the acquisition was to help it distribute its online ads to websites. However, Ali Partovi, who then ran

LinkExchange, tried to sell Microsoft on the idea of Keywords, originally developed by Banister. He made monthly trips in 1999 for this purpose, trying to persuade his bosses to auction off keywords that could be placed next to regular results of search (similar to what Google currently does). "This is the next big thing," Partovi is supposed to have told Bill Bliss, the leader of the online group's Web-search team.[14] Bliss was sympathetic to the idea.

However, at the time, the threatening spot on Microsoft's radar was the rapid growth of AOL. Microsoft's top leaders thought that Internet revenues would come through user subscriptions for such sites as AOL or MSN, or from banner ads on these sites. The leaders did not see the future in paid search. Bliss was also skeptical of mixing search results with paid ads because he feared the ads would compromise the quality of the offering.

In 2000, a new leader of the online group finally got permission for Partovi to run a live test program of Keywords on Microsoft MSN. Advertisers began to place sponsored links on the service and advertising revenues flowed in. However, some managers feared that this service would cannibalize the main advertising revenues on MSN, which at that time came from banner ads. So they placed a restriction on Keywords. The minimum bid was set at $15. (Though this might appear low, Google currently has a five-cent minimum on bids.) Partovi believed that the $15 limit was too high and would drive away many advertisers. On paid search, revenues came from a large volume of low bids for keywords. Partovi even ran an unauthorized test without this price restriction. That test outraged bosses at MSN. The leader of the online group asked Partovi to end the test and stay away from company headquarters for a while.

Then in May 2000, after Keywords brought in about $1 million in revenues, Microsoft shut it down. "In retrospect, it was a terrible decision," said the manager of the online group who had obtained Partovi's permission for the live trial of Keywords. "None of us saw the paid search model in all its glory."[15] The lack of vision was in not realizing that revenues came from a large volume of low bids. Ironically, Microsoft's overt reason for the shutdown was that the revenues were lower than the company's other revenue streams. Yet, the minimum bid restriction on Keywords prevented it from realizing its true potential in revenues! Ultimately, fear of cannibalizing other advertising revenue streams had killed the great potential of Keywords.

In October 2000, Google launched its own version of combining search with auctioned keywords, called AdWords. It went on to become the most successful model for revenues on the Web, propelling Google to grow into one of the highest valued corporations on the stock market. Google is so large today that it poses a threat to Microsoft. In particular, Google is considering office software and web browsers that would threaten some of Microsoft's core revenue sources. In the meantime, Microsoft continues to struggle to develop a paid search service that matches Google's.

Crippled by Fear of Piracy: Sony MP3 Player

In the summer of 2001, Kunitake Ando, then president of Sony, had a vision that was pretty good for its time. He predicted that "the personal computer was quickly losing its status as the heart of the information revolution. The real action in information technology would migrate to the living room, the family room, the automobile, the beach, the holiday retreat . . . net-capable audio and video gadgets, cell phones, and games would keep [people] entertained and in touch."[16] The average consumer might have half a dozen gadgets, each with a hard disc and be able to zap information to each other and to and from the Web, making life rich, fast, and exciting. Ando wanted Sony to reinvent itself for this age.

However, by early 2003, the executives at Sony headquarters were facing a problem which was "small enough to fit in their pockets" yet "heavy enough to weigh on their minds."[17] The problem in question was Apple's iPod, the cool little MP3 player that had captured the consumer's imagination in the same way Sony's Walkman did some twenty years earlier. Ideally, Sony should have owned the portable music player business because of its creation and domination of that market with the introduction of the Walkman. But the new century's new Walkman belonged to Apple, not Sony.

Ando's vision did not become reality because Sony was hampered by a fear of piracy. An example of this fear was Sony's digital Walkman. Whereas the iPod lets a user synchronize its contents with the user's music on a laptop or personal computer, Walkman users were hampered by "laborious check-in/check-out" procedures designed to prevent illegal file-sharing.[18] When asked about a Walkman with a hard drive, Keiji Kimura, then senior VP at Sony headquarters, said, "We do not have any plans for such a product, but we are studying it."[19] In fact a Sony Walkman with a hard drive was highly unlikely because Sony's copy-protection didn't allow music transfers between hard drives.

Sony was facing a peculiar predicament with its electronic and entertainment divisions facing opposing priorities. Its electronics business understood consumers' needs and wanted to help them move files around freely. However, its entertainment business was concerned about illegal copying and wanted to build barriers to move files freely. "We have many things to resolve," Kimura acknowledged. "Protection is one side of it—of course we have to protect our copyrights. But the challenge is how to excite the user."[20] Electronics companies were aligned with Napster to produce electronic gadgets that enabled free copying of music and videos. However, entertainment companies were aligned with the movie and recording companies to prevent illegal copying. In a way, the priorities of the music and movie businesses (protecting piracy) ran in direct opposition to those of the MP3 player business (ease of use including easy copying!). Sony had let the battle in the marketplace get within the corporation and paralyze its innovative efforts.

At its core, the fear of piracy was a fear of cannibalization. Sony's acquisitions in the last decade had deepened this conflict. In August 2004 Sony set up a joint venture with BMG (Bertelsmann Music Group), the world's third largest music publisher. In April 2005, Sony bought MGM (Metro-Goldwyn-Mayer, Inc.), a well-known motion picture studio in Hollywood. Both these units were in the business of developing and protecting music and movie labels from which they earned royalties. Illegal copying by consumers was a big threat to these businesses. But to prevent illegal copying, Sony also created obstacles to legal copying by a user for himself or herself. Thus, fear of cannibalizing music and movie revenues crippled Sony's efforts to develop a user-friendly MP3 player.

Apple exploited this weakness of Sony with the successful launch of the iPod and the expansion of its family of products. Further, Apple also introduced and has run the successful iTunes Store for downloading songs, even though Sony could have beaten Apple to it, given its ownership of Sony Music, which has the second largest collection of recorded music. Before the iPod, Apple was a fifth of the size of Sony. Five years after the launch of the iPod, Apple grew to be twice the size of Sony in market cap (see Figure 2.4). The iPod platform prompted Apple to launch the

Figure 2.4. Annual Market Capitalization of Sony and Apple After Launch of iPod

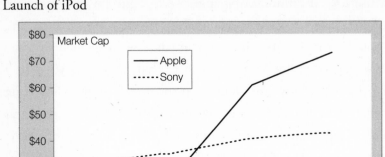

iPhone and then the iPad, other successful products with huge sales and profits.

Sony has made determined efforts at reinventing itself to overcome these problems. One of the radical changes it made was to hire British-born Howard Stringer as CEO of the company in June 2005. But even he struggled with Sony's culture. "The whole security/digital rights management/copyright arena is a critical battlefield," said Howard Stringer. "We all have to invent the business plan for the future. And even though we have sides of Sony that will disagree, finding a consensus is Sony's style."[21]

The deep-seated culture at Sony is a big hindrance to change. Central to this culture is decision by consensus. Such consensus needs to be arrived at within and between divisions. In general, consensus building is a good trait. But when it gets in the way of timely decisions to embrace innovations for the future, it is bad.

Sony was unable to move ahead swiftly and effectively because a commitment to consensus prevented it from resolving the conflict between divisions. Rivals such as Apple are able to move nimbly with new models catering to the needs of the market because they are unencumbered with the size and culture that belong to Sony. Commenting on the swift and decisive decisions taken by Steve Jobs in the development of the iPod, Tony Fadell recalled, "I was used to being at Philips, where decisions like this would take meeting after meeting, with a lot of PowerPoint presentations and going back for more study."[22]

Subsequent chapters will explore practices that can help a company overcome this fear of cannibalization and slow decision making. These practices include empowering innovation champions, incentives for enterprise, and internal competition.

Decline of an Innovator: Eastman Kodak

George Eastman founded the Eastman Kodak company in 1880 based on a relatively simple technology. He designed a box camera and roll film to replace the existing cumbersome glass plate technology for taking pictures. Initially, professional photographers resisted his innovation because of the inferior quality of Kodak's pictures. But lay people picked it up quickly because of its convenience and the product became very successful. Successive innovations over the decades led the company to dominate the photography business, primarily through its superior position in film and prints. The durable camera was the excuse for the consumable film and prints, which provided the majority of Kodak's profits. Kodak built up a commanding position in film that reached 90% in the 1970s before the growth of Fuji.

However, Kodak's great success led to a bloated bureaucracy, generous employee entitlements, and huge overheads. Success created a culture of stagnation. One reporter describes Kodak's culture as follows, "At Kodak this arrogance fueled the growth of a nightmarish bureaucracy so entrenched it could have passed for a government agency. . . . There was an emphasis on doing everything according to company rulebooks. . . . Meetings were held prior to meetings to discuss issues and establish agreement in order to avoid confrontations, which were considered un-Kodaklike."[23] Even with competition from Fuji, some cost cutting enabled Kodak to do well. Its stock peaked on Feb 19, 1997 at $94.75, when the company's market capitalization hit $30.9 billion. Subsequently, the company lost value steadily till its market cap fell below $0.2 billion in December 2011 (see Figure 2.5) and the firm later went into bankruptcy.

Figure 2.5. Annual Market Cap of Eastman Kodak 1996–2011 (US$ Millions)

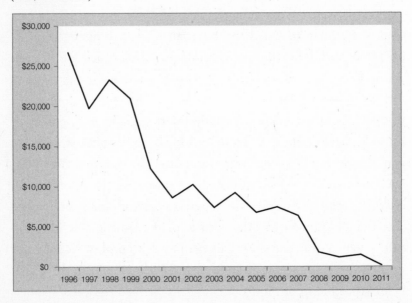

What caused this huge 87% loss in value? It was Kodak's failure to embrace digital photography even after it took off (see Figure 2.6). Ironically, digital photography was not unknown to Kodak. Steven Sasson invented the digital camera at Kodak as early as 1975.[24] Subsequently Kodak produced more than fifty digital products, including the first megapixel sensor of 1.4 million pixels.[25] Sasson has this to say of Kodak's contribution to digital photography: "No matter who makes which digital camera you use today, the camera uses a lot of IP (intellectual property) that Kodak first created. Kodak invented the first megapixel sensor. The first color filter tray was from Kodak. Image compression up to the JPEG standard and, of course, the first digital camera was also developed at the Kodak Labs. One of our

Figure 2.6. Annual Sales of Digital and Analog Cameras (Million Units)

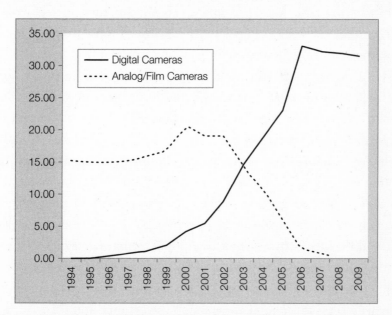

Sources: Prepared by author based on data from GMID, Lucas, and Goh, "Disruptive Technology," and http://www.dpreview.com/news/0401/04012601pmaresearch 2003sales.asp.

cameras was used in the space shuttle mission in the United States in 1991. We also set up the first photo kiosk in 1994."[26] Kodak has over one thousand patents in digital photography.[27] Thus, Kodak was a leader in digital technology. The firm also invested heavily on research in digital technology.[28] So why did the firm lose so much value in the 2000s?

The problem had to do with reluctance to cannibalize the film business. Kodak was used to selling cameras and film but made its profit primarily on film. Film was its cash cow. Digital cameras had the potential to cannibalize that business. The company was reluctant to cannibalize the film business. It hoped digital cameras would not grow to become a very big business. So, in the 1990s, it did not market digital cameras aggressively. In the 2000s, when digital cameras took off (see Figure 2.6), Kodak kept expecting profits from consumables, such as ordering of prints and the distribution and sharing of images via the Internet. Profits from these operations never came anywhere close to those from the film business, causing the decline in sales and market cap (Figure 2.5).

As a result, the company initially was not willing to do the drastic reorganization that would transform the stodgy company, more than one hundred years old, into a small nimble one that can deal with the scorching pace of the digital market. Kodak employee John White describes the clash of current and needed cultures this way: "Kodak wanted to get into the digital business, but they wanted to do it in their own way, from Rochester and largely with their own people. That meant it wasn't going to work. The difference between their traditional business and digital is so great. The tempo is different. The kinds of skills you need are different. Kay and Colby would tell you they wanted change, but they didn't want to force the pain on the organization."[29]

Moreover, when some senior managers realized the need for digital technology and allocated resources for digital products, middle managers kept resisting the change. An article in *Business Week* described the cultural resistance thus: "The old-line manufacturing culture continues to impede [CEO George] Fisher's efforts to turn Kodak into a high-tech growth company. 'Fisher has been able to change the culture at the very top,' says one industry executive, 'but he hasn't been able to change the huge mass of middle managers, and they just don't understand this [digital] world.'"[30]

In this case, the over one-hundred-year success with the old film technology turned into rigidities that prevented the company from embracing the new digital technology. Even when the company reorganized, creating a separate division to handle digital products, infighting between divisions prevented the new division from making a great success with digital technology. In the words of Donald W. Strickland, a former vice president, "The fear of cannibalization always slowed things down."[31] In effect, Kodak never empowered the new division with sufficient independence to compete with and if necessary, cannibalize, and kill off the film division. Unfortunately, the external digital market did that anyway. And a great innovator shrank to a fraction of its value (see Figure 2.5).

A Cycle of Cannibalization: Gillette's Innovations in Wet Shaving

Professor Peter Golder and I analyzed the history of Gillette in the wet shaving market.[32] Our prior analysis and my updated analysis of its recent history suggests that Gillette's story contrasts dramatically with Kodak's in digital photography. Gillette dominated the wet shaving market for over a hundred years. For much of this time, it has had a large, relatively stable market share of 60% to 70%. What is the reason for this great dominance of the market? Figure 2.7 may

Figure 2.7. Gillette's Brand Cannibalization in the Wet Shaving Market

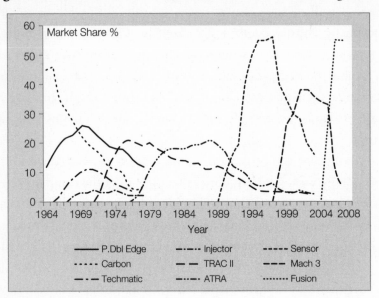

provide a clue. This figure graphs market share of Gillette's brand on the *y* axis against calendar year on the *x* axis. A close analysis of this exhibit reveals an important dynamic. Even though the total share of all Gillette's brands may sum to about a stable 70%, in reality market shares of the individual brands are in constant flux. New brands enter the market at regular intervals while old brands fade away. Indeed, each brand seems to grow rapidly, reach a peak, and then decline. The rate of this rise and fall seems to occur at an increasing pace, providing further support, in addition to Figure 2.2, of the increasing rate of technological change in this market too.

On viewing this exhibit, the casual observer might think that Gillette has acted with great foresight. Just when an older brand is about to decline, it introduces a new brand to take its place. However, the real story may be a little surprising. Gillette introduces a new brand even when the old brand is at its peak. The new introduction cannibalizes the market share of the old brand. Gillette does so, even though in most cases no rival introduces a brand to challenge the position of its dominant brand. For example, in 1972, Gillette introduced TRAC II. This was the first razor with twin blades. Gillette introduced this innovation even at the risk of cannibalizing sales of its older successful brands. TRAC II had five years of rapid growth. In 1976, under the threat of Bic disposable razors, Gillette introduced Good News. Good News had twin disposable blades but was lower priced and cut into short-term profits of the established brands. Then, in 1977, while TRAC II's sales were still rising, Gillette introduced ATRA, with full knowledge that so doing would arrest and cannibalize TRAC II's sales. In 1989, Gillette introduced Sensor, with two independently moving blades. This innovation provided such a big improvement in performance that it commanded a premium price and reversed the losses from the lower priced disposables. While Sensor was still growing, Gillette introduced Sensor Excel that replaced the former brand. Even though Sensor Excel was growing, in 1998 Gillette introduced MACH 3, a razor with 3 pivoting blades. In 2005, Gillette introduced Fusion, a six-blade wonder that did to MACH 3 what it had done to its predecessors.

In hindsight, most of these innovations were big successes. At the time though, each innovation was risky. First, it ran the risk of cannibalizing Gillette's older brands without guaranteeing a higher profit margin. Second, it ran the risk of wasting huge expenditures in research and development and marketing. For example, Gillette spent $700 million in research and development for the MACH 3, and started those investments as much as seven years before launch. In addition, Gillette may have spent $300 million on marketing. Such risks create the fear of cannibalization that afflicts many incumbents. That is not what happened at Gillette, at least for most of its history.

Gillette introduced most innovations in shaving except for the electric razor, the stainless steel blade, and, recently, the home laser kit. It was a fear of cannibalizing its successful products that dissuaded Gillette from introducing the stainless steel blade, even though it owned some of the patents for that technology. When Wilkinson Sword introduced the stainless steel blade in the 1960s, Gillette suffered a steep drop in market share within a year. That experience taught Gillette the importance of cannibalizing successful products before rivals did so. Subsequently, by innovating ahead of competitors, Gillette maintained its dominance of the wet shaving market, even expanded overall market share, and increased profits in some cases.

The culture within Gillette provides some insight as to how it succeeded at innovation.[33] Employees had a passion for the product and an obsession for innovation. At any time, Gillette had over a dozen shaving products under research. The company used its own employees to personally test its prototypes of new products. Using two-way mirrors, the company observed more than one million shaves in a recent year at its research centers.[34] Employees analyzed the consumers' style of shaving, strokes used in shaving, smoothness of shaved skin, and output in shaved hair. A manager commented about his commitment to testing, "We bleed so you'll get a good shave at home. This is my 27th year. I came here my first week. Haven't missed a day of shaving."[35] A vice president of the technology laboratory described Gillette's research passion and culture like this: "We test the blade edge, the blade guard, the angle of the blades, the balance of the razor, the length, the heft, the width. What happens to the chemistry of the skin? What happens to the hair when you pull it? What happens to the follicle? We own the face. We know more about shaving than anybody. I don't think obsession is too strong a word."[36]

This passion for innovation and willingness to cannibalize successful products is responsible for Gillette's unrelenting leadership of and high profits in the wet shaving market. These traits themselves sprang from past mistakes and resulting realization of the fragility of market dominance. While it led in most innovations in wet shaving, Gillette twice failed to innovate and immediately lost market share: it failed to introduce stainless steel blades and electric shavers. From these mistakes, Gillette learned that success leads to complacency that embeds the seeds of future failure. For continued success, it had to strive to develop innovative products and obsolete existing successful products.

However, even with Gillette, innovation was finite. The firm was not the pioneer of laser technology and was not quick in responding to the threat of laser hair removal devices. A small start-up introduced the first home laser hair removal set. Time will tell whether Gillette's failure in this respect will be fatal. (Gillette sold out to P&G, which acquired the entire company in 2005.) The advance of laser technology may have presented a sufficient threat to the company that it sought the support and investment of a giant consumer products company.

Late Move: HP Tablet

Similar to the previous examples, HP Laboratories had a prototype of an e-book reader in the mid-2000s.[37] However, at that time the market for such products seemed small, probably less than $100 million a year. The category may have seemed like a rival to laptops, for which HP had become the major manufacturer after the acquisition of Compaq. Moreover, for a firm like HP with over a hundred billion dollars in sales, mainly from PCs and laptops, pursuing the then relatively minuscule market for e-book readers probably seemed like a distraction. Yet, the e-book reader market got credibility when Amazon introduced its Kindle in 2007. The market took off in the form of tablets when Apple introduced its iPad in 2010 and immediately threatened the PC and laptop markets.

It was only then that HP took this category seriously. HP launched the Slate in October 2010 and the TouchPad in July 2011.[38] But by not aggressively commercializing such a product earlier even at the risk of threatening its own PC and laptop markets, HP may have lost a half decade of valuable product development and in-market experience. As of summer 2012, Apple remained way ahead of all competitors in its share of the tablet market.[39] In September 2011, HP called it quits. It said it would abandon its TouchPad and its mobile phone because of low sales. However, it went further and said it would sell its entire personal computer and laptop business, even though it was the leading manufacturer at the time. Ostensibly, its then CEO, Leo Apotheker, said he was doing that because of small and declining margins in those businesses.[40] However, the real reason would have been the growth of the mobile and tablet businesses at the cost of personal computers and laptops.

HP's failure to aggressively embrace, commercialize, and lead in the tablet market had taken the shine off the personal computer and laptop markets. Without a strong position in tablets, the future of personal computers and laptops seemed dim.

CONCLUSION

This chapter makes the following important points.

- Many incumbents fail to commercialize radical innovations due to a fear of cannibalizing successful products. Success is a curse. When successful products are still profitable, it is difficult to envisage the threat from an unprofitable, seemingly small, new innovation. In particular, economic and organizational factors come in the way of cannibalization.

- Economic considerations seem to weight current successful products over radical innovations. The huge investments, high failure rate, uncertain returns, and distant payoffs for radical innovations all count against them and in favor of current successful products. In addition, specific sales and profit thresholds often screen out radical innovations when compared against the scale and profits of existing firms.

- Organization hurdles include committee and procedures for approval, perceived invulnerability, and resistance from internal stakeholders. In the case of Microsoft, a few enterprising junior managers championed the search. But senior managers failed to see the light. In the case of Sony, divisional conflict and a concern for consensus failed to make a success of the design and marketing of the MP3 player that the firm had developed and commercialized. In the case of HP, the businesses were too focused on the huge PC and laptop market to pay much attention to the e-book reader that the labs had produced. The most surprising case is Kodak. The company was already the world leader in the new digital technology. Senior management, brought in to help with the transition, was in favor of the new technology but was not willing to undertake the deep organizational changes necessary to market it successfully.

- Ironically, firms overlook innovations even when they emerged in the bowels of the firm's organization. Case histories of Microsoft Keywords, Kodak digital technology, the Sony MP3 player, and the HP e-book illustrate this point. Note that in all these four cases, the new technology was developed and, in one case (Kodak), pioneered by researchers in the incumbent firm's own labs.

- Given a monopoly, focusing on current successful products may be preferable to costly innovations that may cannibalize them. But real markets are fairly competitive. If the incumbents will not innovate, competitors will. The preceding case histories show how the incumbents suffered, in some cases fatally, by not pursuing innovations.

- The driving rationale for cannibalization is technological evolution. Such evolution has certain distinct characteristics: (a) in any market, new technological platforms constantly emerge; (b) each such technology introduces one or more new dimensions of performance; (c) as a result, at any point in time multiple technologies compete on multiple dimensions to serve certain consumer functions; (d) improvements in performance of these technologies causes their performance paths to cross multiple times; and (e) the rate of technological change is increasing exponentially over time.

- Technological innovations open whole new markets and obsolete established ones. Thus, monitoring technological evolution with an eye on future growth markets may help counteract the lure of current successful products.

- Some economists have shown that the seemingly counterintuitive principle of cannibalizing one's successful products may be the optimal strategy in a competitive market.[41] It is basically a principle of protecting one's market by preemptive cannibalization. Hence the logic in the saying, "Eat your own lunch before someone else does."[42]

- To be unrelentingly innovative, firms must be willing to cannibalize their successful products, not only when the product is in decline, but even when it is at its peak. Gillette illustrates this strategy in the wet shaving markets. The goals, culture, and organization were all geared for such cannibalization. However, even in the case of Gillette, when a new platform in the form of laser technology emerged, the firm was not the first to commercialize it.

How can a firm instill this willingness to cannibalize as a routine attitude within the corporation? The next two chapters describe two traits—focusing on the future and embracing risk—which help promote a willingness to cannibalize successful products. In addition, subsequent chapters spell out practices that help in providing incentives for enterprise, instituting internal markets, and empowering champions.

CHAPTER 3

Embracing Risk

For us innovation means being willing to bet hundreds
of millions of dollars on a new drug, labor to bring it
out over a decade, fail, and then be willing to try all over
again.

—KEVIN SHARER[1]

THIS QUOTATION FROM FORMER Amgen CEO Kevin
Sharer, who grew the company's revenues from $3.6 billion to
$16 billion in about ten years,[2] reveals a deep understanding of
an essential feature of innovation and risk taking: that failure is
intrinsic to the process and the innovator's best attitude is to
embrace it! Taking risks really means embracing failure, in order
to learn from it and do better in the future.

Innovations may fail at any of the stages of idea screening, development, prototype testing, market testing, commercialization, and
post commercialization. Risk is due to the uncertainty of success
during the stages of developing and commercializing an innovation.
That is, risk is proportional to the degree of uncertainty about the
outcome of the innovation and the costs involved in the innovation.

Sources of Risk: Innovation's High Failure Rate

The riskiness of innovations arises from at least five sources.

First, the loss or failure of projects increases as they move from
the stage of ideation to that of ultimate commercialization. A new

product normally goes several stages of development. Managers start off with a large numbers of ideas, screen these to a smaller set, research the promising ones, develop a still smaller set, realize prototypes of some of these, test market a few, and launch one or two new products. There is a tremendous loss as the firm goes from ideas to successful launches. One study across a large number of industries found that it took over three thousand ideas to arrive at a few successful products; thus, the loss function for innovations is very steep (see Figure 3.1). This loss is extremely high in the pharmaceutical industry. For example, in order to produce the one highly successful cholesterol drug, Zocor, Merck screened about ten thousand chemical compounds, ran clinical trials for more than a dozen, and tried out a handful in human subjects.[3] When bringing new ideas to fruition as new products, managers incur increasing costs without being certain which idea will be the best. This is the first source of risk.

Figure 3.1. Innovation's Loss Function

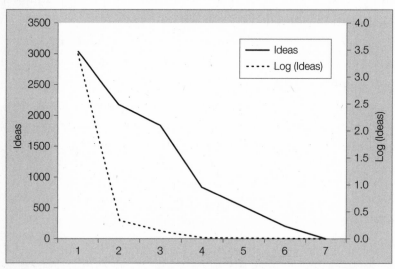

Source: Adapted from Stevens, Greg A., and James Burley (1997), "3,000 Raw Ideas = 1 Commercialized Success!" *Research Technology Management*, 40, 3.

Second, numerous studies suggest that the failure rate for even commercialized new products is very high. Here failure would mean that the new product is not ultimately profitable and has to be withdrawn or discontinued in the market. Estimates of the rate of failure range from as low as 20% to a high of 90%.[4] A recent survey of 416 respondents across industries finds that firms on average commercialized only one successful product out of every eleven projects started.[5] Thus, even after all the screening, research, testing, and marketing, a new product may not become an ultimate success in terms of profit. This is another source of risk.

Third, innovations vary greatly in their commercialization profile. Some innovations can be slowly launched in the market over time from segment to segment (waterfall strategy). Others need to be launched on a large scale to whole market in one go from day one (sprinkler strategy). For example, Fred Smith, who launched Federal Express needed to start with a large countrywide network of costly planes, trucks, and employees (see case history later in this chapter) so that mail could be picked up and delivered as required by the sender. A waterfall strategy reduces risk as it allows for a slow build-up in expenses, which can be covered with growing revenues. A sprinkler strategy requires an enormous investment up front. This need for massive investment with no guarantee of revenue is a third source of risk.

Fourth, the takeoff in sales of a new product is an early sign of ultimate success. However, sales of a new product may take several years to take off. Estimates of the time from introduction to takeoff vary from a few years for digital products to several years for household durables.[6] However, these estimates are for successful new products. In the case of any radically new product that is now being launched, the manager does not know whether it will fail or succeed. In my discussions with managers, I have found that junior managers who are immersed in the new product are willing to wait. But senior managers may be impatient with a long time to takeoff because expenses keep mounting during the wait. This wait for takeoff is the fourth source of risk.

Fifth, some innovations need to grow very rapidly to be viable in a fast-changing environment. For example, Jeff Bezos, who launched Amazon, figured that his start-up needed to grow very rapidly in order to be viable in the rapidly growing Internet world (see case history later in this chapter). Rapid growth requires huge investments that exceed the revenues generated initially. Increasing growth during the first few years after commercializing may be euphoric but involves increasing losses with no guarantee of ultimate success. This is the fifth source of risk.

This discussion shows that risk arises from a variety of sources. Most important, an innovation has a high probability of failure at one of several stages of development; that is, innovation is inherently risky. Innovation tends to lose its glamour when people realize its high failure rate and inherent risk. As one scholar commented, "The popular (and sometimes the scholarly) enthusiasm for risk taking in the entrepreneurial process wanes considerably at the prospect of failure."[7] Moreover, society looks unfavorably at risk, considering failure to be shameful, more so in some cultures than others.[8] Two scholars on the issue put it this way, "Society values risk taking but not gambling. And what is meant by gambling is risk taking that turns out badly."[9]

Thus, embracing risk really means embracing failure. Amgen CEO Kevin Sharer says of failure, "We fail most of the time even when we get the science right."[10] Thomas J. Watson Sr., the former CEO who grew the Computing-Tabulating-Recording Company into a worldwide industry we know as International Business Machines (IBM), once said, "The fastest way to succeed is to double your failure rate."[11]

Specifically, how do most people handle risk? Research indicates that response is not quite rational but still predictable, as seen in three phenomena called the reflection effect, the hot-stove effect, and the expectations effect.

The Reflection Effect: Asymmetry in Perceived Risk

Consider a choice from the following two alternatives:

A. An 80% chance of receiving $4,000 with a 20% chance of receiving nothing
B. A 100% chance of receiving $3,000

Two psychologists, Daniel Kahneman and Amos Tversky,[12] found that when faced with this choice, 80% of subjects in experiments preferred alternative B even though alternative A had a higher expected value of $3,200. The latter payoff comes from multiplying .8 into $4,000. The authors explained that people prefer a sure gain over a gamble in which they could win even more but also lose everything.

Now consider a choice of the following two alternatives:

C. An 80% chance of losing $4,000 with a 20% chance of losing nothing.
D. A 100% chance of losing $3,000

When given this choice, 92% of subjects chose C over D even though C has a greater expected loss ($3,200) than the loss of $3,000 in D. The reason is that people prefer to gamble on a big loss if there is even a small chance that they may lose nothing.

Interestingly, the preference for sure versus uncertain payoff reverses when the payoff is stated in losses (C, D) rather than gains (A, B). The psychologists called this reversal the *reflection effect*. This effect is part of a theory of risk that they called *prospect theory*, for which Kahneman later received the Nobel Prize.

On the one hand, successful incumbent firms with a reasonably secure profit stream can be said to be operating in the domain of gains, as in alternatives A and B.[13] They prefer the surety of a small steady stream of profits to the gamble of innovations, in which they might win big but also win nothing. On the other hand, start-ups or new entrants (or failing incumbents) can be thought of as operating in the realm of losses, as in alternatives C and D. They are willing to gamble on innovations with the potential of a big win, rather than do nothing and face no gains at all or continued losses. Thus, successful incumbents and start-ups may have opposite propensities to risk. Incumbents, who typically have a steady cash stream, look skeptically at potential innovations and ask, "Why? What do I have to gain?" They are risk averse. Entrepreneurs and new entrants look hopefully at the same innovations and ask, "Why not? What do I have to lose?" They are risk seeking. The two parties are at either end of the reflection effect.

The high failure rate of innovations suggest that developing innovations requires committing resources without certainty of outcomes, patience in the face of mounting losses, and willingness to accept failure. The reflection effect suggests that these traits may not come naturally to incumbents. In particular, incumbents may tend to have the opposite traits: low tolerance for uncertainty, impatience with losses, and low tolerance for failure. The latter traits result from incumbents' satisfaction with the current stream of profits from their products and their belief that carefully nurturing current products will ensure continued profits in the future. Subu Goparaju, senior vice president at Infosys, encapsulates the problem this way, "The tendency is to defend what you have already achieved. . . . Everyone is empowered to say no and no one is empowered to say yes."[14] Start-ups, which have no such stream of profits, may be more likely than profitable incumbents to commit funds to innovations, tolerate uncertainty, and be patient with losses.

For example, during the 1970s, prior to the onset of digital cameras, Kodak had a continuous stream of profits. That success brought risk aversion and lack of innovation. Kodak's "executives abhorred anything that looked risky or too innovative because a mistake in such a massive manufacturing process would cost thousands of dollars. So the company built itself up around procedures and policies intended to maintain the status quo."[15]

Apple became one of the most valuable companies in the world due to a string of highly innovative products under the leadership of Steve Jobs. Jobs explains how he overcame the reflection effect at Apple, "Almost everything—all external expectations, all pride, all fear of embarrassment or failure—these things just fall away in the face of death, leaving only what is truly important. Remembering that you are going to die is the best way I know to avoid the trap of thinking you have something to lose."[16]

The Hot-Stove Effect: Learning from Failure

The term *hot-stove effect* was coined by two professors, Jerker Denrell and James G. March, to explain incumbents' risk-aversion.[17] It is a complementary explanation to the reflection effect. They justify the term from the following quotation by Mark Twain:

> We should be careful to get out of an experience only the wisdom that is in it—and stop there: lest we be like the cat that sits

down on a hot stove lid. She will never sit down on a hot stove lid again—and that is well; but also she will never sit down on a cold one.[18]

Innovations represent novel but risky options. Succeeding with innovations involve errors. In the course of exploring alternatives, firms may make mistakes, encounter setbacks, or fail. Moreover, if the firm is testing a new and unfamiliar technology, such mistakes and failure may be more common, especially if performance improves with experience. In such situations, early experiences with a new technology may be less favorable than its long-term average or the average that comes with experience. Similarly, in the face of very risky innovations, with a large variation in results, a small sample of initial tests may well come up with greater failures than that from the long-term average of tests. It is imperative that the innovator learn the right lessons from the failures. Proper and deep reflection on the failure may be necessary to uncover the true lessons. However, the hot-stove effect leads to a bias against alternatives and innovations that are very risky (variable returns) or that require experience for success.

For example, in the last few minutes of a close basketball game, players on a team normally try to give the ball to their clutch players, the players who shoot baskets with a supposedly high success rate during the intense pressure of the last few minutes of a close game. Such players are also much higher paid than regular players. However, research shows that clutch players are not better in shooting performance in the last few minutes of a close game than at other times of the game.[19] Why then does the myth of clutch players persist? It does so because clutch players *want the ball and are unafraid to take risky shots* under pressure. They do fail in those moments and they probably know they failed in those moments in the past. However, they learn from the failure—not that taking a shot could result in a loss as in the past but that taking a shot with cool focus and proper position could result in success. Michael Jordan says in a Nike ad, "I've missed more than 9,000 shots in my career. I've lost almost 300 games. 26 times I've been trusted to take the game winning shot and missed. I've failed over and over and over again in my life. And that is why I succeed."[20] From his failures, Jordan learned what to avoid and what to strive for to achieve success.

In his book *To Engineer Is Human*, Henry Petroski details the failures and disasters that occurred with numerous designs, mostly of bridges but also of buildings, ships, and planes.[21] The learning from the ensuing disasters is not that engineers should not design new bridges or buildings, nor is it that people should refrain from using them. Both such lessons would suffer from the hot-stove effect. However, the real lesson is to understand and learn from the failure and design better structures in the future.

Similarly, the initial stages of conceiving and developing an innovation contain a great deal of uncertainty where failures are inevitable. David Kelley, founder of IDEO, one of the most successful design companies, encourages employees to, "Fail early and fail often."[22] Doing so presents many opportunities for learning; doing so late may be fatal. For example, in the research towards developing the multibillion-dollar drug Lipitor to treat high cholesterol, the research team led by Roger Newton encountered four failures in a row. The management of Lipitor had had enough and wanted to call off the research. However, Newton argued strongly to persist with the research. Like Twain's cat, management reacted superficially to the failures and saw research as going down a blind alley. However, Newton learned from the failures: he acquired a deeper understanding of cholesterol treatment and saw more clearly what specific features the new drug should contain and where to look in terms of drugs that could provide those features. Lipitor went on to become the most profitable drug as of 2012—but Newton went on to lose his job because of management's displeasure with his persistence (see Chapter 7).

The Expectations Effect: Hope Versus Reality

Expectations about innovations tend to be higher than reality for two reasons. First, once people start on the project, they tend to hope for quick results. As Alexander Pope wrote, "Hope springs eternal in the human breast." Second, involvement in a project leads the innovator to overcount its positives and undercount its negatives. These two biases lead to expectations that may rise beyond reality. These expectations are most pertinent along two dimensions, sales and profits. On each of these dimensions, returns from innovations may be slow or fast (see Table 3.1).

What distribution of growth and profits can firms expect for their innovation? How often does a firm get rapid sales? Rapid profits?

My experience and research suggest that the most common outcome is a slow-slow combination.[23] That is, both profits and growth are slow in coming. Examples are that of FedEx and Prius described later in this chapter and the iPod discussed in Chapter 7. Sometimes, growth comes fast but profits come slowly. Examples are Amazon and Facebook (described later in this chapter). Even rarer is the occurrence of slow growth and fast profits. The rarest

Table 3.1. Payoff to Radical Innovations

		Profit	
		Slow	**Fast**
Growth	**Slow**	Common e.g., FedEx	Rare e.g., Collector items
	Fast	Rare e.g., Amazon	Very rare e.g., iPad

68

outcome is fast growth and profits. An example is the iPad. However, the recency and popularity of this example may lead innovators into false expectations for their innovations. Patience is essential. Jeff Bezos, founder and CEO of Amazon.com, noted, "The landscape of people who do new things and expect them to be profitable quickly is littered with corpses."[24]

For example, some great innovators (Steve Jobs of Apple) have had seeming, immediate success with one radical innovation (iPad took off and was profitable in the first year), slow success with another (iPod took three years to take off), and failure with still others (such as Newton and Rokr). Given this distribution of outcomes, it is difficult to draw sweeping generalizations. But if any generalization is possible, it is that innovators need to be patient with growth especially for radical innovations. Innovators usually also have to be very patient with profits.

However, innovators need not have to be patient for growth in a vacuum. My coauthors and I have developed a hazard model to predict the takeoff in sales of a new product given characteristics of the product, country, launch price, and launch year. A synopsis of how to use this model for prediction is in Chapter 8 and details are in three published articles.[25] My coauthors and I have also developed a hazard model to predict the likely time of disruption of one technology by another, given characteristics of the technologies and the market. Again, a synopsis is in Chapter 8 and details are in a published article.[26]

Innovation's Gain-Loss Function: Type 1 and 2 Errors

Any innovation decision involves two types of successes and two types of errors (see Figure 3.1). The two successes are a successful launch and a successful screen. We can call the two errors Type 1 and Type 2. Type 1 error is betting on an innovation that turns out to be a dud or does not really pay off. The loss here is real costs in the development or commercialization of the innovation less any profits that it generated. Type 2 error is failing to adopt or commercialize an innovation that is eventually developed by a rival and turns out to be successful.

Table 3.2 displays the two types of successes and errors. The columns describe the decision that the firm has to make about an innovation, whether to Go or No Go. The rows describes the outcome in the marketplace, whether the innovations succeeds or fails. The crossing of these two factors results in four outcomes: a) a successful launch; b) a failed innovation (or Type 1 error); c) a missed innovation (failure to launch what becomes a successful innovation, or a Type 2 Error); and d) a successful screen of a bad innovation.

Type 1 and Type 2 error rates are intrinsically linked by the criteria set to screen for new innovations. As one increases the stringency of the criteria to screen for innovations, Type 1 error rates (failed innovations) drop. But Type 2 errors (missed innovations) go up; that is, the firm fails to introduce some innovations that would have been successful. As the firm decreases the stringency of criteria to screen innovations, the reverse occurs. That is, the firm pursues more innovations, some of which are successful. But doing so also increases Type 1 errors (failed innovations) and decreases Type 2 errors (missed innovations).

Table 3.2. Innovation's Gain-Loss Tradeoff

| | | Innovation Decision in Firm | |
		Go	No Go
Innovation's Performance in Market	**Succeeds**	A: Successful Launch	C: Type 2 Error Missed Innovation
	Fails	B: Type 1 Error Failed Innovation	D: Successful Screen

The downside to Type 1 errors (failed innovations) tends to be finite. However, the upside of a highly successful innovation is huge. Innovations have changed entire markets, propelled small outsiders into market leaders, and created enormous wealth to the firms that introduces them. Thus, the costs of Type 2 errors (missed opportunities) are huge.

The three effects described above (reflection, hot-stove, or expectations effects) may cause incumbents to pay too much attention to Type 1 errors and their costs. In contrast, incumbents may not pay enough attention to Type 2 errors and their costs. Type 1 errors are visible and involve immediate, tangible costs; thus incumbents may tend to minimize these errors by setting stringent criteria for screening innovations. Type 2 errors often are in the remote future and involve invisible opportunity costs; incumbents may underestimate and tolerate them until it is too late to remedy the situation.

For example, consider the following declines in market capitalization of some leading incumbents as relevant innovations marketed by a rival took off. Nokia, a leader in mobile phones, lost $95 billion in market cap between 2007 and 2012, as Apple's touch-screen iPhone took off. Similarly RIM, a leader in smartphones, lost $60 billion in market cap between 2007 and 2012 as Apple's touch screen iPhone took off. HP lost $43 billion in market cap between 2010 and 2012 as Apple's iPad took off. Sony lost $6 billion between 1995 and 2006 as Samsung's LCD TVs took off. Yahoo!, a one-time leader in Internet search, lost $27 billion as Google's search took off. Moreover, in each of these cases, the firm that introduced the innovation had gains in market capitalization in the billions of dollars (see Table 3.3).

Critics may quibble about the details of these examples. In particular, the gain in the innovator's market cap could be due to multiple other innovations that were introduced. But the broad lesson from these examples is that missed innovations involve two

Table 3.3. Real and Opportunity Costs from Type 2 Errors (Missed Opportunities)

Incumbent	Missed Innovation	Innovator	Real Loss in Incumbent's Market Cap	% Drop in Incumbent's Market Cap	Est. Gain in Innovator's Market Cap[27]	Time Period
Yahoo!	PageRank search	Google	$27 billion	60%	$98 billion	2005–2012
HP	Touch-screen tablets	Apple	$43 billion	47%	$258 billion	2010–2012
Nokia	Touch-screen smartphones	Apple	$95 billion	87%	$195 billion[28]	2007–2012
RIM	Touch-screen smartphones	Apple	$60 billion	90%	$195 billion[29]	2007–2012
Sony	LCD screens	Samsung	$6 billion	23%	$144 billion[30]	1996–2006

losses: the gain in market cap that goes to a rival (that introduced the innovation) and the drop in market cap from an incumbent that failed to innovate. Each of these losses can be huge.

Because these two losses are not easily measured, incumbents may tend to make larger Type 2 errors than is optimal in the quest to reduce visible Type 1 errors. Cognizant of Sony's many missed opportunities in mobile music, smartphones, LCD monitors, and tablets, Masahiro Fujita, president of Sony's System Technologies Laboratories and its Chief Distinguished Researcher, says of risk, "the risk of not innovating is greater than the risk of innovating."[31] What he probably meant is that Type 2 Errors are greater than Type 1 Errors. Thus, a full understanding of risk in innovation must take into account both Type 1 and Type 2 errors.

This discussion also suggests another way to look at innovations. The firm can consider innovations as an option on future growth and profitability.[32] Investing in each innovation and each stage of innovation is really buying an option on a future growth market whose full potential is not well known in the present. A firm may need to buy a large number of these options. Most of them would result in a failure with little or no return. But one option out of many may result in a big payoff. The investment is relatively small, tangible, and current. The payoff is in the future, quite rare, but huge.

Estimating the payoff from a future radical innovation involves a great deal of uncertainty, both in timing and size of payoff. As noted earlier, with various coauthors, I have done extensive work on trying to predict the timing of the takeoff of new products and the timing of the disruption from new technologies, and thus reduce uncertainty (see Chapter 8).

Firms do not have to wait for future payoffs entirely in a vacuum. Publicly traded firms have a means of gauging what these payoffs may be by how their stock price responds to announcements about various events in an innovation project (see Chapter 8 for details). From a large-scale study of responses to such announcements, Ashish Sood of Emory University and I found the following patterns:[33]

a. On average the stock market responds positively (not negatively) to announcements about innovation and R&D, including those made at the start of innovation projects, such as the opening of a lab.
b. The returns to announcements about innovation projects are positive even though they are made on average of about 4.5 years before the actual launch of a new product emerging from the project.
c. Negative events, such as canceling a research project or cutting funding for research, result in negative returns.
d. The negative returns for negative announcements is steeper in absolute values than the positive returns for the corresponding positive announcements.
e. In a few cases for which we had cost or investment data, total returns to the research effort were about *three times* the value of the funds invested in the research effort.

Thus, contrary to popular misconception, the stock market does react negatively to announcements about investment in research, even if such investments involve large outlays of funds many years before fruition. Publicly traded firms can use such analyses to get an early indication of how the stock market views their investments in innovation at every stage of an innovation project and thus an idea of what the likely payoff may be.

Case Histories

The subsequent case histories of the origins and struggles of some radical innovators emphasize the need for understanding the gain-loss function and being patient for growth and profits. The four case histories also illustrate different aspects of embracing risk for innovation. Toyota shows the risk of pursuing an embryonic market with no certainty of growth or profit. Amazon shows the risk involved with the need for rapid growth and slow profit. Federal Express shows the risk involved with needing to start on a large scale with a huge investment. Facebook shows the risk involved in holding off against short-term gains to realize a vision. All the examples reiterate the importance of understanding and embracing risk in order to make a success of an innovation.

Three of the four examples show that the founder took the big risk—initially with forming the start-up, and subsequent risks through its growth. This observation reinforces the lesson of the reflection effect, that start-ups or firms that are led as start-ups have a higher propensity to risk than do incumbents.

Gambling on an Embryonic Market: Toyota's Prius

In 2008, Toyota snatched the leadership from General Motors as the world's biggest car manufacturer. Among all Toyota's car models, the snazzy and environmentally friendly Prius is Toyota's flagship of innovation. Since its launch in 1997 until mid-2012, Prius sold over 2.5 million units worldwide, with about half of them in North America.[34] It brought back numerous trophies, including the prestigious awards of "Fortune Magazine 25 Best Products of the Year" and "North American Car of the Year." The

Prius had become a powerful "social statement" and an "object of cult-like affection."[35] Despite its global recall woes and the 2011 tsunami in Japan, Toyota's Prius retained its status as the best-selling car in Japan for the third straight year.[36] In many respects, the Prius has become a symbol of innovation in automobiles.

However, Toyota's image as a technological innovator and responsible corporate citizen had not always been so. On the contrary, before its success with the Prius, Toyota was seen as a "fast follower," "a copycat," and a stodgy, "risk-averse company" with a rigid system of seniority and hierarchy. It seemed to outdo its competitors only through its lean production system. Indeed, Toyota depicted itself as the Japanese "Volkswagen," trying to appeal to its customers with its affordability and down-to-earth style. The "birth of the Prius," therefore, was revolutionary not only for its hybrid technology but also for its repositioning of Toyota from a backward, risk-averse company to an innovative risk embracer.[37] Every stage of the development, from sketching the model to post-commercialization, involved risk. So how did a company known for careful risk-averse moves gain respect for rapid, risky innovation?

Initial Stage: Striving for Kakushin ("Rapid Innovation")—Aim High

The idea of the Prius dates back to 1993. That year, the Clinton administration founded Partnership for the Next Generation of Vehicles, a ten-year project in which the federal or state governments would fund research to develop family-sized vehicles that could deliver 80 mpg—three times the fuel efficiency of the normal sedan at the time.[38] The Partnership invited all American automotive companies to participate. Despite the unfriendly exclusion, Toyota, discerning that soaring oil prices and a growing middle class would create a demand for a more fuel-efficient vehicle, secretly started a project of its own, known as the G21 (for global twenty-first century).

But no one at Toyota knew what the team was aiming for or how much financial resources the project would take. "I was trying to come up with the future direction of the company," said Katsuaki Watanabe, then head of corporate planning, "but I didn't have a very specific idea about the vehicle."[39]

The engineering team initially targeted to create better fuel economy by refining its existing engine and transmission systems. With its popular and fuel-efficient model Corolla E110 running at 30 mpg, the engineering team aimed to boost fuel efficiency by 50% to 47.5 miles per gallon.[40] But that was not audacious enough for Akihiro Wada, executive vice president of Toyota. "Don't settle for anything less than a 100% improvement," he told his team, "otherwise competitors would catch up quickly."[41] Japanese cars were commonly known as "econoboxes"; such a label would not be fitting for the caliber of the avant-garde vehicle that Wada envisioned. He wanted the new car not only to change Toyota's image as an efficient copycat, but also revolutionize the way the world looks at the Japanese car industry.

Eager for a breakthrough, Wada turned his attention to the hybrid technology, a system that would lower petrol consumption by combining the conventional internal combustion engine with an electric motor. Although the idea of mass-produced hybrids was new, the concept of the engineering system itself was not. In the early automotive history, cars powered by electric motors, steam, and internal-combustion engines all had a competitive share of the market. When American engineer H. Piper invented a petrol-electric hybrid engine that could achieve the thrilling speed of 25 mph in 1905, hybrid cars became the leader of the market.[42]

However, competitors came up with cheaper and simpler gas-fueled vehicles just a few years later, which killed the hybrid soon after. The idea of a hybrid system was not brought back until the 1970s, when the oil crisis created a demand for more fuel-efficient or even entirely fuel-independent cars. Major carmakers such as Toyota and Honda began to dabble with the hybrid system.

Indeed, Masatami Takimoto, then an executive vice president of Toyota, who was developing a hybrid minivan at the time. That project, however, was hampered by the separation between engineers and sales executives. "Engineers had the firm belief that the hybrid was the answer to all those questions—oil depletion, emissions, and the long-term future of the automobile society—but the business people weren't in agreement," said Takimoto.[43] It came as no surprise that Wada's suggestion of developing a hybrid vehicle came under fire from sales executives and investors alike. Some attacked the idea as an impossible task; others argued that even if Toyota brought the hybrid vehicle to life, the vehicle's profit would not be able to make up its astronomical cost. Despite vehement opposition, Wada went ahead with the risky investment.

Once Wada had set his heart on the hybrid, he wanted it fast, lest his competitors release a similar model before he did and humiliate Toyota for being a "copycat." Wada gave a twelve-month deadline to his team, scheduling the release of the prototype at the 1995 Tokyo Motor Show, which he believed would be the best showcase for the new car. Though many engineers thought Wada was demanding too much at the time, they nevertheless made the deadline and unveiled the world's first hybrid concept car in October 1995.[44] It was aptly named "Prius," the Latin word for "prior" or "before," signifying its vision and leadership in innovation. But a greater mission lay ahead—turning the concept into reality.

Experimentation—Undaunted by Failure

While the neighborhood of Tsutsumi was still in a festive mood following the Prius' introduction, Hiroshi Okuda, the ebullient new president of Toyota, received an unwelcome phone call from his engineering team: the engine would not start.

Okuda was concerned. He had just boasted about Toyota's revolutionary development of a hybrid engine at the Tokyo Motor Show. Since 1993, the company had spent 1 billion dollars on the development of the hybrid. He was anticipating the final product to be released by December 1997, giving the team only two years—two-thirds the time for a conventional vehicle. Now the vehicle was not starting. What should he do?

Project failure looms large in the automotive industry, especially during initial development. Facing the skeptical eyes of sales executives and the pressure from Toyota's shareholders, Okuda decided to persist. How could he possibly tarnish Toyota's respect from the world and also Japanese pride? The Prius was a project that he could not afford to let fail.

Determined to succeed, the Prius team designed unrelenting experiments. "On the computer, the hybrid power system worked very well," said Satoshi Ogiso, the team's chief powertrain engineer, "but simulation is different from seeing if the actual part can work."[45] Even when the team finally fixed the software and electrical problems the car moved only a few hundred yards. The battery continued to fail due to extreme fluctuations in temperature. During the Prius's road test with the executives, a team member had to sit with a laptop to prevent the temperature from soaring.[46] To find the right hybrid system, the team went through 80 alternative hybrid engine technologies and 20 different suspension systems before focusing on four designs, which were then refined in extensive detail.[47] Although a thousand Toyota engineers were racing day and night to fix the problems, the team still found itself running short of time. "Ordinarily we get two to three months to make sketches and prepare models," said designer Erwin Lui, "for Prius we got two to three weeks."[48]

Despite facing unceasing technological difficulties, Okuda continued to press on with the Prius. Some analysts estimated that Toyota had invested more than $1 billion on the power controller alone.[49] If you consider this gamble, then few projects can match the stakes of the Prius. With patience and persistence, the team eventually cleared the obstacles. It added a radiator to an electronic component to prevent overheating; it installed a redesigned semiconductor to keep the vehicle from breaking down.[50]

Finally in October 1997, Toyota unveiled its first-generation Prius, two months ahead of schedule. Its performance? It logged an impressive 66 miles per gallon—the 100% improvement Wada had targeted.[51]

Slow Takeoff—A Testament of Toyota's Faith and Patience

Just as Okuda could finally take a breather after the successful development of the Prius, a new challenge lay ahead. Commercialization of the car proved to be just as difficult as its development. Despite the Prius's unprecedented achievement—the first serious competitor to the internal combustion engine since the early 1900s—not everyone was enthusiastic about the invention. Sales managers in the United States were extremely skeptical. They weren't sure if the Prius was really a car. Uncertain that a better fuel economy could attract consumers at the premium price, they wondered if having both the Prius and the Corolla in their lineup would necessitate selling the former at a loss.

In fact, marketing research supported the sales executives' skepticism. Chrysler Corporation's research showed that fuel economy ranked 19th among reasons to buy a car, right after "quality of the air-conditioning."[52] Skepticism and unfamiliarity of the hybrid's technology frightened consumers: when the Japanese government sponsored a festival for people to try out these vehicles on a rainy weekend, many people declined the offer in fear that the electric car would electrocute them.[53] "It's difficult to build consumer technology awareness," said Chris Hostetter, then vice president of advanced-product strategy. "Consumers would have to be taught that the car didn't come with an extension cord. Dealers would have to be trained on how to sell the car and service it."[54] When Toyota invited people in Orange County to try out the Prius, unfavorable reviews soared. Drivers complained about the feel of the brakes, the cheap interior look, and its small. "It was a Japan car," said Bill Reinert, national manager of advanced-technology vehicles, "and it seemed out of context in the U.S."[55]

Initial sales statistics proved the sales managers right. Although the Prius enjoyed some encouraging reception at its launch in Japan, its prospect in the United States was dismal. When the Prius entered the United States in July 2000, oil and gasoline prices hit a record low in the United States. Worse, although the Prius was the first hybrid car introduced in the world, Honda's hybrid, the Insight, reached the U.S. market first. Due to competition from its major rival and low demand, Toyota had to sell the car at a loss, pricing it at $19,995, two-thirds the production cost.[56] It initially lost between $10,000 and $16,000 per car, amounting to about a $100 million loss per year.[57] With scant volume and low profit, Toyota could hardly afford to advertise the car. The marketing of the car was based mostly on word of mouth, public relations, and the Internet. Foreseeing a gloomy start for the hybrid, the U.S. sales team drafted a contingency plan of issuing cut-rate leases, rental coupons, free maintenance, and roadside assistance to boost sales.[58]

As a comparison, GM's first hybrid model, the EV1, incurred a loss of between $1,000 and $2,000 per car after its launch in the United States in 1996. GM eventually withdrew the model from the market seven years later, in 2003, due to its heavy losses.[59] With the EV1 as its precedent, no one knew how long the Prius could stand in the market before it drained Toyota's financial resources. Toyota was risking big.

Eventual Success

Toyota's patience and persistence eventually paid off. As the wave of environmentalism and green energy in the United States continued to grow, the Prius eventually caught on. The company finally began making a profit on the current third-generation Prius, *no less than ten years* after its initial launch in the United States.[60] The eco-friendly car became the new fashion statement. The purchase of the Prius by celebrities such as Leonardo DiCaprio and Cameron Diaz made the car an overnight sensation. A survey conducted by CNW Marketing Research of Bandon, Oregon, in 2007 shows that about half of the Prius owners said they bought the Prius because the car "makes a statement about me" rather than because they were concerned about "lower emission."[61] Built from the ground up as a hybrid, the Prius's distinct design enabled it to outperform its hybrid competitors, such as Honda Civic, Ford Escape, and Saturn Vue, whose appearances were almost indistinguishable from their gas-guzzling counterparts.

Corporations were quick to take part in the Prius hype. Bank of America launched an environmental program that would subsidize its employees $3,000 for a purchase of a new Prius. More than 185,000 Bank of America employees were eligible for this program.[62] Farmers Insurance Group offered up to 10% of insurance discount to customers with a hybrid car. Hyperion, a software company, committed over $1 million a year toward its hybrid purchase initiative that would offer its employees $5,000 for each purchase of a hybrid.[63] Godfrey Sullivan, CEO of Hyperion, believed that the message that the program delivered outweighed the cost: "We are not necessarily going to change the world through this initiative, but it's our aim at Hyperion to get people thinking about change, about making a difference."[64]

Facing the outcry for environmental protection and CO_2 emission reduction, governments worldwide offered various incentives to encourage the sale of the hybrid car. In an effort to promote green energy and boost consumption, Obama's stimulus program, "Cash for Clunkers," offered buyers a rebate of as much as $4,000 on the purchase of the Prius. That promotion tripled sales of the model.[65] While Los Angeles and San Jose, California, exempted hybrid owners from high-occupancy vehicle lane restrictions and street parking fees, Prius drivers in New York State got the special "E-Z pass" that would give them 10% discount on tolls for using the New York Thruway System.[66] In the United Kingdom, hybrid owners had to pay only £15 a year for road tax and £10 to register for an annual exemption from the £8 daily London congestion charge (£1 is about $1.6).[67] In the Netherlands, companies that own the Prius paid only 14% of car tax as opposed to the regular 25%.[68] Pride of ownership combined with its short supply made the Prius a much sought-after item on the market. The Prius retained 57% of its value after three years and only 2% of buyers opted to lease.[69] In 2010, the Prius had the best resale value of all hybrid cars.[70] The numerous awards that the Prius has won are testimonies to its success (see Table 3.4).[71] However, the glory of success can easily mask the long road, the numerous obstacles, the tough marketing, and the great risk that developers of the Prius endured.

Table 3.4. Awards for Prius

2003	"Business Leader of the Year" *Scientific American*
2004	"Car of the Year" *Motor Trend*
2004	"Ten Best List" *Car and Driver*
2004	"North American Car of the Year"
2004	"International Engine of the Year"
2004	"Best Engineered Vehicle"
2005	"European Car of the Year"
2006	EnerGuide Award
2006	Intellichoice Best Overall Value of the Year for Mid-Size Cars
2007	Intellichoice Best in Class Winner: Best Retained Value, Lowest Fuel, Lowest Operating Costs, Lowest Ownership Costs
2008	"Green Engine of the Year"
2009	"Most Dependable Compact Car" JD Power & Associates
2010	"Best Vehicle of the Year" *MotorWeek*

Gambling on Growth: Amazon.com

In 2010, Amazon seemed like a tremendous success story. This case is based primarily on research in Gerard J. Tellis and Peter Golder, *Will and Vision: How Latecomers Grow to Dominate Markets* (New York: McGraw-Hill. 2001). Beginning as a start-up in 1994, it has grown rapidly to a huge corporation. By early 2010 it had sales of $9.5 billion, gross profits of $2 billion, and a market capitalization of $69 billion, much larger than Sony and 69 *times* the size of the leading brick-and-mortar bookstore, Barnes and Noble.[72] How did Amazon.com achieve this amazing success? What is its secret to success? In brief, the answer would be: growing rapidly by fully satisfying shoppers and innovating in every facet of the business to do so. However, achieving these goals required massive investments while tolerating repeated losses. Indeed, the company's innovations and investments kept incurring losses all the way from its founding until 2004, when it posted its first profitable year.[73]

Nick Hanauer, an early investor in the company, said of this strategy, "What few people understood was that the reason that they [we, Amazon.com,] didn't make money was that for the previous five years every time there was a trade-off between making more money or growing faster, we grew faster. It wasn't that there weren't lots of opportunities to make money. It was just that we had consciously foregone those opportunities to reach scale and make it impossible to duplicate what we had done."[74] But growth was not an end in itself. The overriding goal of the company was to make the customer's experience of purchasing through Amazon.com as complete and satisfying as possible. Jeff Bezos sums up this goal very well, "The better you can make your customer experience . . . the more customers you'll attract, the larger share of that household's purchases you will attract. You can become a bigger part of a customer's life by just simply doing a better job for them. It's a very, very simple-minded approach."[75]

Amazon.com was not the first Web bookstore.[76] What made the company unique was Bezos's philosophy, summed up in his own words above, and his effort in achieving it through innovations and investments while sacrificing immediate profits. A review of Amazon's history describes the dedication with which founder and CEO Bezos implemented this strategy. From the very beginning his priority was to make the customer's experience as enjoyable as possible by assuring a wide selection (of books), low prices, speedy delivery, and guaranteeing satisfaction. He stated, "I think the main thing that has differentiated Amazon.com from conventional retailers is its obsessive/compulsive focus on the end-to-end customer experience. That includes having the right products, the right selection, and low prices."[77] Bezos incorporated the company in 1994 and launched the Web site in 1995.

Jeff Bezos first got the idea of an Internet bookstore when doing research as a vice president for D. E. Shaw & Company in New York. He came to the conclusion that books would be a good item to sell online because of the then rapid growth of the Internet (2300%) and the massive inventory returns in the current distribution system (34%).[78] He then put his thinking into deeds by deciding to abandon his current profession and start up an online bookstore. David Shaw, the company's founder, asked him to reconsider his plan to leave the security of a generous salary and the status of vice president. However, Bezos was unafraid of the risk, as he told *Time*, "I knew that when I was 80 there was no chance that I would regret having walked away from my 1994 Wall Street bonus in the middle of the year.... But I did think there was a chance that I might regret significantly not participating in this thing called the Internet that I believed passionately in. I also knew that if I tried and failed I would not regret that."[79]

Innovations were central to the success of Amazon.com. For this purpose, Bezos hired the most talented employees he could identify and challenged them to high standards of performance. Employees' creative abilities were an important criterion for recruiting. Says Bezos, "People here like to invent and as a result other people who like to invent are attracted here. And people who don't like to invent are uncomfortable here. So it's self-reinforcing."[80] Bezos supported a "Just Do It" program which rewarded employees for developing and implementing innovations even without the permission of their bosses.[81] One of his earliest innovations was owning and operating large warehouses to inventory the books (and later other products) that he sold. Subsequently, the company innovated by relying on other suppliers' warehouses. One of the early innovations that greatly facilitated customer satisfaction with the website was one-click buying. Amazon.com has the patent for this innovation,[82] though it is widely copied in one form or another by other websites.

Another major innovation of the company was enabling readers' reviews and ratings of books (that was later extended to other products). This feature created a growing body of user-generated content on each product, which was convenient to use, relevant to the customer base, and always current. Having readers rate the reviews facilitated ordering of reviews by rank and usefulness, adding further value to this feature. This feature created one of the first online communities. A related innovation was the ranking of each book or product on Amazon sales. This innovation was another community feature that gave a direct measure of popularity and indirectly, a crude measure of quality. Scott Lipsky, a former Amazon executive said, "Amazon was probably the first truly worldwide community that was built online. They happened to sell books. But the simple fact that everyone was sharing their thoughts and book reviews made it a community unto itself."[83] A continuous stream of innovations was the company's offering of other consumer products on the same website. Initially it was CDs and movies, then toys, electronics, video games, software, and home improvement. Later they added apparel, sports, outdoors, and gourmet food. More radical innovations were the diversification into auctions and co-vendors of merchandise.

Perhaps the most radical, recent innovation has been the introduction of its own product, the Kindle, an electronic reader. The risks of doing so were twofold: Amazon was a service company, not a hardware company. Moving away from its expertise was a huge risk. Also, success of the Kindle ran the risk of cannibalizing its primary business—print books. Nevertheless, Amazon not only moved ahead, but did so by launching versions of the Kindle at a fraction of the price of rival models. The lowest price was $79 as of 2011. The highest-priced version, Kindle Fire, was $300 less than the lowest priced iPad and sold at a loss. However, sales of Kindle books justified the bold and risky strategy.

Thus, Amazon's success grew from its unrelenting and highly risky innovation. These innovations made the site a one-stop shop for consumers and provided them with a complete and satisfying experience.

Bezos originally forecast profitability in the second or third year.[84] However, introducing all these innovations and especially extending into all these product categories was an investment-intense undertaking. The company did everything on a large scale. As such, investments had to be huge. In the first few years, there were no profits to show. The company kept growing by borrowing or selling equity for investments while steadily increasing the size and riskiness of the enterprise. Bezos started the company in 1994 with an investment of $50,000 from his savings. The following year, he persuaded his parents to invest $250,000 from their savings. Sales for the first year were good at $511,000. However, due to marketing expenses, product development, and other expenses, the company had a loss of $303,000.[85]

Still Bezos decided to increase and not decrease the scale of operation. In 1996, he raised $8 million from KPCB for a 12% share of the equity in the company. However, he invested about $6 million in marketing and $2 million in product development for a massive loss of $ $5.8 million despite revenues of $16 million. All these losses were not accidental. The company's prospectus for the 1997 IPO stated quite clearly, "The Company believes that it will incur substantial operating losses for the foreseeable future and that the rate at which losses will be incurred will increase significantly from current levels."[86]

In 1997, Bezos had two figures to be proud of. He raised $45 million through an IPO and reached sales of $148 million. However, he spent $40 million in marketing and $13 million in product development, in addition to other costs of goods and distribution, so that he had another losing year with losses totaling

$28 million.[87] That year Barnes and Noble entered the online business with lower prices than Amazon. Bezos decided to fight the competition head-on and not be outdone in prices, even at the cost of further losses. His letter to the shareholders outlined his philosophy, "We will continue to make investment decisions in light of long-term market leadership considerations rather than short-term profitability considerations or short-term Wall Street reactions.... We will make bold rather than timid investment decisions where we see sufficient probability of gaining market leadership advantages."[88]

In the next two years, Bezos continued to build the business aggressively, growing sales to $610 million in 1998 (growth of 313% over 1997) and $10 billion in 1999. This growth involved massive levels of borrowing and investing in marketing, product development, and warehousing to support this level of rapid growth. However, due to aggressive marketing, sales, pricing, and product strategies, losses grew to $125 million in 1998, a 346% increase over 1997. This pattern of growth continued in 1999, with sales reaching $294 million and losses amounting to $36 million.

In subsequent years, the company still did not have profits, while it came under tremendous pressure to do so. Analysts criticized the strategy of growth without profits, believing that "Amazon's Get-Big-Fast strategy was doomed."[89] Things took a turn for the worse with the bust in Internet stocks in 2000 and the ensuing recession. The worst year was 2001, when Amazon.com showed a total loss of $1.4 billion for the year. The company began many cost-cutting measures, including layoffs and trimming product offerings. However, innovations did not stop. The situation began to improve slowly and subsequently Amazon.com posted its first profitable year in 2004 (see Figure 3.2). Although the company again became the butt of jokes when the stock market crashed in

Figure 3.2. Amazon's Losses Relative to Sales Over Time

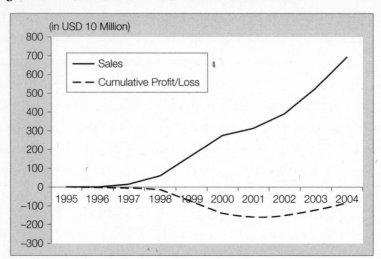

2008 and 2009, it had a quick turnaround toward the end of 2009 and early 2010.

In hindsight, Amazon's story is one of amazing growth and success. Beneath the surface, that initial growth and subsequent profit were bought with massive, risky investments in marketing, product development, and warehousing. The road to success was rocky. Bezos showed tremendous courage and undertook huge risks to realize his vision for the company.

Gambling on Vision: Facebook

Since its origins in 2004, Facebook grew in six years to become the second most visited site on the Internet. That success is due primarily to a continuous stream of innovations introduced under constant risk. The risk arose from internal pressure about the dangers of those innovations and external pressure to sell out to venture capitalists and other buyers for a quick gain. At times the founder, Mark Zuckerberg, almost caved in. But he ultimately resisted all those pressures to realize his vision of a transparent, open, and highly accessible social networking site. A brief review of the rise of Facebook reveals the many tough tradeoffs Zuckerberg regularly faced.

Hatch of an Idea in a Dorm Room

One October in 2003, Mark Zuckerberg, a sophomore in computer science at Harvard, thought up a nifty idea.[90] He compiled ID photos of his fellow residents by hacking into nine Harvard Houses' online face books. With these photos he created a website called Facemash, where viewers can vote for the hotter of two randomly chosen photos or rate the looks of students in a particular House against other residents. Within four hours, 450 students visited the site and voted at least 22,000 times.[91] The site lived for only a few days before students' outrage over the site's privacy violation compelled Zuckerberg to shut it down. Zuckerberg was almost expelled from Harvard for his unauthorized access of the school's network. Nevertheless, the unexpected success of Facemash validated the popularity of such networks and prompted him to start his next project—The Facebook.

At the time, Harvard did not have a student directory with photos.[92] "Everyone's been talking a lot about a universal face book within Harvard," Zuckerberg said. "I think it's kind of silly that it would take the University a couple of years to get around to it. I can do it better than they can, and I can do it in a week."[93] A son of a dentist in New York, Zuckerberg displayed his talent in computer programming at an early age. As a high school senior in Phillips Exeter Academy, Zuckerberg and his friend Adam D'Angelo built a plug-in for the MP3 player Winamp that would customize users' playlists based on their listening habits, much like today's radio site Pandora.[94] They offered the service online for free, attracting thousands of users and catching the attention of AOL and Microsoft, which both offered them a job. However, Zuckerberg and D'Angelo opted for colleges.[95]

Indeed, Zuckerberg coded thefacebook.com in a week and launched the site on February 4, 2004. Within 24 hours, twelve hundred Harvard students had signed up and it took only two weeks for it to reach half of the Harvard student body.[96] Zuckerberg's roommates, Dustin Moskovitz and Chris Hughes, soon joined in to help Zuckerberg add features such as "poking"—a flirtatious alert to attract a recipient's attention. They paid $85 a month to a Web-hosting company to maintain the service free to Harvard students. However, the infectious appeal of the site soon exceeded the host's limit. By May, Zuckerberg had expanded the network to more than thirty elite schools. Banner ads had generated a few thousand dollars to the project.[97]

But that still would not sustain Facebook's rapid growth. (It was then known as thefacebook.com. The company later purchased the shorter domain name facebook.com for $200,000). Knowing Facebook's need for funds, a well-connected classmate of Zuckerberg introduced him to several financiers in Manhattan, one of whom offered $10 million on the spot for the site.[98] Such an offer would be tempting for any 20-year-old college student whose website was only four months old, yet Zuckerberg was willing to forego this quick gain to gamble on something bigger. He headed to Silicon Valley that summer to put his ideas to a test.[99]

Bet on Silicon Valley

"We just wanted to go to California for the summer," recalled Zuckerberg, perhaps masking the uncertainty and hope in the move.[100]

Zuckerberg, Moskovitz, and Hughes arrived with no car, no job, and no connection. They sublet a four-bedroom house as an office and bunkhouse.[101] As Facebook's exponential growth necessitated more servers, the team found itself in a dire financial situation. Zuckerberg spent his savings of about $20,000 in the first few weeks in Palo Alto.[102] But this was far from enough to sustain the site's swelling growth. He risked having to spend more or shutting down and going home.

That was when Sean Parker came into the picture. Parker was the cofounder of Napster and later of Plaxo, an online contacts management network that had raised millions of dollars. Parker was moving out of his apartment to find a new place to stay.[103] As he was unloading from his boxes into his white BMW, he bumped into Zuckerberg and his colleagues. Zuckerberg, who had long admired this Internet entrepreneur, asked him to crash in with them.[104] So through this accidental encounter, Parker joined the team. By September, Zuckerberg made Parker the president of Facebook.

Besides providing a decent car and buying alcohol for house parties—since he was the only one in the group over 21—Parker brought in connections and valuable advice during the early stage of Facebook. Parker's prior conflicts with and losses to venture capitalists sensitized Zuckerberg of the risk of losing control of the start-up to gain capital. He was subsequently very wary of venture capitalists. Parker's connection in Silicon Valley brought in the first investor to the company—Peter Thiel, a one-time CEO of PayPal. After Zuckerberg's presentation on Facebook, Thiel agreed to lend $500,000 to the kids in exchange for a 10.2% of the company, leading to a value of $4.9 million.[105] Although the valuation was lower than what Zuckerberg had previously got in Manhattan, he appreciated how Thiel, unlike other venture capitalists, trusted him with complete control over the young company.

As the 2004 fall semester approached, Facebook continued to grow, doubling its membership to 200,000. Zuckerberg now faced a life-changing dilemma. He had just secured funds of $500,000 and a foothold in Silicon Valley. To sustain Facebook's growth, he needed greater commitment and funds. Should he continue the risky summer project in Silicon Valley or go back to school to earn a secure degree?[106] Many of his colleagues wondered if Facebook was merely a fad and questioned whether this dorm project was worthy enough a cause to drop out of school. Despite the risk, Zuckerberg gave up the security for his dream, aspiring to make real social change through Facebook.

Risk-Loving Hacker Culture

One of the keys to Facebook's rapid expansion was its embrace of risk. Even though the company expanded over time to a point where staffers could no longer tap on each other's shoulder, Zuckerberg kept the company's pipeline short. Its tolerance of failure allowed its engineers to experiment freely and iterate innovations in real time. Zuckerberg encouraged his engineers to move fast, pushing new code to be tested daily: "We think eventually you get judged not by how you look but by what you build. I think there's a lot of pressure inside of companies where people want to optimize for a launch to go smoothly. But really you want to be the best over time. Take more risk. If we do those, we have a good shot of succeeding."[107] Although Facebook, with serious investor support, could no longer operate like a frivolous dorm project, its hacker culture lived on. "What most people think when they hear the word 'hacker' is breaking into things," said Zuckerberg, "but in Facebook, it's about being unafraid to break things in order to make them better."[108]

Zuckerberg kept his commitment to small teams where an individual voice could be heard and innovative ideas could be realized quickly through collaboration. He maintained weekly product updates, but if his team desired to test an idea, it could push the code to a group of users daily. To Zuckerberg, hacker culture is the collective effort to build something "bigger, better, and faster" than individuals can do alone. "The root of the hacker mind-set is 'There's a better way,'" said Paul Buchheit, the developer of Gmail at Google and cofounder of FriendFeed who joined Facebook after it acquired FriendFeed. "Just because people have been doing it the same way since the beginning of time, I'm going to make it better."[109] The risk-loving hacker culture of Facebook indeed manifested itself through rapid deployment of new features. For example, in September 2004, the team added group applications and its idiosyncratic "wall," a summary page on which you and others could write.[110] By December 2004, ten months after its creation, Facebook reached one million users.[111]

It was soon apparent that Thiel's money would not be enough to sustain Facebook's growth. In May 2005, with the help of Thiel, Zuckerberg raised $12.7 million from Accel Partners, allowing him to expand Facebook's service to more than eight hundred college networks.[112] Every expansion was fraught with risks. One risk was in diluting the elitist origins of the network, especially when it expanded beyond the Ivy League. The other risk was of overloading the network with traffic, without any immediate increase in revenues or apparent benefit. Always on the founders' minds was the demise of Friendster, an older, hugely successful network that failed when traffic unbearably slowed down service. Supporting Facebook's expanded traffic required thousands of dollars in new, more powerful servers.

In the summer of 2005, Facebook entertained expanding the network to high school students. This move had several risks. First, there was again the danger of being overwhelmed with traffic. Another potential problem was the negative reaction of college students who would find their network populated with high school kids. Then there was the risk of allowing e-mail addresses that did not have the certainty of identity of college e-mail addresses. In addition, many parents were opposed to their schoolchildren being on Facebook due to the exposure of minors to online predators. Nevertheless, Zuckerberg prevailed in his arguments to expand the network. In September 2005, Facebook included high school students, resulting in 5.5 million active users. The following month, Facebook added a photosharing feature onto the site. That move almost burned down the site's infrastructure due to the exploding technical demand.

Nevertheless, the growing popularity of the site with added features convinced Silicon Valley's venture capitalists to continue investing, allowing Zuckerberg to bring in $27.5 million in April 2006.[113] Zuckerberg then increased its users by adding work networks.

In September 2006, Zuckerberg made a highly risky move of opening the site to everyone with a valid e-mail address. Students were not happy with the swarms of people who joined the site. They may have been uncomfortable being friends with parents and relatives from whom they wanted to maintain a separate identity and life. While some students rushed to delete their X-rated party pictures, others joined online petitions threatening to leave Facebook. The expansion, which diluted Facebook's exclusive appeal, risked the site becoming the second MySpace. "I didn't realize it from the outside, but the change in going from a [college-student-only] site to being open to the world was extremely controversial," said Paul Buchheit. "Most people [at Facebook] thought it was a bad idea and was going to ruin the site."[114] Despite the strong opposition, Zuckerberg persisted on his vision to make the world more transparent, open, and connected. His missionary zeal steered Facebook clear of all hurdles that would derail its growth. Students eventually adapted to the change. Facebook's user numbers skyrocketed.

News Feed Crisis

Zuckerberg's tolerance for risk at times blinded him to Facebook's users' sentiments. The rashness showed up when Facebook introduced News Feed, which broadcasts users' online activities to everyone they have friended on Facebook. This set off a backlash in the Facebook community, particularly college-bound users, who felt that the new feature had intruded upon their privacy, never mind that their eagerness to share their personal information was the mainstay of Facebook's existence. Taking advantage of the new issue-oriented feature—"global groups"—angry users created a group called "Students Against Facebook News Feed," ironically attracting more than seven hundred thousand users through News Feed ("Your friend has just joined this group") in less than 48 hours.[115] Zuckerberg rushed to install a privacy option three days later that allowed users to control their information flow. "We really messed this one up," Zuckerberg wrote in his open apology letter.[116]

The crisis eventually cooled down. Zuckerberg later claimed that News Feed had been the most successful move for the site. "Once people had the controls and knew how to use them, they loved News Feed," said Zuckerberg.[117] The News Feed crisis did not discourage Zuckerberg from taking risks. "Regardless of what we do, if it changes the site, there will be reactions. Change is really disruptive for people, especially if you're providing a web service that people aren't opting into directly," Zuckerberg said. "Values are worthless unless they're controversial. We want to move quickly. We're willing to give up a huge amount of stuff in order to move quickly."[118]

To Sell or Not to Sell

It did not take long for Facebook to whet the media giants' appetite. In fall 2005, just as the site was reaching five million users, Zuckerberg started getting instant messages from Michael

Wolf, president of Viacom's MTV network, expressing his interest to meet with Zuckerberg in Palo Alto. In December, Wolf offered Zuckerberg an attractive opportunity to get together while he was visiting in San Francisco. Wolf offered Zuckerberg a ride home to New York for the holidays, in Viacom's corporate jet.[119]

Zuckerberg fell for the bait. Because Viacom's corporate jet was in fact unavailable, Wolf chartered a first-rated Gulfstream V to take him to the east coast. During the five uninterrupted hours with Zuckerberg aboard, Wolf discreetly suggested his intention to acquire Zuckerberg's firm. But the 21-year-old Zuckerberg maintained a healthy distance, interrogating Wolf about his MTV business instead, with particular interest in advertising.

Finally, before the plane landed, Zuckerberg said, "This plane is amazing!" Wolf took the opportunity and replied: "Maybe you should just sell a piece of the company to us. Then you can have one for yourself."[120]

Over the next few months, Wolf continued to pursue Zuckerberg. He made a cash offer of $800 million and provisions that could make it worth as much as $1.5 billion.[121] For a small business that was just a year old and involved small investments by the cofounders, this sum must have seemed astronomical.[122] Selling the company would solve the site's financial problems, for the site was running at a loss. Zuckerberg, who still lived in his sparsely furnished rented apartment, could take home a handsome sum of money.[123] He could cut short the uncertainty and walk away with a sure, huge monetary payoff. But Zuckerberg had an ambitious vision in mind. He wanted to build a comprehensive "social graph" that would revolutionize how people interact with each other. He wanted to change the world. "I don't really need any money," he told Wolf. "And anyway, I don't think I'm ever going to have an idea this good again."[124]

A few months later, Yahoo!'s CEO Terry Semel offered $1 billion in cash to buy Facebook.[125] Zuckerberg agonized about the offer, facing intense pressure from cofounders, employees, and board members to accept. Looming over Zuckerberg's decision was the fallen giant that preceded Facebook—Friendster. It was the first social network phenomenon, and it had struggled to manage growth. Friendster ultimately failed—after turning down Google's $30 million offer in 2002 (which, if paid in stock, would have been worth about $1 billion in 2007[126]). A few weeks later, due to disappointing second quarter earnings, Yahoo! lowered its offer to $850 million. Zuckerberg was relieved and easily turned down the offer with board approval. That night he went out with his colleagues for a beer. The deal was off.[127] Paul Buchheit saw Zuckerberg's spurning the Yahoo! offer as a defining moment, "They basically gambled the whole company on that one step."[128]

"Can this kid be for real?" asked Ellen McGirt, former editor of *Fortune*, now a senior editor of *Fast Company*.[129] For those who remember the ambitions crushed and fortunes lost during the dot-com boom, selling the company for a pile of money seemed to be lucrative exit strategy for any young innovator. With founders' sales of start-ups like MySpace to News Corp for $580 million and YouTube to Google for $1.5 billion, many wondered about Zuckerberg's judgment. Zuckerberg, a member of the Google generation, seemed to be too young to have learned from the dot-com bubble.

Moreover, the competition in this market was growing intense with the entry of tech giants. Cisco acquired Five Across, which sold social networking software to corporate clients. Yahoo! built a social networking site called Yahoo! 360. Microsoft jumped into the market with the introduction of Wallop. Google dabbled with the idea of integrating social networking into its e-mail service, known as Buzz. Even Reuters tried to get into the game by developing a social network that targeted fund managers and traders. Could Facebook survive against these corporate giants? The offers from Viacom and Yahoo! seemed like sure, easy money relative to a highly uncertain future.

But Zuckerberg calmly focused on his vision. He was playing a different game. "I am here to build something for the long term," said Zuckerberg, "Anything else is a distraction."[130] An advisor to Facebook described it this way, "A lot of people say there are problems with having a 22-year-old C.E.O., but one thing that is good about it is that he doesn't remember the boom and the bust that followed. That has distorted the thinking of a lot of people. If they have a good product or service, they sell way too early and they don't stick with it."[131] Indeed, Zuckerberg stayed with the founding motto of the site: openness, transparency, and collaboration. Although many pundits in Silicon Valley deemed this precocious kid naive and foresaw a falling trajectory, Zuckerberg was steadfast with his vision, reluctant to give it away for greenbacks.

Facebook needed to grow quickly to keep itself competitive in the fast-paced Internet world. But it kept running short of funds to support the site's rapid expansion. Then, in the summer of 2007, Microsoft CEO Steve Ballmer approached Zuckerberg with a proposal. Zuckerberg knew Ballmer's intent and took him for a walk outside his office in Palo Alto. He told Ballmer that they were raising funds for Facebook's expanding infrastructure at a $15 billion valuation.[132] Zuckerberg thought the lofty $15 billion was more than any company of its size could ask for. A moment of silence ensued. But Ballmer had a more ambitious goal. He said, "Why don't we just buy you for $15 billion?"[133]

Though, Microsoft's offer was fifteen times that of Yahoo!'s, Zuckerberg's response was negative. Zuckerberg, staunchly and naively optimistic as some might argue, would rather risk his site overloading than losing full control of it. Moreover, he was determined to pursue his vision. Ballmer tried to buy the company in stages but Zuckerberg resisted all these moves.[134] Ballmer ended up paying $240 million for 1.6% share of the company. That gave Facebook the value of $15 billion, the lofty figure Zuckerberg had lobbed to Ballmer.[135]

Opening the Site to Third-Party Applications

"Crushing the competition has freed the company to gamble even harder," wrote reporter Ellen McGirt on describing why Facebook was rated as the most innovative company in 2010.[136] In May 2007, Zuckerberg redefined the level of risk for its company by opening the platform to third-party developers, allowing them to take advantage of Facebook's people connections, which grew to 41 million. In just a few months, some 80,000 developers added more than 4,000 new applications.[137] What was Facebook's return for hosting the service? None, not a cent! To outsiders, Zuckerberg seemed to be missing out on a big financial potential, but he was just fine with it. He reinforced the principles of hacker culture: "It's good for the ecosystem, good for the product, and good for the users. We want a system where anyone can develop without having our permission. There are things that we will never think of, or get around to, that would really make the user experience better."[138] To encourage developers' involvement in Facebook applications, Zuckerberg even rewarded $25,000 to $250,000 for the most innovative programs. Zuckerberg's vision of openness, transparency, and collaboration has defined social networks in the current age and fueled Facebook's growth.

This vision, however, did not come without risk, and even that is an understatement. "We've had a lot of scalability problems in the past," D'Angelo said. "If you are not careful, you can overwhelm your engineering team to the point where your servers die and your service fails."[139] As ads were still minimal and outside developers paid no fee to put their applications on the site, many investors were wary about Zuckerberg's lofty vision and his indifference to financial risks. Zuckerberg's response? "In a world that's moving quickly, you know that if you don't change you'll lose. Not taking risk is the riskiest thing you can do. You have to do things that are kind of bold even if they're not obvious."[140]

Risk Rewards

On its sixth birthday, Facebook celebrated worldwide users of almost half a billion—that's one in every twelve persons in the world! The three musketeers expanded their team to twelve hundred engineers and their territory to a new 135,000-square-foot office space in Palo Alto. The social site became so viral worldwide that it has been translated into more than seventy languages. In 2008, Collin English Dictionary declared "Facebook" as their "Word of the Year." The following year, the New Oxford American Dictionary added the verb *unfriend*, defining it as "to remove someone as a 'friend' on a social networking site such as Facebook." In September 2009, Facebook finally announced that it had turned cash flow positive for the first time, soothing the nerves of some agitated investors.[141] In April 2010, Facebook took Google's crown as the most visited website in the United States, accounting for 7.07% of U.S. Web traffic.[142] Facebook is supposed to have played an important role in the revolutions and protests in Tunisia, Libya, Egypt, Syria, and Russia. Indeed, Facebook is so powerful a social utility that some authoritarian governments, such as China, Syria, Iran, Vietnam, and recently Pakistan, have been blocking the site intermittently to prevent political uprisings. Especially satisfying to the founder must be the voice for millions of people seeking liberation.

Facebook might have a long way to go in reaching real financial success, but its enduring social influence has already manifested itself. This influence was achieved by Zuckerberg's unrelenting innovation with a risk-loving culture that he cultivates inside his company. Had Zuckerberg taken the $10 million from Manhattan six years ago, or the millions and billions offered subsequently, Facebook might never have gone so far. Had Zuckerberg not taken the risk of successively opening the site to new segments of the public, it might have been forgotten by its passionate college students once they graduated. Had Zuckerberg not been unrelenting in innovations, any competing site or Internet giant would have surpassed Facebook in audience. Zuckerberg gave up opportunities of quick gains to achieve his goal to make the world a freer and more connected place.

Gambling on Scale: Federal Express

Fred Smith conceived of Federal Express in a now-famous term paper he submitted in a class at Yale in 1966. This case is based primarily on research in Gerard J. Tellis and Peter Golder, *Will and Vision: How Latecomers Grow to Dominate Markets* (New York: McGraw-Hill, 2001) and Robert A. Sigafoos, *Absolutely, Positively Overnight!* (Memphis, TN: St. Luke's Press, 1983). After a short but successful military service in Vietnam and some work to build up his inherited business, in June 1971, Smith founded Federal Express. In July 1975, the company had its first profitable month. In 1976, the company became the dominant shipper in the small-parcel airfreight business. That was also its first profitable year (see Figure 3.3). From then on, shipments and profits increased rapidly. Despite increasing competition, Fred Smith maintained leadership of the market he started through highly risky but unrelenting innovation.

However, the great success of Federal Express masks the enormous risks that Fred Smith undertook to commercialize his

Figure 3.3. Early Growth of Federal Express

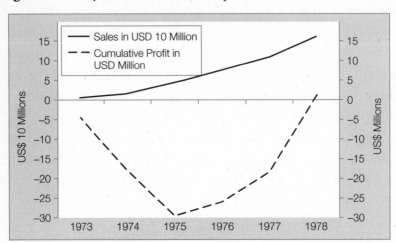

innovation. Smith envisaged a system with dedicated trucks, planes, and warehouses so that the entire shipping business promised fully controllable and reliable overnight delivery.

Also, for overnight delivery all over the United States (or at least the major cities), the system had to start with a minimum number of trucks, planes, and professional employees, including pilots and mechanics. Thus, the company had to start off on a huge scale involving massive initial investments even without any revenues. Making a success of this enterprise was a gigantic undertaking fraught with great risks that Smith himself never foresaw. The glory surrounding Smith's ultimate success often overlooks the difficulties of establishing Federal Express. Smith's term paper did not envisage the costs of implementing the new system. It did not provide details of the new system. The market research studies he commissioned barely covered the difficulties of the task and grossly underestimated the financing required. Indeed, the project almost collapsed or failed several times. Success emerged only through his fearless embrace of risks and dauntless efforts to bring the enterprise to fruition.

For example, over a year after July 1972, when he raised $52 million in financing, Smith's entire time was consumed trying to gain fresh funding or ward off previous financiers demanding repayments or threatening foreclosure. Smith describes the hardships of this time, "No man on this earth will ever know what I went through during that year, and I am lucky I remember my name much less the details that you are trying to ask me. With the trauma that year, the pressure was so great on me, and there were so many events that went on, and so much travel and so many meetings with investment bankers, General Dynamics, and a hundred different people who came down to Memphis, I just don't recall specifics of virtually anything during that period of time, in addition to trying to run a company at the same time."[143]

In addition to seeking funds for his start-up, Smith had to carry out numerous other tasks in a short time period. He thrice had to negotiate with government agencies for relief from regulations: to reduce the weight limitations for cargo jets, to get adequate gasoline during the oil embargo, and to fly larger jets. He also had to negotiate with local Memphis officials for routing air traffic at his new hub. He had to modify the Falcon jets, for which he purchased an aircraft shop in Little Rock. He had to supervise the recruitment and training of pilots, truck drivers, salesmen, office staff, and managers. For this, he could only offer hope of a brighter future rather than a big salary. Most important, he had to win new business. Art Bass, company president, says this of Smith, "This Company should have died five or six times in its first three or four years, but Fred refused to give up. Boy, was he tenacious. With sheer bull and courage he pulled off a miracle. That's the only way to express what he did."[144]

CONCLUSION

This chapter makes a number of important points about innovation and risk, which is essential to succeeding with innovation.

- Risk occurs because of the heavy up-front investment, the long gestation period of innovations, the great uncertainty of success, and especially the high failure rate.

- The failure rate of innovations is steep and occurs at all stages. One may need to start with thousands of ideas to yield a few successful innovations. Thus, at its core, embracing risk implies embracing failure and learning from it.

- Incumbents and new entrants have opposite propensities to risk that can be explained by the reflection effect. When faced with an innovation, incumbents who have a steady stream of profits from current products ask, why, what do I have to gain? New entrants who have no such profits ask, why not, what do I have to lose? Thus, successful incumbents are risk averse while new entrants are risk seeking.

- The risk aversion of incumbents can also be explained by the hot-stove effect. When faced with a new technology, incumbents may have many small failures and missteps. They could respond by avoiding all future work on the innovation. As such, they learn the wrong lessons from failure. Alternatively, we can say they fail to learn from errors, like Mark Twain's cat that avoids all stoves for life because she once sat on a hot stove.

- Another effect that explains risk aversion toward innovation is that of expectations. Innovators often approach innovations with high expectations, for early profits, or early sales, or both. In effect, for most innovations, both sales and profits are typically slow in coming. False expectations may lead to prematurely aborting a promising innovation.

- All of these effects translate into a failure to make the optimal risk tradeoffs. Innovations have two types of error rates, Type 1 (failed innovations) and Type 2 (missed innovations). These two errors are linked by the criteria used to screen innovations. Due to the effects listed above, incumbents tend to set too high a screen to minimize failed innovations. As a result, they may miss important innovations, despite having abundant resources in terms of talent, knowledge, and finances.

Mark Zuckerberg, cofounder and CEO of Facebook, states the risk tradeoff succinctly: "So many businesses just get so worried about looking like they might make a mistake that they get afraid to take any risks."[145] However, "the biggest risk you can take is to take no risk."[146]

CHAPTER 4

Focusing on the Future

Samsung's future hinges on new businesses, new
products, new technologies. As a member of Samsung,
we should see failure as a new opportunity and
constantly take on new challenges.

— SAMSUNG CHAIRMAN LEE KUN-HEE[1]

FUTURE FOCUS MEANS KEEPING an eye out for the mass
markets of the future. Despite transforming Samsung into one
of the world's largest and richest tech companies, Chairman Lee
Kun-hee realizes the transient value of current success. His quote
at the start of this chapter expresses his desire that Samsung
never lose sight of the future that belongs to new products,
businesses, and markets. A focus on the present mass market is
highly limited and at times can be fatal because current success is
highly transient. Firms need to focus on the future so that they have
a good handle on what consumers of the future will demand and
what technologies of the future will make possible. The firm that has
such a grasp is eminently capable of being prepared or even shaping
the future rather than merely reacting to it. Chairman Kun-hee
gets it. Despite success, he inculcates among his employees a sense
of urgency and a "culture of impending doom." He is "adamant
that Samsung could disappear in an instant if it misjudges the next
big trend."[2]

Looked at in reverse, every mass market today was once a
struggling niche market. And many a large, successful incumbent

was once a struggling start-up catering to a niche market. However, markets are constantly in flux and many a niche market grows to be mass market. Such growth occurs for two reasons. First, consumer tastes change. Every generation of consumers has its own favorites, hot items, and legends that cause those of the prior generation to appear dated. Niche tastes in one generation could well become mainstream in another. Second, new technologies are constantly advancing in performance at an increasing rate.[3] This progress causes new products to emerge, improve in price or quality, and serve ever-larger segments of consumers (see Chapter 8).

For example, diet soda started as a niche market for diabetics. Disposable diapers started as a niche market for travelling parents who did not want to mess with cloth diapers. Air conditioners started as a niche market for establishments that did printing. Microwaves started as a niche product for restaurants. Microcomputers started as a toy for hobbyists who wanted to build and program their own personal computers. Facebook started as a niche network for Harvard students (see Chapter 3). In all these cases, either consumer tastes changed (diet drinks) or technology improved (the other categories) to reduce costs and increase quality so that the niche market of today became the mass market of the future.

Recent research suggests that through a future focus, CEOs have a long-term impact on how firms detect, develop, and deploy new technologies over time.[4] The same study argues that CEOs' attention is a critical driver of innovation even when they focus on future events per se and not on innovation and when the outcomes are in the distant future. Further, firms whose CEOs attend to the future are faster at detecting, developing, and deploying new technologies and products than firms whose CEOs lack that attitude. That perhaps explains the success of Samsung.

Future focus is easy to understand and its importance is easy to appreciate. Yet, Professors Vijay Govindarajan and Chris Trimble of Dartmouth College suggest that most firms (and CEOs) overwhelmingly focus on the present rather than on the future.[5] Invariably, a future focus is difficult to embrace and implement. Why so?[6]

Why Future Focus Is Tough

Four psychological biases prevent firms from focusing on or correctly predicting the future: the hot-hand bias, availability bias, paradigmatic bias, and commitment bias.

Hot-Hand Bias

The hot-hand bias occurs when consumers wrongly project into the future a trend that is essentially random. One example of the hot-hand bias is the public's prediction of continued success for a "hot" basketball player who shoots a string of baskets. As a result, players, audiences, and commentators will yell, "Give 'em the ball." However, rigorous research shows that this belief is false because shooting spells of basketball players are essentially random and thus unpredictable.[7] Nevertheless, players, the public, and many sports commentators continue to believe in the hot hand because they use successful shots as evidence of the hot hand while they ignore failed shots. More generally, the hot hand occurs because decision makers project past information sequences into the future when making current decisions.[8]

How does this apply to innovation? In order to appreciate the application, one needs to understand the growth pattern of radically new products. My coauthors and I have followed the growth pattern of a large number of such products as they evolved across numerous countries. These products have spawned entirely new categories, including refrigerators, TVs, VCRs, DVDs, PCs, mobile phones, or tablets. The sales of each of the product categories include sales of all brands in a market in each of many countries of the world from the time the products *first emerged* in a market. As of now we have over seven hundred categories × countries in our database[9] and have documented our findings in a series of peer-reviewed articles.[10] The striking feature of the growth of all these new products is that they are mostly reverse Z-shaped (for example, see Figure 4.1).

Figure 4.1 shows the typical pattern of early sales growth of a radically new category in any one country of the world. What's the significance of the reverse Z-shaped curve?

The curve initially has a long period of low, almost flat sales followed by a steep growth in sales from a point we call the takeoff. When sales are low for consecutive periods, firms project the same pattern indefinitely in the future, due to the hot-hand bias.[11] As a result, the category seems to be of low potential and of little consequence. Focusing only at current flat sales prior to the

Figure 4.1. Typical Growth in Sales of Radically New Product

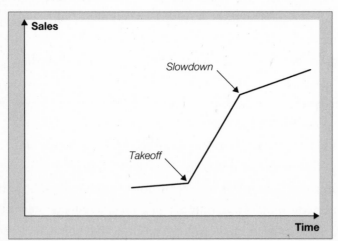

potential takeoff and ignoring the takeoff will either lead to not introducing an innovation or to prematurely pulling the plug on a promising innovation.

When the new product takes off, all hell breaks loose. Typically, the takeoff is engineered by one firm that has been persistent and innovative with the category. At that point, numerous competitors rush in to try to get a piece of the cake. A few succeed but most, including big players, fail. The firm that triggered the takeoff is in the best position to exploit the situation. It has the technology, manufacturing, and marketing to harvest the fruits of the growth of the new category. Competitors that dismissed the category have to play catch-up.

Examples will bring home this point. In the last decade, Apple has reinvented itself and become one of the largest corporations in the world because of its innovations in three categories: mobile music, smartphones, and tablets. Ironically, in each of these categories, Apple was not only not dominant—it wasn't even a player. Prior to Apple's entry, each of these categories seemed to have low potential. As a result, major incumbents in these categories either ignored them or underinvested in them. For example, Sony, the pioneer of mobile music, had an MP3 player in mobile music prior to the iPod (see Chapter 2). Blackberry, a leader in mobile phones, had a smartphone prior to the iPhone. HP, the leader in PCs and laptops, had an e-reader prior to the iPad (see Chapter 2). In all three cases, these categories probably seemed of low potential prior to Apple's entry that triggered a takeoff of the category. In the case of MP3 players, the category took off three years after the entry of the iPod. In the case of HP, the firm did not even introduce a tablet prior to the iPad. In all three cases, an analysis of the potential of the takeoff might have motivated the incumbents to have been better prepared for or even to have upstaged Apple's entry.

Many firms are unaware of the phenomenon of the takeoff, the extensive evidence in support of it, and the model now available to predict it. As a result, they tend to undervalue and underinvest in a radically new category prior to its takeoff. When the takeoff does emerge, they are unprepared. They then tend to rush into the category, which then attracts a large number of competitors.

A future focus means realizing that radical innovations often have a slow start. It is imperative to ascertain the likelihood of a takeoff and predict it. Fortunately, we have developed both a model to predict the takeoff and have identified drivers that affect and can control takeoff. The section "Planning for the Future" in this chapter will explain these issues.

Availability Bias

The availability bias (or availability heuristic) refers to a phenomenon in which people wrongly provide a higher probability for the occurrence of an infrequent event than of a frequent one. This phenomenon was first documented by two well-known psychologists, Amos Tversky and Daniel Kahneman.[12] Consider the following examples:

Which is a more frequent cause of death:

- Homicide or emphysema?
- Tornadoes or lightning?
- Vehicular accident or lung cancer?
- Shark attacks or sand hole collapse?

When asked these questions, a majority of people (as perhaps the readers) answer the first option in these pairs, homicide, tornadoes, vehicular accident, and shark attacks. In fact, as a cause of death, emphysema is 1.01 times as likely as homicide, lightning is 1.15 times as likely as tornadoes, lung cancer is 1.28 times as likely as vehicular accidents, and sand hole collapse is 1.45 times as likely as shark attacks.[13] Why does this happen? The simple reason is that people consider the likelihood based on examples of these events that come to mind.[14] The media report those events that are sensational precisely because they are infrequent and make for good news. In these examples, media reports are much higher for homicide than emphysema, tornadoes than lighting, vehicular accidents than lung cancer, and shark attacks than sand hole collapse. Thus, people wrongly consider the more heavily reported events as more likely even though in reality they are less likely.

What has this got to do with innovation? The availability bias afflicts managers in one important way. Managers are immersed in the products, technologies, and consumers of the present. They have to meet schedules, analyze performance, and resolve crises for current markets. Often, managers move from crisis to crisis merely out of necessity. Thus, the present is more available to managers. The future seems remote because it is further off and does not impinge on them immediately; that is, the present looms larger than the future, the current looms larger than the distant. However, innovations are typically about future products, technologies, and customers. Radical innovations are about a future that is quite hard to envisage. But because of the availability bias, managers end up emphasizing the present over the future and focus on decisions about the present over those about the future.

Further, at the time that new technologies first emerge, many of them are inferior in performance to the dominant technology being used to meet consumers' needs[15] (see Chapter 8). Still, the new technologies are important for two reasons. First, they are superior to the dominant technology on a secondary dimension that serves a small niche of consumers. This niche could well grow to be large in the future. Second, the emerging technologies may improve in performance in the future and attract the attention of the future mass market. Because both these attributes of new technologies are about the future, due to the availability bias, managers of the current dominant technology tend to discount them. Thus, the availability bias may lead managers to discount important emergent technologies that could disrupt them in the future. Later in this chapter we will discuss tools and strategies to compensate for this bias.

Paradigmatic Bias

Paradigmatic bias (or perceptual bias) refers to the phenomenon by which people's perception and interpretation of evidence is strongly colored by their priors. These priors may be their nationality, ethnicity, beliefs, or behavior. For example, Republicans and Democrats often interpret the *same evidence* about the performance of the economy with diametrically opposite explanations. On close cases (5 to 4 majorities), justices of the U.S. Supreme Court often vote according to their political leanings, even though both sides will cite the same constitution, evidence, and sometimes even case law. Paradigmatic bias is not restricted to current issues, politics, and justice. It also afflicts religion. For example, religious zealots often call faithful adherents of another religion infidels based on their own scriptures, whereas the recipients of this label return the compliment based on their own scriptures. This practice is a good example of paradigmatic bias.

Paradigmatic bias afflicts the sciences. The physicist Thomas Kuhn showed this effect in his classic book, *The Structure of Scientific Revolutions*.[16] Indeed, he is the one to whom we owe the contemporary meaning of the term *paradigm*. Though Kuhn did not give a single definition of the term, he used it to mean a shared body of problems, theories, values, and methods of research. Kuhn argued that proponents of one paradigm continue to adhere to it even in the face of mounting evidence that it fails to explain all available evidence—and even when a rival paradigm begins to better explain such evidence than the dominant paradigm. Indeed, proponents of the dominant paradigm might never abandon it! The dominant paradigm dies off because new recruits to the discipline adopt the new paradigm. Kuhn shows quite powerfully that even a field as supposedly objective as science is riddled and tormented with the paradigmatic bias.

What has this got to do with innovation? A great deal! Indeed, Thomas Kuhn's book at the surface describes the history of scientific revolutions. But what he describes as happening to revolutions in science quite neatly applies to revolutions caused by disruptive technologies. Incumbents that dominate a market often have grown large and successful based on mastery of particular technology. Professors Christine Moorman and Ann Miner find that organizational knowledge and memory about current or prior technologies can work against innovation.[17] Such knowledge can trap managers into an obsolete line of thinking that biases them against innovations for the future. Likewise, Professor Paul Leonardi of Northwestern University finds from his research that people who use a particular technology develop frames through which they view current problems and design solutions.[18] As a result, innovators from different departments using different technologies disagree about problems and solutions. As engineers are steeped in their own paradigms, they are unable to understand their disagreements. Leonardi concludes from his study, "Innovators were blind to the reasons why others disagreed with them. As discussions become more focused . . . innovators moved further away from being able to recognize the true nature of their disagreement."[19] This is a classic situation of paradigmatic bias.

For example, IBM grew to be a giant firm on the success of the mainframe computer, Xerox on dry coping, Kodak on film technology, and Microsoft on the PC operating system and office software. Such incumbents see the world through the paradigm of the dominant technology. The emergence of a disruptive innovation appears to such incumbents as an inferior means of solving current customers' needs. Indeed, on some dimensions it may well be (see Chapter 8). However, the emerging technology represents an entirely new way of solving problems that is quite different than the old way represented by the current dominant technology. Unfortunately, the paradigmatic bias prevents managers of the dominant technology from appreciating this difference and realizing the future potential of the emergent technology.

Consider some famous quotations of managers of dominant technologies when presented with an emergent technology. In 1876, Gardiner Hubbard offered to sell Alexander Graham Bell's patent for the telephone to William Orton, president of Western Union. In response, Orton said, "What use could this company make of an electrical toy?"[20] When sound first came to silent movies in 1927, Harry M. Warner of Warner Brothers said, "Who the hell wants to hear actors talk?"[21] When TV first appeared in 1946, Darryl Zanuck, head of 20th Century Fox, said, "Television won't be able to hold on to any market it captures after the first six months. People will soon get tired of staring at a plywood box every night."[22] When told of the personal computer, Ken Olsen, president and founder of DEC, a leading minicomputer maker, said in 1977, "There is no reason for any individual to have a computer in their home."[23] Once personal computers took off in the 1980s, DEC's position quickly eroded.

Soon after the iPhone's launch, RIM's cofounder Mike Lazaridis said, "The iPhone has severe limitations when it comes to effortless typing."[24] RIM (Research in Motion) was the maker of the then popular BlackBerry that dominated the smart phone market. However, in a few years, consumers took up the iPhone in large numbers, making Apple a leader in the smartphone market and shrinking RIM's share. By their choice, consumers showed that touch screens really provided effortless typing.

All these great leaders of great technologies failed to see the future because of either the availability bias or a paradigmatic bias. The second half of this chapter will discusses tools to mitigate these biases.

Commitment Bias

Commitment bias (or escalation of commitment or sunk cost fallacy) is a phenomenon in which decision makers continue to invest in a failing venture with the false hope of recovering past investments, even though evidence suggests that all future payoffs are less than the cost of future investments. Barry M. Staw may have been the first to describe this bias, in 1976.[25] The bias exists because decision makers wrongly believe that abandoning the venture at the current moment will certainly waste past investment. However, they do so even when objective analysis suggests little chance of recovering past or sunk costs. The term *commitment* is used to describe this bias because of the commitment that decision makers feel towards the venture, even when it is failing. The term *escalation of commitment* is used because in practice, the more that decision makers invest, the harder it gets to abandon the venture. The term *sunk cost fallacy* is used because the decision maker fails to see that at a current point in decision making, all past costs are really sunk, can never be "recovered," and should never be considered in the current decision about new investments. The only things that matter are new or marginal costs and new or marginal revenues.

119

Examples for the sunk cost fallacy include managers persisting in failing projects, political leaders continuing in futile wars,[26] and CEOs supporting failed mergers.[27] In all these cases, fear of writing off the loss or a false hope of recovering past investments sustain the projects far beyond justifiable time and cost. In the case of the U.S. war in Afghanistan, the presidents and generals have explicitly said that abandoning the war would mean that lives already lost would have been lost in vain.

What has this got to do with innovation? Incumbents often grow large and successful on a dominant technology. Sometimes they themselves may have pioneered that technology. When threatened with a new emergent technology, the gut reaction of incumbents is to shore up the dominant technology, reinvest in it, and use it to fight the emergent technology.[28] To a certain extent, this reasoning is logical. New technologies are constantly emerging and not every one of them will be a winner. But the right attitude is to scan the horizon, explore new alternatives, and embrace the new if they are promising. Always fighting the new is self-destructive. Indeed, even when the emergent technology is ascendant and the dominant technology is in decline, incumbents continue to invest in the dying technology. They suffer from a commitment bias. As a result, many incumbents die because of their strong commitment to a dying technology.[29]

A good example of this problem is Thomas Alva Edison. Edison is arguably the foremost innovator of all time, having over 1,090 patents to his name. He invented such innovative products as the incandescent light bulb, phonograph, movie camera, film projector, electricity generator, and DC (direct current) standard for electricity. Initially, until about 1880, DC was the standard for all electricity production and distribution in the United States. During Edison's lifetime, inventors in Europe developed the AC (alternating current) standard. Although DC was adequate initially for purposes such as light bulbs, AC became a superior standard for the more advanced uses of electricity and the higher level of production and distribution that ensued. George Westinghouse was an early believer in AC and partnered with Nikola Tesla to introduce it in the United States. Tesla himself was an employee of Edison and recommended AC to Edison. However, Tesla left when Edison rejected AC and did not compensate him enough for his contributions. Westinghouse and Tesla's efforts on behalf of AC triggered what has come to be known as the Battle of Currents of the 1880s. Numerous firms on both sides of the Atlantic were drawn into this battle with heavy investments and their survival on the line. The battle has come to be personified as a battle between Edison and Tesla.

Edison had a huge investment in DC due to his being its inventor and DC's being the basis of his business model and revenues. Because of his investment, and despite AC's superior performance, Edison worked hard to discredit it. He ran a publicity campaign for this purpose. As part of this campaign, Edison developed an electric chair to run on DC and succeeded in having it adopted for a death sentence in New York. The chair did not work well and the condemned prisoner died a slow and horrendous death. The effort to discredit AC backfired, tarnished Edison's reputation, and discredited DC. AC soon won the battle and became the dominant standard for electricity the world over. In the end, Edison regretted not having accepted Tesla's advice to switch to AC from DC. What is amazing is that even a great inventor like Edison, steeped in the merits of innovation and the cycle of creative destruction, denigrated the superior AC due to his investments in DC.

Planning for the Future

Future focus is really a mind-set that is essential for innovation. However, adopting such a mind-set is neither simple nor automatic. Certain tools and practices can help managers to get a handle on the future. More important, use of these tools or strategies on a regular basis can slowly mitigate the biases we have just described and instill future focus in the minds of managers and in the firm as a whole. Four such tools and practices are discussed next: predicting and managing takeoff, targeting future mass markets, predicting technological evolution, and analyzing emergent consumers.

Predicting and Managing Takeoff

As stated earlier in this chapter, sales of a radically new product are initially low for a long time prior to takeoff but rise dramatically after the takeoff. A deep appreciation of this phenomenon can have a profound effect on planning for a radically new product. It prevents unjustifiably high expectations early on. It increases the need for patience. Most important, it forces managers to think about the future and how they may predict and change it. Indeed, my coauthors and I have found that takeoff is partially a predictable event. We have used the hazard model for such prediction. The hazard of an event is the probability of an event given that it has not occurred as yet. It is calculated as the ratio of two probabilities (current odds of occurrence divided by cumulative odds of nonoccurrence). The hazard model comes from the medical and actuarial sciences, where it is used to predict the hazard of some event such as death or the recurrence of cancer. In innovation, we use the hazard model but in a reverse sense—to predict the new life of an innovation at the moment of takeoff. With the data we have collected and the specific context of a new product, managers can predict the time to takeoff of such a product.

To begin with, analysts need to focus on the underlying product category rather than a single brand that may have triggered the takeoff. For example, the category of MP3 players existed several years before the iPod, and tablets and e-readers existed years before the iPad. If an analyst focuses on the successful, individual brand that takes off rapidly, then he or she wrongly assigns too short a period of takeoff and wrongly raises the threshold for future products. So it's best to research all the prior brands that were launched in the category. Next, it is imperative to properly research and describe the long period of time that existed between the year of launch of the first brand in the product category and the year of takeoff. Established databases like those of GFK or Euromonitor may not always document this time period because they often track categories after or just before takeoff.

Our past research has found that some variables can influence the hazard of the takeoff of a new product. Among these are year of introduction, type of product, country of introduction, product accessories, and price. The year of introduction has an effect on time to takeoff. New products take off more rapidly now than in prior generations. For example, the average time to takeoff used to be eighteen years before World War II and is about six years in recent decades. The probable reason for this change is that information dissemination, media penetration, and technological improvements are all faster now than they were decades or half a century earlier. The type of product also influences takeoff. In particular, entertainment or what we call "fun" products generally take off faster than kitchen and laundry or what we call "work" products. The probable reason is that fun products are more visible, more talked about, and satisfy the needs of more members of the family than work products do.

The time to takeoff varies a great deal across countries. Japan and Scandinavian countries show the fastest time to takeoff. Next in time to takeoff are the United States and the midwestern European countries such as Belgium, Germany, Austria, and newly developed Asian countries such as South Korea, Taiwan, and Singapore.[30] Table 4.1

Table 4.1. Takeoff of New Products by Country

Country	Mean Time to Takeoff	Products Studied
Japan	5.4	14
Norway	5.7	15
Sweden	6.1	15
Netherlands	6.1	16
Denmark	6.1	15
United States	6.2	14
Switzerland	6.3	15
Austria	6.4	15
Belgium	6.5	16
Canada	6.9	12
Finland	7.0	15
Germany	7.1	15
S. Korea	7.2	12
Venezuela	7.3	12
United Kingdom	8.0	14
France	8.2	15
Italy	8.3	15
Spain	8.5	14
Chile	8.5	11
Mexico	8.7	11
Portugal	8.8	15
Greece	9.0	14
Brazil	9.3	11
Thailand	10.2	12
Egypt	12.1	13
Morocco	12.3	12
India	12.4	14
Philippines	12.6	13
Indonesia	13.6	15
Vietnam	13.9	14
China	13.9	16

Source: Adapted from Chandrasekaran, Deepa and Gerard J. Tellis, "Global Takeoff of New Products: Culture, Wealth or Vanishing Differences?" *Marketing Science*, 27, 5, (September–October), 844–860.

provides a full listing of differences in time to takeoff across countries as ascertained by our recent research.

There is some evidence that certain accessories are responsible for the takeoff of some products. In the high-tech world, the term used for these accessories is "killer app." For example, the availability of spreadsheets like VisiCalc may have triggered the takeoff of the personal computers.[31] The availability of browsers, especially Mosaic, may have triggered the takeoff of the World Wide Web.[32] The availability of iTunes may have triggered the takeoff of the iPod.[33]

The most important determinant of the hazard of takeoff—and one that is also controllable by managers—is price. New products take off when the price drops by 50% to 70% of the introductory price. Thus, introductory price setting is an important aspect of new product strategy. Setting a high price can help to establish a high reference price against which all subsequent price drops may serve as an incentive for new groups of consumers to buy the product. However, setting too high a price may turn off consumers, lead to unacceptably low sales, and destroy credibility when steep price drops occur, as happened with the iPhone 8GB. Also, certain price points may reflect thresholds below which a price needs to drop before the new product takes off.[34] Table 4.2

Table 4.2. Price Points at Which Some Radically New Products Took Off in the United States

$1,000	$500	$100
Home VCR	Color TV	Calculator
Camcorder	CD Player	Answering Machine
Automobile	Microwave Oven	Disposer
Cellphone	Black and White TV	Digital Watch

Source: Adapted from Golder, Peter N. and Gerard J. Tellis, "Will it Ever Fly? Modeling The Takeoff of New Consumer Durables," *Marketing Science*, 1997, 16, 3, 256–270.

Figure 4.2. Change in Hazard of Takeoff at Three Rates of Annual Price Drop

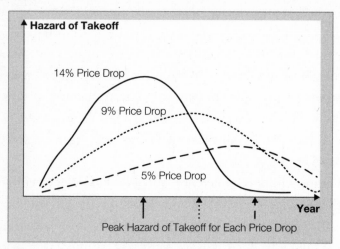

Source: Adapted from Golder, Peter N. and Gerard J. Tellis (1997), "Will It Ever Fly? Modeling the Takeoff of New Consumer Durables," *Marketing Science*, 16, no. 3, 256–270.

gives examples of new products that took off in the United States when their prices fell below certain price thresholds.

One of the advantages of the hazard model is that it can be used the predict the hazard of the takeoff of a new product as one changes certain marketing variables such as price. For example, Figure 4.2 shows how the likelihood of takeoff increases and shifts to the left (earlier) as we drop annual prices from 14% to 9% and 5%. Such simulations are a powerful means of planning for the future takeoff of a new product.

Targeting Future Mass Markets

When first introduced, new products often serve a niche. After takeoff, they begin to serve the mass market. Growth, sales, and profits increase dramatically after takeoff. Indeed, takeoff may be considered the point when the new product moves from appealing to a niche to appealing to the mass market. Thus, an essential aspect of new product strategy is to target future mass markets. Often, the firm that pioneered the new product and first commercialized it is not the one that triggers the takeoff. The reason is that the pioneering firm is often heavily focused on the new technology and the niche and does not foresee the potential of the future mass market. A later entrant to the market sees this potential and is responsible for the takeoff. Thus, a vital responsibility of managers of new products and of firms involved with innovation is to envision the mass market and realize the price, accessories, product quality, or features that will appeal to the mass market and trigger takeoff. Some examples, old and new, illustrate this point.

As the owners of Pampers, Procter & Gamble (P&G) is one of the largest manufacturers of disposable diapers.[35] Yet it was not the pioneer of this category. The pioneering brand was Chux, which was owned by Johnson & Johnson (J&J). Chux entered the market in 1935 and dominated the market with a premium brand that sold for 8.5 cents apiece. In comparison, laundry service for cloth diapers cost 3.5 cents per change, while home washing cost 1.5 cents per change. Because of its premium price, parents used Chux only when traveling, accounting for just 1% of the market. P&G decided to enter the market only in the 1950s. They targeted the mass market. But to do so, the firm had to bring down the price of manufacturing disposable diapers. P&G realized that the secret lay in a good automated manufacturing process and low-cost but high-quality materials. It took the firm five years to bring the manufacturing cost down to 3 cents a unit and another five years to produce a sufficiently good quality product, but when Pampers was launched in 1966, the product category took off. Sales of the category increased from $10 million to $370 million by 1973 and Pampers became a household name. J&J tried for a decade to recapture the lead from P&G but never quite succeeded. It finally exited the market. This case illustrates how P&G's focus on a future mass market paid off, while the pioneer J&J's focus on a niche led ultimately to market exit.

Automobiles have been around for over a hundred years. But the mass market for automobiles opened up when Henry Ford introduced the assembly line and brought the manufacturing price low enough so he could sell a car for $850 versus the going price of $2,000 to $3,000. With that radical innovation, automobile sales expanded rapidly in the United States and the western world, until the automobile reached very high penetration levels in these countries. However, for most of the developing world, the automobile was too expensive. In particular, in India, penetration of the automobile was just .7% in the early 2000s. A large fraction of the population travels on two-wheelers. Even a family of four may travel on a two-wheeler with father driving the scooter, mother in the passenger seat at the back, one child standing in front of the father, and another seated at the back on the mother's lap. Ratan Tata, CEO of Tata & Sons, a holding conglomerate that includes an automobile company, was saddened by this dangerous mode of transportation. He vowed to do something about it. That would mean manufacturing and selling an automobile for the price of $2,500, when the going price at that time was over $5,500. With resolve, persistence, and extensive innovation, his firm managed to introduce a car at that price in March 2009, after six years. As of 2011, the car has the potential to open the mass market for automobiles in the developing world and revolutionize how cars are made and sold all over the world. Here again, focus on the future mass market led to a highly innovative product and price.

Apple's introduction of the iPod, iPhone, and iPad represented late entry into markets with large, highly successful incumbents with deep pockets and extensive research and development (R&D)

investments: Sony in mobile music, Nokia and RIM in mobile phones, and HP in computers. The success of these products can be attributed at least in part to Steve Jobs's better envisioning the needs of the future mass markets for these products than the established incumbents.

These examples all go to show the critical role of targeting future mass markets when planning for radical innovation. Even though estimation of the future may not always be accurate, the discipline of thinking about and trying to predict the future forces on managers a future focus that is priceless. Lack of such a focus allows managers a false sense of security in the present as the final state of the future. Such a lack of focus can be disastrous. Moreover, the tools of predicting takeoff discussed earlier and of predicting technological evolution discussed next provide managers with some help in focusing on future markets.

Predicting Technological Evolution

Competing for the future often boils down to developing and commercializing the next big innovation. But especially in the high-tech markets, innovations are developed on one of various competing technological platforms. So, developing the next big innovation requires predicting the technological platform that is going to be the best in the future. For example, which technology for auto batteries will win out in the future: lead acid, nickel cadmium, fuel cell, or lithium ion? Similarly, which is the technology for display monitors will win out in the future: LCD (liquid crystal diode), LED (light emitting diode), plasma, or OLED (organic light emitting diode)? Should printer makers focus on laser, thermal, or ink-jet technology? How will homes of the future be lit, by fluorescent, LED, or MED (microwave electrodeless discharge) technologies?

How should firms choose among competing technologies of the future?[35a] This is one of the fundamental questions facing managers of technology and innovation.

My coauthor, Professor Ashish Sood, and I have grappled with this issue for many years. We discovered four novel findings: (a) multiple technologies compete at any time period; (b) each does so along multiple dimensions of performance; (c) the evolution in performance is due to innovations in design or components; (d) the evolution in performance of each technology forms a distinct pattern (see Chapter 2). Although each technology has its own unique path, technologies share certain common features in their evolution. Thus, by combining knowledge gained from the historical path of one technology with that from all other technologies, we have succeeded in partially predicting the future path of a technology, especially the crossing of the paths.[36] Such prediction is essential for developing future innovations.

For example, Professor Ashish Sood and I analyzed how these principles apply to the automobile engine market.[37] Manufacturers in this market are racing to develop an automobile engine that is efficient, inexpensive, and non-polluting. An electric motor that does not need gasoline seems ideal. But on which technology should such a motor be built? In the first part of the 2000's GM may have spent over one-billion dollars trying to develop such an engine. It invested most if not all of this money on a single technology, the hydrogen fuel cell. But hydrogen fuel is costly, corrosive, and dangerous. GM could not overcome these problems despite the huge investment. It has so far failed to market an automobile based on hydrogen fuel technology.

In contrast, a new entrant, Tesla Motors, attacked the problem with an entirely different solution. Its motor was based on a radical configuration of 6831 lithium-ion batteries. Tesla spent about $105 million to develop a new car based on this engine. The

Lithium-ion battery is superior to the hydrogen fuel cell because it is safer, cheaper, and more easily recharged. The beauty of this radical innovation is that the car accelerates from 0 to 60 in four seconds, reaches top speeds of 130 miles per hour, and has a range of over 200 miles, with a fuel efficiency of two cents a mile and a recharging time of two hours. It can also be recharged from a home outlet. Tesla started marketing the car based on this engine in 2008. After the Tesla's successful launch, GM also developed and marketed an electric car, the Chevy Volt, using a Lithium-ion battery pack. However, in this case, as in others described in this book, a small start-up beat a giant incumbent to market with a radical innovation.

In this case, the incumbent GM's error was not the absence of investment in research but the heavy focus on only one alternative technology, hydrogen fuel. It apparently did not consider other competing technologies and did not try to predict the future path of these technologies. Our framework of analyzing competing technologies (see Chapter 2) and our model to predict the path of alternate technologies will reduce the likelihood of such errors.

For example, an analysis of the automobile battery market shows three platform technologies: galvanic cells, fuel cells, and flow cells (see Figure 4.3A). Hydrogen belongs to the fuel cell platform while lithium-ion falls in the galvanic cell platform. We evaluate these alternate technologies on the important performance dimension of efficacy in miles per kilowatt. Galvanic cell starts below fuel cell in performance but improves rapidly, especially in the mid 2000s.

Within each of these technologies, performance improves based on innovations in design and components. For example, lead-acid, nickel-metal-hydride (NiMH), and lithium-ion fall within galvanic cells. Proton exchange membrane fuel cell (PEMFC) and zinc-air fall within fuel cells and flow cells, respectively (see Figure 4.3B).

Figure 4.3. Technological Evolution in Auto Batteries

(A) Evolution of Platform Technologies in Auto-Battery

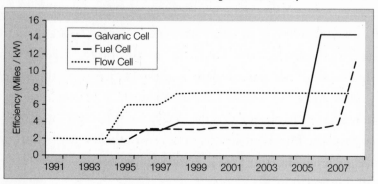

(B) Evolution of Components Technologies in Auto Battery

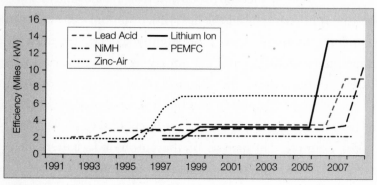

(C) Evolution of Component Technologies in Portable Battery

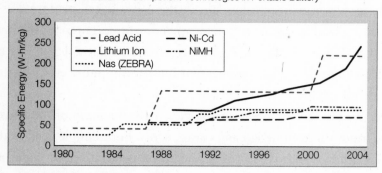

Source: Adapted from Tellis, Gerard J. and Ashish Sood, "A New Framework for Choosing the Right Technology," *Visions*, 34, no. 3 (October 2010).

Here again, lithium-ion starts off low, but improves sharply in 2006. While this increase may seem sudden in the auto-battery market, its improvement in performance was well known in the portable battery market (see Figure 4.3C). In this market, lithium-ion starts improving as early as early as 1992. Thus, scanning related markets for alternate technologies can be very fruitful. A framework and model such as the one we propose provides firms with options when investing in technological innovation. It provides early warnings of the emergence of new technologies and of their potential future paths. Thus, choosing technologies need not rely on gut feeling or raw creativity but can benefit from scientific analysis as explained here.

Bob Lutz, then vice chairman of GM, reveals the firm's reluctance to experiment with rival technologies in a very telling blog post, "GM had the technology to do hybrids back when Toyota was launching the first Prius, but we opted not to ask the board to approve a product program that'd be destined to lose hundreds of millions of dollars. In the end, it cost us much more than that; it cost us our reputation for technology leadership and innovation."[37] He seems repentant and resolved to change, writing, "We made that mistake once. We won't make it again." However, he did not indicate how he would avoid such a mistake in the future. Our research suggests a framework and model to make such a decision.

The framework consists of identifying four key aspects of technological innovation: (a) the levels of innovation (whether design, components, or platform), (b) the competing technologies at each level, (c) the dimensions of performance on which to compare them, and (d) the patterns of evolution on each dimension (see Chapter 2).[38]

Importantly, Professor Ashish Sood and I have developed a hazard model to predict technological disruption.[39] The prediction can be done in terms of either performance of the technologies on one of several dimensions or total sales of all products sold on a technology. We have found that a number of variables help in the prediction, including characteristics of the rival technologies, the number of technologies in the market, who introduced them, and the order of introduction. Even if these predictions do not always pan out, the exercise forces managers to focus on the future and more thoughtfully evaluate the alternatives they face.

Analyzing Emergent Consumers

Radical innovations have the paradoxical trait that mainstream consumers are unaware of their benefits and may also find little need for them when first encountered.[40] Thus, market research for radical innovations is difficult and potentially misleading if carried out indiscriminately. Indeed, when asked about marketing research, Steve Jobs once said, "People don't know what they want until you show them. That's why I never rely on market research. Our task is to read things that are not yet on the page."[41]

However, analyzing customers who tinker with or adapt existing products to serve their own needs may provide valuable clues about future products and future markets. For example, modern dishwashers may have descended from the invention of Josephine Cochrane, who developed a hand-powered model to wash dishes because her servants were chipping her fine china. The Linux operating system was initiated by Linus Torvalds and developed as open source code by those dissatisfied with the price or quality of the Windows operating system. The drink Gatorade was developed by a trainer of a college football team.

Emergent consumers are those who can envision innovations of the future, experience needs before the mass market, or who like to tinker with products to fit tangential rather than mainstream needs. Looking for these consumers has great potential in the development of radical innovations because they foster a future orientation as well as provide clues about customers and products of the future. As such, a firm may be better prepared to cater to the mass market when an innovation takes off. For consumer goods categories, recent research suggests a specific scale to identify emergent consumers.[42]

MIT Professor Eric Von Hippel and others suggests four steps that may be useful in analyzing emergent consumers that he called "lead users":[43]

1. *Start the process*. For this purpose the firm would build an interdisciplinary team, define the target market, and define the goals of the analysis.

2. *Identify needs and trends in the defined market*. For this purpose, the emergent consumer team would need to interview experts in the market or the underlying technology, scan the relevant literature including a search of the Web, and identify the most important trends. In recent years, the Web has become a powerful tool for identifying and monitoring emergent consumers. The team can do so by tracking Web chatter for products and services on blogs, user groups, forums, and review sites. Recent research has shown that such electronic conversations contain useful information based on their ability to predict stock prices.[44] If so, monitoring them should be an essential component of the analysis. Customers' online criticisms of current products and services indicate directions for new products. Customers' online suggestions of desirable features of products and services should constitute important leads regarding the ideal to which the market is aspiring. Indeed, in the current environment, analysis of Web chatter could

constitute the most important aspect of the identification and analysis of emergent consumers. With those leads, the team can identify all new products or new technologies that have already emerged or are likely to soon emerge. The team can then develop predictions as to when the new products are likely to take off and when the new technologies are likely to pass the old ones in performance on specific dimensions, as described previously.

3. *Identify the segment of emergent consumers.* Stage 2 would provide the names of at least a few emergent consumers. If not, the team could research early adopters or very heavy users of the current generation of products to get the identities of a few emergent consumers. Identifying the segment of users would involve tapping into the emergent consumer network based on names that the team has obtained up to that point. In addition, emergent consumers themselves may be aware of other emergent consumers who are more knowledgeable or have more acute needs. When tapping online chatter and online forums, recent research indicates that the distribution of customer comments and suggestion involves a small head with a very long tail that can reach in the thousands.[45] Researchers should focus on the long tail as much as on the small head of the list of comments. Emergent consumers are more likely to fall in the long tail, whereas mainstream customers are more likely to fall in the small head.

4. *Design the innovation concept.* In this step, the team would learn from ideas or prototypes from emergent consumers about the most pressing needs or solutions for the present. Although these needs and solutions are those of only emergent customers, there is a high likelihood of their becoming mainstream in the future.

Table 4.3. Studies of Users Building Own Solutions

Year	Market	Users Sampled	% Own Solutions
2011	Computerized commercial banking	36	55%
2011	Computerized retail banking	36	44%
2004	Outdoor sports	153	10%
2003	Medical surgery	261	22%
2002	Extreme sports	197	38%
2002	Kite surfing	157	26%
2002	Mountain bike equipment	287	19%
2000	Library search	102	18%
1992	Pipe hangers	74	36%
1988	PC-CAD	136	24%

Source: Adapted from Luthje, C., and Herstatt, C. (2004), "The Lead User Method: An Outline of Empirical Findings and Issues for Future Research," *R&D Management*, 34, no. 5, 553–568.

Only a few formal studies exist on the usefulness of analyzing emergent customers in developing innovations. However, the results of these studies indicate that the concept has high potential. Results suggest that the percentage of users who developed solutions for their own use varied from 10% for outdoor sports equipment to 38% for extreme sporting equipment (see Table 4.3). Firms that have benefited from the use of emergent customer analysis include 3M, HILTI AG, Nortel, and Johnson & Johnson.[46]

Analyzing emergent customers has some limitations. First, the method may not be useful in certain high-tech industries where product cycles are short and turnover in technology generations are high. Second, highly secretive industries (for example, defense, communication) may not be suited for this method, because emergent customers may feel uncomfortable revealing information and knowledge. Third, the method is more suited to industrial goods than consumer goods, because the former can be identified more reliably and easily.

Nevertheless, the analysis of emergent customers should be an important exercise in innovation development because it helps to foster a focus on the future.

CONCLUSION

This chapter explains the importance of future focus, the biases that prevent it, and the tools that mitigate the bias and foster such a focus.

- Future focus is essential for innovations because markets are in a constant flux. This flux occurs because consumers' tastes are changing constantly and technologies are evolving at an increasingly rapid pace. Today's industry leaders are unlikely to remain leaders or even survive if they do not focus on the future and adapt accordingly. Incumbents especially need to look for future mass markets.
- Future focus is difficult because of four biases that firms face:
  - The availability bias describes how deep involvement in current pressures and crises causes firms to exaggerate the present and discount the future.
  - The hot-hand bias causes firms to wrongly project the current slow growth of radical innovations and the rapid growth of successful products into the future. As a result they wrongly weight current products over future innovations.
  - The paradigmatic bias arises from viewing future innovations through the lens of current products. As a result, the innovations suffer a poor evaluation.

- The escalation of commitment (bias) leads firms to invest more in current products and technologies even when such products are past their prime. All these biases cause an emphasis on present over the future.
- Four methods can help firms mitigate these biases and foster a future focus in firms: predicting takeoff of radically new products, targeting future mass markets, predicting technological evolution, and analysis of emergent customers. None of these methods is flawless. The predictions of these methods are probabilistic and not deterministic and provide input for discussions about the future. The methods and the predictions thus foster a focus on the future.

Beyond these methods, subsequent chapters describe general firm practices that can also foster a future focus: incentives for enterprise (Chapter 5), internal markets (Chapter 6), and empowering innovation champions (Chapter 7).

CHAPTER 5

Incentives for Enterprise

> Changing the attitude and behavior of hundreds of
> thousands of people is very, very hard to
> accomplish. . . . You can't mandate it, can't engineer it.
> What you can do is create the conditions for
> transformation. You can provide incentives.
> —Lou Gerstner, Former CEO of IBM[1]

INDEED, INCENTIVES ARE the most powerful practice for
creating a culture of innovation. However, traditional incentives
in many organizations may be aligned for seniority, loyalty, or
sales productivity, but not for innovation. We may believe that
rewards for seniority and loyalty increase productivity and retain
good employees. Our instinct is to treat failure as bad and success
as good. So we reward success and penalize failure. Even for little
children, we use rewards to motivate good behavior and penalties
to discourage bad performance. But are these beliefs, instincts, and
practices good for innovation? This chapter shows why traditional
incentives stifle innovation, why failure must not be shunned, and
why incentives for enterprise promote innovation. Incentives for
enterprise are asymmetric, with strong rewards for success and
weak penalties for failure in innovation. This chapter discusses the
power and characteristics of incentives, including their economics
and psychology.

Traditional Incentives: Winning Loyalty

Traditional incentives are often based on longevity in the organization, with perks and rewards increasing based on the number of years of employment. This incentive scheme has many motivations. First, it is based on a simple, easily measured and implemented scheme. Second, it motivates loyalty to the organization and reduces the costs of employee turnover. Third, unions prefer it perhaps because it is objectively tracked and fosters social equity (in contrast, enterprise-based incentives can lead to much inequity). However, traditional incentives based on longevity do not foster innovation. Such incentives reward employees even when their performance falls below average so long as they put in the years. Longevity-based incentives motivate employees to hang on to an organization even when they are underperforming. Over time, organizations with longevity-based incentives will be left with loyal employees but not their innovators, who would have jumped ship to join organizations that better reward innovation.

Traditional incentives are often tied to seniority in the organization, with higher incentives reserved for senior managers and lower incentives for junior managers. If seniority itself is based on longevity, then such incentives have all the disadvantages of longevity-based incentives. Moreover, rewarding seniority rather than enterprise stimulates envy and status flaunting but not innovation.

Traditional incentives are also often tied to sales of existing products or satisfaction of current customers. However, even such performance-based incentives do not foster a culture of innovation. Focusing on existing products instead of new products encourages attention to current details but hampers new ideas and innovations for the future. Linking incentives to current customer satisfaction limits development of new markets and customers that may become important in the future.

To foster innovation, firms need incentives for enterprise. Such incentives, unlike traditional ones, reward employees for developing and implementing innovations: new ideas, products, services, or businesses. In such a system, bonuses, raises, promotions, and perks are all tied to the quality and number of innovations. Even young or new employees may do better than veterans in this system.

One important characteristic of incentives for enterprise is that they are asymmetric in their reward structure: strong rewards for success with weak penalties for failure. An asymmetric incentive structure encourages employees to take on risky projects, a prerequisite for innovation (see Chapter 3). Failure naturally elicits shame. Reinforcing or even maintaining such natural reactions to failure suppresses risk taking. Embracing and learning from failure can be powerful and encourages risk taking.

Asymmetric Incentives: Turning Failure into Success

For many incumbents embracing failure goes contrary to the grain of good management practice. Progress is measured by good results. Failure is penalized. Executives from organizations have told me that their organizations do indeed have asymmetric incentives, but they are the opposite of that proposed here: they offer weak or no rewards for success and strong penalties for failure! Why does this come about? Success is part of the implicit contract in employee hiring; so is avoiding failure. Thus, the incentive structure takes success for granted and does not especially reward it, but punishes failure. In particular, one senior executive of a major multinational corporation once lamented that his employees were risk averse.

On further discussion I found out that the problem was not with the employees but with the corporation. It had low rewards for success with innovations but penalties for failure. The result was risk-averse employees.

A formal study by Professors Gina O'Connor and Christopher M. McDermott found a pervasive reward structure that was not conducive to innovation.[2] Over six year, the authors studied ten large established firms including IBM, 3M, DuPont, GE, Texas Instruments, and Nortel Networks. The authors found that in most cases, firms provided what I call perverse incentives: strong penalties for failure but weak rewards for success. As one innovator told them, "The origin of the breakthrough success is often forgotten, but an R&D effort that does not succeed is never forgotten." In another case, when sales forecasts of an innovation were not met, a team member was "put in the penalty box." Most team members viewed innovation projects as career risks, given the low probability of success and high penalties for failure. As a result, key team members threatened to quit (and often did) during or after the project or were fired during the project.

In sharp contrast to this practice, the asymmetric reward structure that I call incentives for enterprise involves strong incentives for success with weak or no penalties for failure. Such an incentive structure motivates innovation. Innovation requires exploring new possibilities, traveling unexplored terrain, and investing in uncertain options. Failure is common (see Chapter 3). In an environment where the individual is allowed to fail and learn from failure, innovation thrives. In a culture where errors are shamed, innovation suffers. Jeffrey Pfeffer of the Stanford School of Business warns, "Companies that want to encourage innovation and entrepreneurship therefore have to build a forgiveness culture, one in which people are not punished for trying new things."[3]

In practical terms, to create innovations firms must allow for a process of trial and error in which unsuccessful innovations are redesigned or discarded in favor of ultimately successful ones. If employees are not assured that failures will be tolerated, they may hesitate to take risks. Without risks, there will be less trial, experimentation, and endeavor, which are essential for success. Raj Shah, a director of engineering at Google, echoes that view: "Our philosophy at Google is fail early, fail often, move on. If the innovator took a risk, failed, and admitted failure, then we keep investing in him or her; while if the risk taker *fails to admit the failure* [italics added], we stop investing in him or her."[4]

Research shows that the fear of real or possible sharp criticism about work or failures undermines creative and innovative activity.[5] Feedback and evaluations that provide balanced corrective information, however, enhance creativity.[6] Further, to encourage innovations, innovators must be protected from any monetary penalties for failure. Incentive schemes geared to fostering innovation must tolerate and even reward failure, especially in the early stages of the innovative process.[7]

For example, Steve Jobs is well known for his fanatically high standards for quality in Apple's innovations. Yet even with these high standards, Jobs had a simple rule for failure that eschewed penalties: "Sometimes when you innovate, you make mistakes. It is best to admit them quickly, and get on with improving your other innovations."[8] Jobs is celebrated for his successes. But he also had numerous failures, including the over-priced iPhone 8GB, the faulty iPhone antenna, the hardware produced by NeXT, the initially slow sales of the iPod, the failure of the Apple III, the over-heating of MacBooks, and most notably the failure of Lisa. The latter two failures resulted in his biggest failure, being fired from the company he founded. It was a low point of his career. But reflecting on it later, Jobs said, "I didn't see it then, but it turned out that getting fired from Apple was the best thing that could have ever happened to me. The heaviness of being successful was replaced by the lightness of being a beginner again, less sure about everything. It freed me to enter one of the most creative periods of my life."[9]

Attitudes to failure vary substantially by culture. Failure seems to be shunned more in traditional or eastern societies than in modern or western societies. Countries with a tradition of exploration and enterprise seem to have the greatest tolerance for failure. Actually, the tolerance for failure may well be a primary driver of such exploration and enterprise. In this respect, two countries seem to stand out, the United States and Israel. Of all large countries in the world, the United States is a bastion of entrepreneurship. Several factors account for that. Not the least is its tolerance for failure, especially in entrepreneurial pockets such as Silicon Valley. For example, in the Valley, bankruptcy is a badge of honor.[10] Steve Jobs had this to say about entrepreneurship in the Valley, "The penalty for failure, for going and trying to start a company in this Valley, is nonexistent."[11] In contrast, in Europe and especially in Japan, failure is penalized. For example, German law does not allow anyone who declares bankruptcy to become the CEO of a corporation.

Steven Sasson, the inventor of the digital camera, has this to say about nurturing invention:

> The ideal way is not to just look to the experts, look to people
> who have a passion to explore and those who are not afraid
> of making mistakes. . . . Thomas Edison was a prolific inventor
> and he was always surrounded by people who thought they were
> all better than him. Inventors spend most of the time being
> wrong and liking it, being comfortable with failure, because
> that is how you learn. Inventors have to be resolute and the
> environment should be tolerant to you. You have to spend a lot
> of time being wrong than being right.[12]

146

Israel is another country with a high tolerance for failure, which fosters a highly entrepreneurial climate. Two reporters describe the culture as follows: "Israeli culture and regulation reflect a unique attitude to failure, one that has managed to repeatedly bring failed entrepreneurs back into the system to constructively use their experience to try again, rather than leave them permanently traumatized and stigmatized."[13] Much of this culture is fostered in the military, in which all citizens must serve. Recruits are trained early to face unexpected dangers, make quick decisions, and take responsibility for their actions. However, the reward system encourages risk taking, as one air force officer said, "We don't finish you off permanently for a bad performance."[14] In Israel, laws regarding bankruptcy are lenient enough to make it one of the easiest places in the world to start a fresh company after a bankruptcy.[15] That tolerance is critical. Research shows that failed entrepreneurs have a 20% chance of success in their next enterprise, higher than that of new entrepreneurs but not much lower than that of successful entrepreneurs.[16]

Perks are also a major means of incentivizing innovations. In some established corporations, perks such as fancy offices, reserved parking, company cars, and company jets are tied to rank, seniority, and longevity within the company. Indeed, the corner office or 27th-floor glass office can become symbols to flaunt. But in some highly innovative corporations, even the CEO has only a cubicle. When Gordon Moore, cofounder and CEO of Intel, who was worth billions, was once asked why he had no more than a cubicle without a door or window, he replied, "In a business like this, people with the power are the ones with the understanding of what's going on, not necessarily the ones on top. It is very important that those people who have the knowledge are the ones who make the decisions. So we set up something where everyone who has the knowledge has an equal say with what was going on." Moore's implicit message was that the lowly engineer working on routine innovations was valued as highly as the CEO and founder. Windowed offices, heavy doors, and gold-plated fixtures were not symbols of achievement. Facebook has gone a step further with open working spaces that do not even have cubicles. It has peeled away status, perks, and walls to create an atmosphere of openness, equality, and intense interaction for innovation.

Thus, incentives for enterprise must be based on innovative performance and not on seniority or longevity or even performance on current products. Such incentives must be asymmetric, with strong rewards for success and weak penalties for failure. Constructing such incentives requires constant watchfulness and deliberate intent, because the natural human tendency is just the reverse: to shame failure and overlook success or take it for granted.

Making Incentives Work: Economics and Psychology of Incentives

Economic theory suggests that human behaviors (activities) can be priced and that desired activities can be motivated by suitable monetary incentives. Positive incentives consist of monetary incentives (salary, bonus, stock options), perks (titles, office, planes, and so forth), and nonmonetary incentives (awards and honors). A major challenge with incentives is deciding which metric to link them to. Incentives tied to sales of current products will lead to a focus on and increase in sales of current products. Incentives tied to current publications will lead to a focus on and increase in publications. One chief technology officer of a major multinational corporation said to me of their one-time strategy, "We judged people on papers, so they wrote lots of papers." Incentives tied to patents will lead to an increase in patents. Incentives tied to innovation will lead to an increase in innovations. That is surely important, but may not be enough. A vice president of research labs for another major multinational said to me, "We have innovations sitting on the shelf." In this latter case, incentives were even designed for developing innovations, but not for commercializing them.

Incentives for enterprise must be tied to commercialized innovations. Possible metrics may be a percentage of sales of new products developed in the last few years, a percentage of sales from new markets, or long-term growth. A combination of metrics is better than any single one, so as to avoid employees' gaming the system.

Research suggests that in general, linking salary, bonus, and stock options to a firm's innovativeness enhances the overall performance of the firm. In particular, recent studies of the relationship of incentives to innovation found the following results:[17]

- The ratio of long-term incentives (for example, stock options) to total compensation for senior executives (for example, CEO and R&D head) varied from 42% to 32%, being higher for more senior executives.
- For firms with centralized R&D, more long-term incentives are associated with greater innovation productivity (such as citations, filings, and originality of patents).
- The greater the technological intensity of a firm, the more the CEO bonuses are tied to financial results and the more CEO total incentives are linked to evidence of influential innovations.
- As technology intensity increases, aligning bonus with financial results better predicts firm performance.

Monetary incentives also have limitations. The psychology of incentives suggests that providing a monetary incentive (that is, putting a price) on some behaviors is costly, less effective than nonmonetary incentives, and can backfire. Four examples reveal counterintuitive principles of the psychology of incentives.

Moral Incentives

Two economists wanted to see if small penalties could prevent parents from arriving late to pick up their children from day care.[18] So they designed an incentive system that fined parents $3 per late pickup of a child. This was small compared to the monthly fee of $380 for the service. Instead of tardiness decreasing, it doubled. The economists next tested what would happen when they stopped the fine. However, the number of late-arriving parents did not decline from the new higher rate. What explains this economically irrational behavior?

To understand this, one must realize there are three types of incentives: monetary, moral, and social.[19] In this case, the penalty of $3 was a monetary incentive. But there was a more powerful moral incentive at work. That was the guilt of being late. When the penalty was imposed, the $3 fine absolved parents of the guilt of being late, but was too small to serve as a monetary disincentive—substantially less than it would cost for a babysitter. Moreover, a parent could be late every day of the month and only incur an additional $60, much less than monthly service. Financially, it was cheaper to be late! So, the incentive backfired and did not achieve the goal intended.

Once instituted, removal of the penalty did not provide any new incentive to be on time. The small fine had put a value on the parents' guilt—$3. So, when it was removed, they could still arrive late, pay no fine, and now feel no guilt!

A large penalty of $100 for each time late would have worked better than the $3. But that would also have caused much ill will, as parents would have felt that the day-care center was profiteering from uncontrolled events that caused them to be late.

So what should have been done? The day-care center could have heightened the guilt for being late and worked with parents who were repeatedly late. This example shows how moral incentives can be more powerful than some monetary incentives. It also shows how the psychology of incentives is as important as their economics.

Social Incentives

In 1993, the Swiss government identified two small towns as potential repositories of the country's nuclear waste program.[20] Many of the townspeople were deeply concerned about the prospect of living so close to a nuclear waste repository. Two researchers tested the effectiveness of incentives in motivating people to accept the repository. They first surveyed respondents to ascertain their base receptivity to the repository. Fifty-one percent of the people agreed to the location. To increase receptivity to the repository, the researchers repeated the survey with three different levels of compensation: $2,175, $4,350, and $6,525. However, the receptivity to the repository declined by about half when the incentive was offered, without significant difference across the three levels. All those who rejected the first incentive were then made a fresh offer with a higher incentive: from $2,175 to $3,263, from $4,350 to $6,525, and from $6,525 to $8,700. Only one new person was willing to accept the repository at the higher offer. What explains this economically irrational behavior?

The first 51%, who were receptive to the repository, probably did so out of a sense of social obligation—a feeling of national pride or a sense that it was the fair sacrifice for the common good. When money was introduced into the equation, it may have put a monetary value on the choice. For some, this value was probably less than the social obligation. For others, it may have appeared as a choice of making quick money versus the dangers of the dumpsite. This case shows that the power of social incentives was more effective than the pull of economic incentives.

What could have been done? A better strategy would have been for the government to more clearly explain to residents the social benefits of the repositories of the nuclear waste program that motivated the scheme in the first place and appeal to their sense of social obligation.

Firms can use moral, social, and monetary incentives to motivate employees. As the previous examples illustrate, moral and social incentives are more powerful than monetary at reasonable price levels and can cost less. Thus, a public award ceremony (costing $1,000) to acknowledge the innovator of the year can do more than a private prize of $1,000, because of the huge social payoff from the former. When firms are seeking deep commitment from employees for work beyond the usual hours or creativity beyond the normal, social incentives can play a big role. Unpriced perks at work such as gourmet meals, free drinks, and massages can build a social contract with employees that can motivate them to give beyond their monetary hiring contract. Behavioral economist Dan Ariely says, "Money, as it turns out, is very often the most expensive way to motivate people."[21]

Fairness of Incentives

Recently in the United States, the federal government has encouraged states throughout the country through strong incentives to conduct standardized tests on math and science. Federal funding for education has been offered to encourage adoption of such tests and improve quality of education for low-performing schools. However, one school district found that its incentive system caused its teachers to cheat on the test that had multiple-choice answers.[22] Teachers could cheat in several ways. A teacher could write the answers to the test on the blackboard during the exam. Other teachers could prepare students for the questions on the test if they had early access to the test. Still others could erase the incorrect answers and replace them with correct answers on their students' answer sheets. The corrections were probably done once the exam was over, the children had left, and the teachers had time before they had to turn in the papers.

Why did the teachers cheat? Aside from the moral issue of integrity, teachers probably cheated because the incentives were strong but they lacked the means of meeting targets in the short term. Teachers whose students did badly on the tests were likely to be sanctioned. If the entire school did badly, federal funding could be withheld for the school. Moreover, the school could fire low-performing teachers. But if students did well on the tests the teacher would likely be lauded and promoted. In the short term, some teachers may have been unable to improve students' performance on the tests due to weak students, limited resources, limited time, or their own limited abilities. Under pressure to perform, teachers may have cheated to avoid penalties and gain rewards for themselves and their schools.

The cheating was detected by studying unusual answer patterns and correlations among students in a given classroom, strange patterns within any one student's answers, and a comparison of how the students performed on the tests the year before and after the alleged cheating. The school district also conducted mock tests and had students retake the test under close monitoring. The intent was to see if students did as well on the test the second time, when no chance for cheating was allowed. The school district found that students whose answer sheets were initially determined to have been modified by errant teachers did not do as well on the tests the second time around. After making allowances for general differences in student performance, the school confronted the teachers and eventually fired those who had cheated.

This example shows the harm of strong penalties for failure coupled with difficult conditions for compliance: a system in which participants do not have a fair chance to meet goals within the time and recourse constraints. What could have been done? The incentive system could have emphasized rewards for improvement over penalties for failure, it could have been coupled with adequate training for low-performing teachers or students, and it could have set performance standards that were relative to the starting point of the teachers and the students. In that way, weak teachers, or those with weak students, could have a fair chance of winning the rewards that were offered in the stipulated time.

Framing Incentives

At one time, if you bought a book on Amazon anywhere in the world, you paid $3.95 on shipping. Many years ago Amazon instituted a policy of free shipping for sales over $25.[23] The firm found that sales increased dramatically in response. Consumers were probably buying from Amazon when they otherwise would not have and also increased amounts they bought so that they crossed the $25 threshold. However, this increase did not happen in France. Investigations revealed that in France, instead of dropping the cost of shipping from the prior level to free, the French division had charged patrons 1 franc or about 20 cents for shipping. Would a 20-cent cost difference be high enough to induce such a strong difference in consumer behavior in France relative to the rest of the world?

To find out, Amazon changed its promotion in France to include free shipping. France, like the other countries in the world, showed a dramatic increase in sales as well. Thus, a drop from 20 cents to "free" caused a dramatic shift in national sales volume, whereas a drop from about $3.95 to 20 cents did not. The pull of "free" was powerful enough to create a whole new surge in sales.

"Free" suggests a huge gain as opposed to the 20 cents, which though small, suggests a real loss.

Thus, small shifts in framing incentives can cause disproportionately large changes in response behavior. In general, setting up or framing incentives as rewards (gains) rather than penalties (losses) are likely to be more powerful and motivate positive behavior. So the psychology of incentives reiterates the needs for an asymmetric incentive system.

Stories of incentives at IBM, Google, GM, and 3M illustrate these principles and pitfalls of providing incentives for innovation.

Power of Incentives: IBM's Transformation

In the mid-1990s, IBM was about to implode. This giant of the computer era, with thousands of new patents each year, was near death. There was tremendous pressure to break the company into smaller sustainable parts or do a fire sale of its assets, because the company seemed too large, bureaucratic, and lethargic to survive as one piece on its own. At this point, the board hired Lou Gerstner, CEO of RJR Nabisco and former president of American Express Company. In an enlightening book, Gerstner describes the problem at IBM as one of a stultifying culture rooted in dysfunctional incentives.[24]

IBM became a highly profitable giant from its dominance of the mainframe computer market in the 1960s and 1970s. Tom Watson Jr., the CEO who took the firm to that position of dominance, established a strong and distinct culture at IBM. The culture permeated all aspects of IBM life, ranging from paternalism towards employees, to a rigid dress code at work, to no drinking at corporate gatherings.[25] Key aspects of the culture included the values of excellence in work, superior service, and respect for individual employees. But with the passing of Tom Watson Jr., the culture became highly codified into rituals that had lost their original meaning, purpose, and usefulness.

For example, superior customer service had become largely administrative, without any passion and innovation in serving changing customer needs. Excellence in everything we do became "a spider's web of checks, approvals, and validation that slowed decision making to a crawl."[26] Respect for the individual "helped spawn a culture of entitlement, where 'the individual' didn't have to do anything to *earn* respect—he or she expected rich benefits and lifetime employment simply by virtue of having been hired."[27] In other words, rewards were given for just being an IBM employee, without any regard for performance. As a result, very technical, competent employees were paid similarly to those less well trained and productive and below the level of compensation in the industry. Individuals could not be terminated for nonperformance because that would show disrespect to the individual, in violation of the IBM culture. As a result IBM became vulnerable to competitors. It lost market share in critical markets. Revenues dropped. It was not able to support its bloated workforce. It had to lay off 125,000 employees.

By the end of his nine-year tenure, Gerstner had transformed the company into a highly innovative, nimble, and effective service provider. In his book, he attributes the transformation to one major accomplishment: a change of culture. At the core, that transformation involved a radical alteration of IBM's incentive structure. Gerstner transformed the culture from an inward one focused on process to an outward one focused on the customer. Everything the company did was organized around serving the customer with innovations, urgency, and superior quality. In line with this organization, the incentive structure was changed from entitlements to rewards for meeting customer needs. The change was not easy, as Lou Gerstner states in the introductory quote of this chapter. Yet, incentives are probably the most powerful of the three practices within the reach of top management for effectively establishing a culture for innovation.

Incentives for Enterprise: Google

From its incorporation in September 1998, Google has grown rapidly to become a behemoth with revenues of $29 billion, over 24,000 employees, and a capitalization of $191 billion for year-end 2010. In just eleven years since incorporation, it had grown to become the 39th largest global company by market cap,[28] ahead of PepsiCo, HP, Samsung, and Intel. Yet it strives to maintain a spirit of an entrepreneurial start-up. Its core product is search. Many people assume that its success is due to its initial highly innovative search engine, PageRank, based on number of hyperlinks pointing to each site. However, it has remained at the top due to its continuous innovation. Just a few major innovations are AdWords, AdSense, Android, Chrome, Earth, Gmail, Picasa, Desktop, and Docs. Sustaining that innovation is a culture that strives for unrelenting improvement in making information available to consumers at a click. At the root of that culture is a system of incentives for creating new ideas, rewarding innovations, and rewarding enterprise. In particular, Google has generous rewards for success with weak penalties for failures in a multilayered incentive system. That culture has enabled it to stay ahead of its numerous competitors, from large corporations such as Microsoft with deep pockets and massive research to countless entrepreneurs the world over who are striving to develop better products than those of Google.

Perks, Options, and Awards

For starters, in addition to standard fringe benefits, Google provides employees with outstanding perks, including fitness centers, gourmet restaurants, haircuts, laundry, dry cleaning, car washes, massages, and babysitting services on its campus. It also offers generous transportation allowances, commuter buses to and from home, and health and retirement benefits. Google ranks high on graduates' lists of most desirable employers.

Part of motivation for this largesse is Google's flush cash position. However, the explicit motive for these benefits is to attract and retain the best employees and pamper and motivate them to give their best to Google. These perks are also meant to remove all distractions and free up employee time and energy, not just for regular jobs but also to be innovative. Google believes this management philosophy gives it an advantage over its competitors because the company makes it easy for programmers to do what they want, which is to write code. Google's Eric Schmidt and Hal Varian say the goal of the perks is "to strip away everything that gets in their [workers'] way." They explain, "Let's face it: programmers want to program, they don't want to do their laundry. So we make it easy for them to do both."[29] Google recognizes the added benefit of increased job satisfaction. And the costs of such perks are minimal relative to the benefits of increased productivity, including innovation.

Initially, Google gave its early employees generous stock options, which made them millionaires overnight when the company went public. These employees are nicknamed "economic volunteers" within the company because the profits they reaped after the firm went public made them financially secure for life.[30] Even today, Google continues to use its high-priced stock to lure and retain talent.[31] Initially, Google's salaries were lower than market rates with an emphasis on such stock options. Many start-ups often use this strategy to ease cash flow and incentivize employees to share in the potentially huge rewards of a start-up. However, subsequently, to attract talented engineers, Google has begun increasing salary levels to make them competitive with the rest of the technology industry.[32] By early 2007, experienced engineers could earn as much as $130,000 a year, in addition to stock options and shares when they join.[33]

Founder's Awards, which run into millions of dollars, are another incentive tool to encourage and recognize employee innovations. For example, Niniane Wang won a million-dollar Founder's Award for an innovative program that searched computer desktops.[34] Wang was only 27 years old at the time. Bret Taylor and Jim Norris won a Founder's Award for innovation on Google Maps, again estimated at a million dollars.[35]

Google's strategy is consistent with research on incentives. For example, a recent study found that talented individuals preferred employment contracts where individual performance was rewarded strongly (with a larger equity component and greater performance-based pay) than employment contracts with weak incentives that pay a "fixed amount reflecting some average level of performance."[36] In the software industry where talent is critical and competition intense, Google's reward structure would be essential to attract, retain, and incentivize talent.

Time Off to Explore: Structure and Fruits of 20% Off

"If you're not failing enough, you're not trying hard enough," says Richard Holden, product management director for Google's AdWords service. "The stigma [for failure] is less because we staff projects leanly and encourage them to just move, move, move. If it doesn't work, move on."[37]

Google places a premium on success but it doesn't punish failure. In fact, engineers at Google can spend 20% of their time working on personal projects unrelated to their primary assignments.[38] This mandate is part of Google's package to employees, "a license to pursue dreams." This mandate has spawned services such as Google News and the social networking site Orkut. "Google is . . . all about individuals fulfilling or exceeding their potential, and employees are given significant license to foster this," says Geoffrey Moore.[39] Outstanding employee projects have a good chance of developing into commercial products. Google News, Gmail, and Google Finance are the fruits of this program.[40]

The development of Gmail is instructive.[41] A Google user complained about inefficient existing e-mail systems and how she had to spend a great deal of time filing messages or trying to find them.[42] Alternatively, she had to consistently delete e-mails to ensure she stayed under the usual limit of four megabytes per e-mail account. Frustrated with these limitations, she asked if someone at Google could help fix the problem.[43]

Paul Buchheit had started work on an e-mail system while he was in college, but never completed the project. Buchheit's college had Internet facilities on campus but, at the time, e-mail was restricted to the user's computer. Buchheit found this policy limiting and realized how much more useful it would be if he could access his e-mail from any computer on campus. He figured if he had a Web-based e-mail account, his information could be online at all times and he would be able to access his data from any location.[44]

When Buchheit joined Google in 1999, he continued to design a method to improve e-mail systems. Fairly quickly, he created a viable Gmail model using existing company technology.[45] But that was just the beginning of the challenge. Gmail also had to make money and be profitable for the company. Buchheit decided to innovate with a concept which was in existence at the time but not believed viable by most companies: linking ads to the content of an e-mail.[46]

Marissa Mayer was then Google VP of Search Products and User Experience. When Buchheit told her of his idea, she shot it down and asked him not to proceed. She theorized it was easier, like their competitors, to start with limited-storage e-mail accounts and then to charge people for mailboxes with increased megabytes. Buchheit, convinced of the potential of this new product, ignored his supervisor's orders, pursued his research, and completed work on the ad integration component.[47]

When Mayer saw the integration of e-mails and ads she almost shut the project down. Mayer thought the "ads were never going to work" and thought that "target[ing] the ads at [people's] email [was] going to be creepy and weird . . . and cause privacy concerns."[48] However, she held off on asking Buchheit right away to remove this feature from Gmail. During this time, she typed an e-mail about hiking and saw an ad for hiking boots. She also got an e-mail about Al Gore's visit to Google and up popped an ad for books about Gore.[49] Mayer then realized that she had been mistaken; Buchheit's ad integration concept could be highly profitable for the company. There is some ambiguity about whether AdSense, a Google product that generates multimillion-dollar advertising revenue, arose from or led to this project.[50]

Buchheit completed a personal project he started in college on his own 20% time. His efforts were, at a point, clearly contradictory to what senior management believed was a viable business model. But, instead of reprimanding Buchheit for disregarding orders on the advertising integration, senior management was willing to accept its error and embrace an employee's innovation. When Mayer realized she was wrong and that Buchheit was right, she did not bury his invention, but promptly accepted the new idea, with resounding commercial success for Google. Buchheit was handsomely rewarded for the innovation and retired from Google at age 30.[51]

Employee innovation with the 20% time also extends to non-software-related areas. Cari Spivack, who used to work on Google's book-search product, got tired of driving to work in rush hour traffic. She thought of the idea of using a company shuttle that would reduce employees' commutes. Spivack found a bus company and worked out possible routes a shuttle might take. She presented her idea to Google management after she researched it. Google rewarded Spivack's creativity by implementing the idea without having multiple committees conduct feasibility studies.[52]

The 20% time is a costly program that is difficult to monitor. Google leaves it up to employees to use their 20% time productively. While there are some outstanding successes, a large proportion of such time may well be unproductive. This failure is the cost for a few successful innovations.

Challenge of Talent Retention

Recently, as Google's employee pool has grown huge, some valuable ideas have been lost in the crowd without getting the needed attention and support. Some of these ideas have left the firm together with their creators. Thus, even with strong incentives for innovation, Google loses talent. To prevent such losses, Google established a system of Innovation Reviews.[53] The Innovation Review allows employees to present new product ideas to Google top management, including the founders and CEO. It ensures that senior management is aware of and involved in the early development of new ideas. It also ensures that the project receives the money and manpower it needs to result in a commercially viable product for Google.

This policy resulted in the development of several new products, including software for facial recognition to use Microsoft Outlook simultaneously with Google's data storage facilities.[54] In addition to generating new revenues for the company, the review meetings recognize employee innovations and use company money and manpower to bring the employee's ideas to fruition.

Google's generous incentive system—where employees are relieved from mundane worries, have ample time to pursue their own interests, are rewarded handsomely for productivity, and are not penalized for failure—has consistently led to Google being ranked as one of the best companies for which to work.[55] More important, it has created an atmosphere where innovation thrives. The wisdom of Google's policy is backed by findings from independent research. For example, research shows that monetary rewards do not deter creativity. However, if the incentives are accompanied by strict guidelines and restrictions on how the work is to be performed, the incentives do have a serious negative impact on creativity.[56] The open atmosphere of 20% time can therefore strongly promote innovation.

Incentives for Loyalty: General Motors

Through innovations in design, segmentation, and management, General Motors (GM) flourished through the first two-thirds of the last century to become the dominant manufacturer and marketer of automobiles in the world. However, during the last forty years, GM began a steady decline to ultimately bankruptcy in 2009. This decline points to a culture that contrasts with that of Google. A consistent theme in GM's decline is a culture that rewarded longevity rather than enterprise, focused on short-term returns rather than long-term growth, and did not persist through obstacles and failure. On his second visit to Congress in December 2008, GM CEO Rick Wagoner finally confirmed these problems, conceding that "GM has made mistakes in the past."[57] Some of these mistakes were not investing in technology for the future, caving in to short-term union demands, and not persisting through errors.

Technology Troubles

GM has frequently, and to its own detriment, refused to take adequate long-term risks with new technology. In its refusal to learn from errors and tolerate the slow and unsure course of innovation and in its shortsighted haste not to fail, it killed the very thing it was seeking—to develop market leadership through breakthrough technology. Over the decades, GM has been unable "to strike a balance between those inside the company who pushed for innovation ahead of the curve and the finance executives who worried more about returns on investment."[58] It has spent billions of dollars on innovations like the Saturn and the EV1 electric vehicle but abandoned the projects early because of a seeming lack of immediate profits.

GM's struggle with electric technology is a prime example of its refusal to take risks, learn from errors, and be patient about success. GM engineers started developing electric car technology as early as the 1970s. In 1990 GM exhibited its first prototype of an electric environmentally friendly car, called the Impact, at the Los Angeles Auto Show. The Impact, eventually renamed the EV1 (Electrical Vehicle), was a battery-operated car, which was released in limited markets in 1996. Although the EV1 became popular, in 1999 GM withdrew the car from the market, citing technical concerns and lack of demand. In 2003, GM recalled all EV1s from the market and had most of the cars crushed in the Arizona desert.[59]

The real reason for the demise of the EV1 is controversial. Some outrage over the death of the EV1 spawned the documentary, "Who Killed the Electric Car?"[60] The documentary blamed, inter alia, GM and the oil lobby. The price of gasoline was low during this time. The documentary alleged a conspiracy between GM and the oil companies, which saw the possibility of declining oil profits if people switched to electric cars.

However, GM attributed the car's demise to its unwillingness to wait for the EV1 to become profitable. Though the electric technology in some form could be profitable in the future, it was not willing to take that risk of uncertain and long-term payoff. In contrast, Toyota did the opposite and pursued hybrid technology (see Chapter 3). John Shook, a manager at a GM-Toyota joint venture plant said, "Toyota is built on trial and error, on admitting you don't know the future, and that you have to experiment. At GM, they say, 'I'm senior management. There's a right answer, and I'm supposed to know it.' This makes it harder to try things."[61]

GM also admitted that in subsequent years it did not put enough resources into developing the hybrid car technology.[62] GM put its fuel-efficient and hybrid technology on hold to focus instead on building large cars with big engines and horsepower, which yielded high profits in the short-term.[63] On the one hand, with cheap gas and the popularity of big cars, GM was not willing to risk investments in alternate technologies of the future to secure future markets. On the other hand, Toyota, as well as other Asian automobile companies, looked ahead and developed smaller, cheaper, more fuel-efficient, and hybrid cars. When gas prices eventually went up, GM's big gas guzzling cars were not the vehicles the public wanted.

GM had the opportunity to be a market leader in this segment. Instead, GM lost this race to Toyota. While Toyota's Prius hybrid sold more than 2 million vehicles globally since it hit the market in 2000, GM's Volt hybrid electric entered the market only in 2011.

Even then, the Volt was much costlier (estimated $40,000) than the Prius, (estimated at $21,000).[64]

GM regrets killing the EV1 hybrid car. "If we could turn back the hands of time, we could have had the Chevy Volt 10 years earlier," regretted GM R&D chief Larry Burns.[65] Just as the EV1 was not immediately profitable, the Volt will not generate profits for a few years. But desperate for a hit and under pressure from the Obama administration, GM is willing to take the risk because it needs the innovations to survive.

Labor and Union Priorities

GM had started with a sound method of incentivizing employees. In 1923, Alfred Sloan, CEO of GM, helped GM employees buy GM stock.[66] However, over time, GM moved away from such incentives. Tragically, in the 1980s, GM's CEO Roger Smith offered unions very generous retirement benefits to buy peace with the unions over not increasing salaries. The strategy did not affect earnings, because at the time, accounting rules allowed a firm to ignore retirement obligations when computing earnings.[67] Ultimately, as thousands of employees retired, retirement obligations became an unbearable financial burden. GM bought short-term peace with long-term trouble. It had created a culture of entitlement, similar to the one at the old IBM.

Recent developments underscore how unproductive this culture was. Even when GM was facing possible bankruptcy, it was unable to reduce its costs and its daily cash burn due to agreements signed with the unions decades earlier.[68] Union agreements prevented GM from shutting down plants or laying workers off without costly penalties. GM factories had to be maintained at a minimum "80% capacity" whether the plant was generating revenues or not.[69] Even when plants stopped production, GM had to pay all workers that were laid off, including their very expensive medical costs and pensions.[70] It had a "Jobs Bank" program for this purpose. For example, an employee who was laid off because the employee's division merged with another in 2000 enrolled in the Job Banks program. By 2006 the employee was still not working for GM. But the employee received his or her salary, with benefits, for nearly the entire period since 2000. The cost to GM in 2006 for salary and benefits (with annual increases) for this one employee alone, who had stopped working for the company over six years earlier, was over $100,000![71]

Tragically, all these generous benefits were longevity-based incentives that motivated loyalty but did nothing for stimulating innovation, as research suggests.[72] Unions favored them because they seemed more equitable than performance-based incentives. Further, these incentives prevented GM from directing much-needed funds into the redesign and updating of its models. These benefits were designed due to a failure to inspire unions to work toward the long-term good of the firm and the employees.[73] The incentives were also the result of a deep cultural malaise at GM. John Z. DeLorean, the legendary car innovator and a GM vice president, alleged that starting from the 1960s, GM's management culture evolved to an elite clique. Executives were promoted not on the basis of performance but on how well they supported the status quo.[74] Managers thwarted DeLorean's efforts to improve the quality of cars by an emphasis on maintaining the existing structure (products, markets, salaries) and short term financial results.[75] This policy was due to a shortsighted focus on quarterly results instead of innovation for long-term growth. Thus, incentives were designed on rewarding mediocrity in management and not on promoting enterprise.

Recent research bears out the futility of a culture such as GM's. Research shows that if CEOs and senior management are rewarded only on short-term revenues and are penalized for delays in profit, the firm would be jeopardizing its long-term growth.[76] CEOs may be averse to taking risks necessary for innovation if there is no immediate possibility of profits, thus jeopardizing the firm's development of future markets.[77] A more successful approach appears to be incentivizing CEOs for creating innovations for long-term growth.[78]

GM's ultimate bankruptcy and government bailout in 2009 was a long time coming. It points to a deep-seated failure to build a culture of innovation. The root cause of this failure was the firm's structuring of rewards to placate unions, support an elite, and achieve short-term accounting profits at the cost of long-term innovation and growth.

Incentives for Innovation: 3M

3M claims it is one of the world's successful new products company. By 2009, its worldwide sales topped $25 billion, with operations in more than sixty countries, and employment over 79,000.[79] 3M has built a corporate culture highly supportive of innovation that has made it well known for invention and creativity. As Ronald Mitsch, senior vice president of Research and Development at 3M in the 1990s, admitted: "Innovation does not just happen unless you make sure people know it is a top priority and then provide them with enough freedom and resources to make it work."[80]

3M incentivizes employees in numerous ways. Since 1920, 3M has followed a policy of allowing researchers to spend up to 15% of their time working on projects of their choice. Many successful products, including the Post-it® note, were results of the 15% rule. The 15% rule also benefits researchers because it gives them an opportunity to shape their own careers on projects that interest them.

3M permits a "freedom to fail" policy that does not penalize employees for trying new products and inventions. Its "dual ladder" policy enables technical people to advance up the technical side of the ladder, taking on increased responsibilities for technologies instead of people and budgets. Scientists who are happiest in the lab can remain there without losing pay or recognition and receive promotions on the technical side of the dual ladder.

3M focuses acutely on developing new businesses and markets. It has a goal that 25% of sales must come from products that did not exist five years earlier. It gives "Golden Step Awards" for products that sell $2 million, at a profit, within the first two or three years of national production.

3M's culture of tolerating failure dates almost to the founding of the company.[81] Dick Drew, one of the architects of innovation at the firm, was an engineering school dropout.[82] One of his first assignments was testing 3M's waterproof sandpaper at the automobile paint shops. He learned of problems body shops were having while painting cars. When the painters tried to remove the protective tape, it would invariably damage the paint job. Drew promised to produce a better, nondrying adhesive tape, even without knowing how to do it.[83]

His boss asked him to drop the project, reminding him that 3M was an abrasives company and not a tape company.[84] However, Drew kept at it. Within two years of working on it within the company without approval, Drew developed the Scotch masking tape in 1925.[85] 3Mers believe that at this point the culture changed at 3M.[86] 3M decided they were going to tolerate failure and they were not going to discipline someone for doing the right thing.[87]

The same principle resulted in the discovery of the Post-it note. 3M scientist Spencer Silver was looking to invent super glue but instead created a semi-permanent adhesive.[88] At the time, 3M was not looking for a semi-permanent adhesive and he found no products within 3M that could use his adhesive.[89] But rather than dispose of the technology because it had no use within the company and reprimand Spencer for wasting time, the technology was stored in the company laboratory and used years later as the basis for the Post-it note.

Five years later, 3M's Art Fry was frustrated by the scrap paper bookmarks that kept falling out of his hymn book and onto the floor during choir rehearsals. Fry decided to make a better bookmark that would stick lightly to paper without tearing the paper when it was removed.[90]

Fry decided to coat the bookmark with Spencer's adhesive. When Fry used the newly conceived bookmark to write messages to his boss, a new idea dawned on him—it was not a bookmark but a note.[91] However, he faced tough problems and marketing resistance within the company toward the product. He used his 15% time for eighteen months to find solutions for the product. Market surveys for the product received lukewarm interest from consumers. 3M managers then conducted a fresh personal sampling of the test Post-it notes and found that 90% of the people who tried the notes would buy them.

Finally in 1980, several years after Fry first conceived the idea, the Post-it note was launched nationally.[92] The Post-it note team won 3M's Golden Step Award. This award recognizes teams that develop profitable products yielding sales for 3M.[93] The team won the award two years in a row in 1981 and 1982. Today, there are more than four hundred Post-it products sold in more than a hundred countries.[94]

This success was facilitated by 3M's tolerance of trial and error in the innovation process. At the outset, Spencer was allowed to create a product which had no commercial value for the company at the time. Spencer spent years showing the product to various departments within 3M but none had use or need for it.[95] "My discovery was a solution waiting for a problem to solve," said

Spencer.[96] Five years later, as noted, 3M allowed Fry to use his 15% time for over eighteen months to work on a product that the company did not believe, at the time, had any commercial value. As Fry said, "At 3M we are a bunch of ideas. We never throw an idea away because you never know when someone else may need it."[97]

Apart from the 15% option and dual career paths, 3M has a number of programs to incentivize innovation. These include:[98]

- Seed capital: money granted to a researcher to further the development of a new idea or technology.
- The Carlton Society Award: "honors employees for outstanding career scientific achievements, their contributions to new technologies or products, and high standards of originality, dedication, and integrity."[99]
- Circle of Technical Excellence & Innovation Awards: awarded for outstanding "contributions to 3M's technical capabilities."[100]

3M's consistent emphasis on developing new products and markets, strong monetary and nonmonetary incentives for innovation, tolerance of failure, and creation of a separate reward and promotion structure to recognize the nonmanagerial scientists within the organization has made it a world leader in the development of new products and innovation.[101]

Structuring Team Incentives: IBM's Learning from Online Gamers

Firms that value innovation are finding they have to be innovative about being innovative. For some it means looking outside traditional research models to study and understand ways to promote innovation and creativity amongst employees. For others, implementing policies that encourage and celebrate failure is a step in the practical direction. IBM Research is a case in point.

Recently, IBM Research, in collaboration with Stanford University and the MIT Sloan School of Management, undertook a study of the online multiplayer gaming virtual world to research whether lessons in innovation and leadership could be learned from observing behavior of the online gamers.[102] Unexpectedly, IBM learned some interesting lessons on incentives and risk taking from the gamers.

In online games, much more so than in the real world, IBM found that the incentive systems rewarded players on the willingness to take risks during the game.[103] In online gaming, risk taking is encouraged and failure is accepted as the cost of doing business. A player was rewarded for enterprise irrespective of the player's age, education level, or position. In the real world, risk taking can be a permanent black mark or career killer.

IBM also found that when incentive systems in online games were openly available to all players, it increased trust and credibility amongst the players. IBM learned that the complexity of the incentive structure was directly affected by the size of the team and the availability of leadership opportunities. For games that needed a guild or team of seventy or eighty people, a complex incentive system was necessary to motivate the team. Whereas, for smaller teams of only twenty or thirty guild members, greater opportunities for leadership were available, and so a less complex incentive structure was necessary for smaller teams than for larger teams.[104] Thus, where opportunities for innovation and enterprise existed, fewer monetary incentives were needed.

In trying to adopt the lessons learned from the online gaming world, IBM researchers found that some elements, such as transparency in incentive structures, were easier to implement in the real world than other elements, such as an inherent tolerance for risk.

Nevertheless, IBM started implementing what it learned from the computer games to address risk taking and failure within the company. It found that allowing employees the space to make mistakes while instilling confidence to try new things far outweighed the risk of failure. The company did so practically by breaking major operations into smaller projects that enabled it to better incentivize employees with leadership roles. The smaller projects also allowed for more failure, because in smaller doses failure was more palatable and affordable.[105]

IBM modified its incentive structure to allow time for risk and failure. IBM Research now evaluates its engineers on one- and three-year time frames: one-year for bonus and three-year for rank and salary.[106] The three-year evaluation cycle demonstrates the company's commitment to investing in the early, risky stages of innovation that take years to show results.[107] The three-year time frame also helps compensate for any one bad year.[108] By rewarding employees on dual criteria, IBM encourages employees to undertake riskier long-term innovation projects which they might not have otherwise chosen to do.

IBM was itself innovative in researching the rapidly growing and exceedingly popular world of online gaming to learn how to deal with risk. And its willingness to step outside the box produced some unusual results to help the company improve innovation and creativity.

CONCLUSION

This chapter highlights the following principles about designing incentives for enterprise.

- Incentives are powerful. They can substantially alter individual and corporate behavior. They are perhaps the strongest organizational practice that drives innovation. They constitute the core practice that firms can control to motivate innovativeness among employees and transform the culture of their organization toward one of innovation.

- Traditional incentives based on seniority, rank, and years of service motivate loyalty but not innovation. They may actually demotivate innovation as innovative or new employees leave and noninnovative or long-time employees stay.

- Incentives for enterprise need to be asymmetric: they should have strong rewards for success with weak penalties for failure. One powerful incentive for innovation is to allow employees a generous fraction of their time to explore their own ideas.

- Perks are incentives. Because young and new talent is often highly motivated and idealistic, offering them generous perks comparable to what senior employees receive can be highly motivating for innovation.

- Failure must be tolerated or even encouraged so long as employees learn from failure. Social penalties, such as shame, should be minimized for failure.

- Monetary (or economic) incentives in the form of salary raises, bonuses, perks, and stock options are strong motivators of performance. Incentives stimulate action along the metrics chosen for evaluation. A mix of metrics avoids perverse response from choosing only one metric. Especially important is choosing metrics that reflect sales from commercialized innovations and long-term growth.

- The psychology of incentives is as important as their economics. Moral and social incentives can be as strong as economic incentives but cost less. Social incentives in the form of praise, employee recognition, awards, and celebrations cost less than economic incentives but could be quite effective. The simple reason for this fact is that most people value the respect, admiration, and esteem of their peers far more than they value money, especially for what one can design with equivalent cost. Moral incentives (appealing to moral values or aspirations) are basically free, but can be powerful. Moral and social incentives thus should always be in the mix with economic incentives.

• Incentives can have negative, unintended effects especially if penalties are strong and participants do not have a fair chance to achieve the positive incentives. Framing incentives as gains is better than framing them as losses.

In sum, incentives are powerful but highly varied. They can be positive, as in honor, or negative, as in shame. They can be tied to success or failure. They can take a variety of forms including monetary, moral, or social. Carelessly designed, they can turn out to be costly and backfire. But skillfully designed they can be quite effective for innovations. Most important, incentives need to be asymmetric, with strong rewards for success and weak penalties for failure.

CHAPTER 6

Fostering Internal Markets

*Internal markets bring external competition inside so as
not be obsoleted by innovators outside.*

IN THE LAST SEVERAL DECADES, Silicon Valley may have
generated more innovations, start-ups, patents, initial public offerings, and wealth per capita than any other geographic region in
the world. In particular, with 1% of the U.S. population, Silicon Valley generates 12% of its patents and 27% of its venture
capital.[1] A recent study finds Silicon Valley ranks first among all
such ecosystems in the world and in terms of start-ups alone it is
three times bigger than the second on the list, New York City.[2]
Moreover, many of these start-ups have grown to become highly
successful, fast growing, and very profitable firms with huge market
caps. One consultant in the Valley summarizes the success of the
Valley thus: "Never has so much wealth been created in so little
time by so few people."[3] The wealth they have created has been a
boon not only to their founders but also to their employees, the
state of California, and the whole U.S. economy. Silicon Valley has
been so successful that cities, states, and countries all over the world
have tried to emulate its success by initiating Silicon Valley–like
clusters of their own: Silicon Alley, Allee, Beach, Bog, Fen, Forest,
Glen, Gulf, Gorge, Hill, Plateau, Slopes, Wadi, are just a few of
the many such imitations around the world.

What most characterizes Silicon Valley is probably a free market
for ideas, funds, talent, and innovations.[4] The entrepreneurial

atmosphere is so intense that it attracts talent from other similar clusters around the world. Even Google, with the most generous working conditions of any corporation in the world, finds it difficult to prevent its talented employees from leaving to form start-ups of their own in the Valley.[5] Would not corporations and even governments benefit from having within the organization a productive culture like that of Silicon Valley?[6] How can one bring the outside market within the organization to ensure its survival, productivity, and growth? That is the subject of this chapter. That is the concept of fostering internal markets.

In reality, the situation within organizations is just the opposite of that in markets. Successful start-ups grow to become large organizations. Large organizations develop bureaucracies, which are characterized by a hierarchy of authority, numerous rules to guide employees' behavior, and numerous procedures to guide activities. Bureaucracies tend to be homogenous and monolithic. That is, various parts of the hierarchy all follow the same procedures and all ultimately report upwards to a single authority. Bureaucracies are not inherently bad. They develop with one predominant goal in mind—to keep the organization running smoothly and efficiently. A large, successful organization must ensure the satisfaction of its current customers and the future continuation of the past stream of profits. Thus, bureaucracies are designed to perpetuate the past that yielded success.

However, for these very reasons, bureaucracies inhibit radical innovations. Innovation is amorphous and risky. Bureaucracies are precise and predictable. Innovation requires embracing divergence. Bureaucracies ensure uniformity. Innovation thrives on quick decisions in response to a changing environment. Bureaucracies are slow moving, requiring numerous approvals for minor deviations. Innovation encapsulates the future. Bureaucracies institutionalize the past. Innovation is about capturing future markets and future profits. Bureaucracies are all about protecting past customers and past profits. Thus, bureaucracies tend to smother innovation. And the more monolithic and homogenous the bureaucracy, the less innovative it is. When a bureaucracy does produce innovations, it favors incremental or sustaining innovations that fit with its current skills, routines, and markets. Bureaucracies tend to overlook radical innovations that can transform markets or cannibalize current products. Chapter 2 underscores with examples how these issues led dominant incumbents to overlook the next big radical innovation that would have sustained and furthered its success.

For example, by 2005, Research in Motion (RIM) was the leading producer of smart phones with a dominant position. Its BlackBerry was a favorite of the corporate market because it offered two unique features, security and a miniature keyboard. A whole bureaucracy developed around phones that perfected these features. Cofounder Rick Lazaridis give this bureaucracy his stamp of approval, saying, "We will always work from the present status of the BlackBerry in terms of reliability and security, because that is what our users expect."[7] As a result, innovation around new evolving technologies and fast-changing consumer needs suffered. "Their overriding ambition was to protect the products instead of adapting to fast-changing customers tastes," is how one reporter describes the culture within the firm.[8] After Apple came out with touch-screen phones, the BlackBerrys with miniature keyboards seemed increasingly archaic and RIM's market cap declined sharply, from $78 billion in May 2008 to $7 billion in April 2012.

Is there an organizational structure that especially fosters radical innovation against the drag of bureaucracies? My research with Rajesh Chandy involving 24 face-to-face interviews and 194 completed surveys of executives responsible for new product development shows that internal markets can serve as an important antidote to bureaucratic structures.[9] A few others have also urged the use of internal markets for this purpose.[10] Internal markets bring into the organization the healthy aspects of the competition that exists outside the organization. Internal markets consist of teams of employees, business units, or divisions that at least partially compete with each other. The rivalry involves the freedom to compete to research, develop, or market alternate ideas, technologies, products, or business models for various consumers. Research teams could write proposals for funds, facilities, and talent to develop promising innovations. Other teams that have developed innovations could lobby business units to commercialize these innovations. Business units themselves would have some freedom to commercialize innovations even though these innovations may compete with existing products of other divisions.

Several caveats are in order at the outset. The selection of technologies or business models on which to compete must be restricted to those that build on the firm's current strengths or are likely to cannibalize the firm's current successful products. As such, the firm still maintains a strong interest and competence in such technologies or business models, so the internal competition does not degenerate into a mad rush into anything and everything. Even then, internal markets have many risks and costs, which this chapter addresses. Further, those employees, teams, or business units that lose out in this competition should not be punished. As Chapter 5 emphasizes, the rewards system in this competition must combine strong incentives for success with weak penalties for failure. Losing teams must be encouraged to "learn and move on."

The structure of internal markets offers firms three important advantages.[11] First, it helps the firm fight obsolescence. Every firm today lives with the prospect of dozens or hundreds of rivals, innovators, or entrepreneurs all over the globe planning on marketing products of the future that might cannibalize the firm's existing products. The essential logic of internal markets is to grow or bring within the firm such innovators that otherwise would flourish independently outside the firm. These innovators may then help the firm cannibalize itself before an outsider in the external market does so (see Chapter 2). Second, internal markets provide the firm with options. In most markets, rival technological platforms coexist. A firm may not be sure which technology will be the most successful in the future. With internal markets, a firm may support two or more technological platforms at the same time so that it has multiple options depending on which takes off in the future. Later this chapter addresses the potential duplication or lack of focus that having these options entails. Third, internal markets motivate employees to give their best. Competition resulting from internal markets spurs individuals or teams to do better than their rivals. Lack of competition leads individuals or teams to coast or, worse still, leads motivated talent to exit the firm. Thus, well-managed competition can lead to an increase in creativity and productivity.

Characteristics of Markets

What are the essential elements of markets? We can think of four primary characteristics of markets.[12] These are:

1. **A forum for choice**. The most important aspect of a market is that it lets consumers choose freely among offerings. That freedom enables only the best ideas and products to survive. Mediocre ones will die out from nonselection.

2. **A forum for competitive offers**. The next most important element of a market is that competitors are free to enter and offer products to consumers for a price. As a result of free entry and consumer choice, firms must constantly strive to satisfy

181

consumers with better products or lower prices. Competition among suppliers will enhance consumer choice. It will also encourage competitors to strive to improve their products and lower their prices to survive and flourish.

3. **A forum for exchange**. A market provides a place or medium where sellers can exhibit their products and services, buyers can see what's available, and buyers and sellers can close the deal. This is typically what we refer to as a marketplace.

4. **A forum for information exchange**. A fourth important characteristic of a market is the availability of information about buyers and sellers, provided by themselves or by third parties. The information is typically about the nature of demand and supply. Information is the lubricant that keeps the market functioning smoothly. However, the price mechanism in markets can also serve as an indirect transmission or signal of information. When prices are on the rise, it may signal increasing demand for a commodity, which may drive investment in that commodity. The reverse is true of declining prices.

These characteristics of markets lead to three important outcomes that are highly beneficial to the community at large.

Markets as Idea Generators

Well-functioning markets abound with fresh ideas. Entrepreneurs are constantly thinking up new and better ways to produce goods and services. They then build prototypes and seek out financing to commercialize these new goods and services. In particular, they tap angel investors and venture capitalists for funding for these ideas. For example, an average venture capitalist in Silicon Valley could get as many as five thousand unsolicited business plans a year.[13] Large corporations that have not internalized the market for ideas may get just a handful. Although markets are rich in diverse ideas, corporations struggle with few homogenous ideas as employees labor under the burden of routines.

Having many diverse ideas is vital for innovation. For any problem, all that's needed is one good solution. The probability of hitting that solution increases with the number and diversity of ideas.[14] The larger the pool, the more likely it will encompass a good idea. The greater the variance in ideas, the more likely it will encompass top ideas, besides the bad ones. Thus, in contrast to quality control, where manufacturers strive to raise the mean and reduce the variance, in idea generating, firms need to raise the number and variance of ideas. The market is rich in precisely what the corporation is poor—diversity and number of ideas. Internalizing the market will ensure that corporations have a rich set of ideas to begin the innovation process.

The firm can reach out to three groups to maximize the diversity and number of ideas: employees, consumers, and suppliers. The larger the corporation, the greater its tendency toward bureaucracy and lethargy; however, if all those employees were incentivized to generate ideas through fairs, contests, and prizes, the firm could harvest a wealth of ideas. With the growth of consumer online activity, consumers can also be tapped for ideas through properly constructed websites. These websites can also be structured to allow voting by consumers of the best ideas, similar to rating reviews in Amazon.com. Consumers can be motivated with prizes for winning ideas or just the honor of being the top idea person. Such idea generation from consumers in online forums has been called "crowdsourcing."[15] A similar system can be set up for suppliers. Thus, by properly incentivizing and organizing idea generation, firms can tap their pool of employees, consumers, and suppliers for ideas.

Markets as Talent Pools

Employees love loyalty. Innovators love adventure. Our experience with corporations, especially large successful ones, is that they succeed in developing a large core of loyal employees. But they struggle with developing innovators. The reason for this situation is the failure to recognize and reward talent within. The reward for talent within organizations typically follows a declining response curve—superior talent earns higher reward but at a declining rate. In contrast, the reward for talent in the marketplace is exponential—superior talent is rewarded at an increasing rate (see Figure 6.1).

Beyond a point, these two curves intersect and then diverge further apart. Before that point, firms exist in the region of loyalty. Here, talent has no reason to leave the firm. Beyond that point, organizations fail to reward talent as much as the market does. That is the region of mobility. In this region, organizations that are not aggressively challenging their talent to innovate and not generously rewarding them will bleed talent to the market. Such talent will seek out organizations that are more innovation oriented

Figure 6.1. The Market for Talent

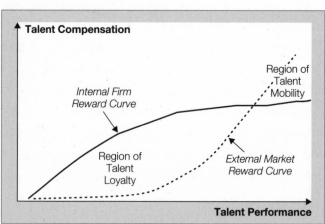

184

or they will launch out on their own. Alternatively, such talent will leave to form start-ups that compete with their former employer. Scott Cook, the chairman of Intuit, had this to say about talent: "I wake up every morning knowing that if my people don't sense a compelling vision and a big upside, they'll simply leave."[16] Tony Fadell, sometimes referred to as the "Father of the iPod," was employed by Philips before he tried to develop a music player on his own, failed, and was subsequently hired by Apple (see Chapter 7). The role of Philips in mobile music may well have been different if it had managed to retain and empower Fadell to develop a mobile music player for them.

To retain talent, some firms, such as Google, pamper their employees with extravagant amenities (see Chapter 5). These are small costs to bear for the highly profitable innovations that those employees could generate. But incentives and amenities are not enough. The most important motivation for attraction and retention of talent is the opportunity to shape the world of the future by working on the next big innovation. Internalizing the market for talent involves giving units adequate freedom within the corporation to attract talent and giving talent freedom to join projects and units that work on innovations that excite them.

Markets as Efficient Resource Allocators

Markets are great forums for the efficient allocation of resources. Essentially, sellers who produce better goods amass profits, which they can invest in even better products. Products that are duds do not sell, discouraging further investment in their production. In contrast, the resource allocation *within* an organization, especially a large one, is sticky. Resources normally flow from top to bottom. Top managers are prone to support their pet projects, the ones they developed, or on whose success they moved up the ladder. In such a process, old products suck resources way past their prime.

Examples are GM's investment in SUVs, Kodak's investment in film photography, Microsoft's investment in MSN, Intel's investment in chips for PCs. However, markets outside are in a constant flux. Old products die out as innovations steal market share from them. Externally markets constantly and smoothly allocate resources to the most promising innovations. The challenge for large corporations is to internalize this efficiency in resource allocation in the market outside. They need to make sure that talented employees within the firm are not shortchanged for resources. Gary Hamel articulates this dilemma well: "It's ironic that companies pay CEOs millions upon millions to unlock shareholder wealth but seem incapable of funneling six- and seven-figure rewards to people who can actually create new wealth."[17]

Large corporations have a thorough screening process to invest in projects. This screening tends to be highly risk averse and geared to avoid losses (see Chapter 3). Big innovations are risky and could easily be screened out in such a process. In contrast, the market outside involves small sums of money that are successively invested in a range of ideas. The market's concern is not loss avoidance but upside gain. Highly risky projects with a huge upside get funded in a portfolio of similar projects, even though many of them could well fail. All it takes is one big success amid many failures. Internalizing the market for resource allocation means replacing the top-down allocation with a bottom-up competition for funds. Innovators, individually or in teams, should be allowed to compete for a pool of funds. Senior managers should serve as referees rather than judges. To fully internalize the external market, at least some of the judges of these competitions should be future-oriented experts in the area, from the outside market—business and academia. Firms should slowly move their funds for research, development, and commercialization from a legacy model of supporting old favorites to a market model of supporting ideas, prototypes, and innovations generated by talent within or outside the organization.

Markets also have some negative outcomes that deserve to be discussed.

Cascades and Bubbles

The phenomenon of cascades and bubbles derives directly from the signaling present in markets. If many buyers are not well informed and make purchases based on the purchases of other buyers, markets can cascade onto some popular choices that are not necessarily good. Those choices become considerably overpriced yet hugely popular, resulting in bubbles. The Internet crash of 1999–2000 and housing crash of 2008–2009 are recent examples of an age-old problem. When the bubble bursts, a large number of buyers and sellers get hurt. Thus, markets are not always a panacea. Within a firm, cascades and bubbles may arise when decisions are based on votes, which themselves are influenced by comments of others rather than in-depth analysis of the options. Such signaling can occur if decision makers have access to others' evaluations or votes, such as occurs in some crowdsourcing setups. Cascades and bubbles can be minimized by encouraging decision makers to evaluate proposals on the merits of each proposal at hand and minimizing their access to signals from others.

Cutthroat Competition

Markets also lead to cutthroat competition. They wean out the inefficient and mediocre and reward the efficient and good. Although this is painful yet acceptable outside a firm, it can be traumatic within a firm and dysfunctional if not managed well. Indeed, the popular press is quite critical of internal markets for this one reason.[18] Many employees join corporations because they do not want the risk, ruthless competition, and insecurity from being independent contractors or entrepreneurs in real markets. They love the paternal attitude and job security of large corporations. As Bob Gatto, vice president of business development at Nestle, says, "People come to a corporation for a [secure] corporate job."[19] Thus, many employees have a strong distaste for internal markets. However, such markets will be highly attractive to the most enterprising and talented employees. Indeed, carefully introducing internal markets into organizations could well stem the loss of talent to entrepreneurial ventures while motivating risk-averse employees to become entrepreneurial. The goal of the firm is to retain its brightest talent even if it means losing the security-minded employees for whom the office is too hot.

Lack of Cooperation

An essential element of the development of innovations within a firm is the sharing of ideas, cross-stimulation, and cooperation among various employees involved with development. Internal markets run the danger of destroying this healthy environment. To minimize this loss, firms can adopt a number of mechanisms to encourage cooperation. First, at quarterly or six-month intervals, various teams can present their research and progress at open seminars within the firm. All parties can then see the progress of the team, provide comments for improvement, as well as learn from advances and failure. Second, employees can be provided with monetary or other incentives for contributing ideas to teams other than their own. Third, all teams involved in serving a particular market, albeit with rival technologies or products, could be provided with some fraction of the reward of the team that does best and succeeds. This reward system would be similar to that within a conference in the NCAA[20] competition. Teams within a conference compete aggressively to win the conference and go to a national bowl championship. But all teams share in the profits that accrue to the winning team. A relevant example is the sharing of a bonus by Andy Rubin, a vice president at Google in fall 2008. With the launching of the first Android phone, Rubin won a multibillion-dollar contractual bonus. He voluntarily shared this with his team of over a hundred employees, who each received between $10,000 and $50,000.[21] In general, the firm needs to emphasize that the goal of internal competition is not for one team or individual to beat another but for the whole firm to explore and advance a variety of avenues due to the uncertainty of knowing which particular one will best succeed.

Failure

One of the results of competition in the market, especially in the development and commercialization of innovations, is that many such efforts fail. All these failure can be costly. However, in the external market, these costs are borne by entrepreneurs and those investors who decided to back the entrepreneurs at their own risk. However, in the case of internal markets, failure is borne by the firm that institutes and supports such internal markets. Because only a few innovations succeed, the cost of failure can be high. But as Chapter 3's discussion on embracing risk reiterated, this cost is one that the innovator must be willing to bear. Reluctance to accept failure and learn from it leads to risk aversion, inertia, and lack of innovativeness. Indeed, internal markets are means by which a firm can institutionalize the trait of embracing risk (see Chapter 3). The question then is not whether a firm should bear such costs, but to what extent it can bear such costs and how much it learns from failure to do better in the future.

Duplication

When internal markets are tolerated, encouraged, and established within a firm, it inevitably leads to higher costs from duplication when two or more groups, business units, or divisions try to serve the same market of consumers with rival products or technologies. To do so effectively, they need resources in the form of budgets, talent, and space. Thus, the firm may have to double the resources it devotes to serving one market. If the outcome is two competing but independently viable units, then this cost will be justified. If the outcome is the successful marketing of an innovation that otherwise would have been overlooked, then the cost is certainly justified. However, if one unit fails to produce a viable or successful product, then the investment in that unit seems wasted.

The firm has to evaluate all such waste against two pros. First, with internal competition comes the potential benefit of bringing within the firm innovations that would otherwise have emerged outside in the open market. One criterion that the firm could use is the danger of cannibalization from outside. How likely is it that a potential alternate technology would be developed and commercialized by a competitor and subsequently cannibalize the firm's successful products? If such a probability is very small to zero, then the firm need not focus on such a technology. The higher this probability, the greater the resources the firm needs to devote to that technology. Second, with internal competition comes the potential benefit that the firm does not focus all its resources on a single technology that subsequently does not bear fruit or becomes obsolete.

Consider, for example, GM. As discussed in Chapter 4, in the 1990s and 2000s the firm spent over a billion dollars on the hydrogen fuel cell as an alternative to the gasoline engine. However, a variety of alternatives to the internal combustion engine were on the horizon, including the hybrid engine, lithium-ion battery, methanol cell, liquid natural gas–based engine, and alcohol-based engine. GM spent most of its resources on the hydrogen cell at the cost of developing or at least exploring alternate technologies. The root problem may have been lack of internal competition.

190

Without such competition, research resources were devoted on the one technology picked by managers at the top. Initial investment in talent and resources would have led to further investments, as talent drawn for one technology would tend to see it as the best. As it turned out, the hybrid technology (pioneered by the Toyota Prius) and then the lithium-ion battery (pioneered by Tesla) made more rapid inroads into the market than the hydrogen cell. In particular, the lithium-ion battery was pioneered by Tesla for less than $100 million. A portfolio strategy, with rival teams focusing on rival technologies, may have initially appeared redundant. However, such a strategy may have led to a more efficient and productive use of the over $1 billion that GM spent on the hydrogen cell with little to show for it.

Lack of Focus

Competition in the external markets means dozens to hundreds of individuals, entrepreneurs, and firms competing to serve a single market with some innovation. Lack of focus in not an issue when the innovation is the primary focus of these entities. However, fostering internal markets within a firm can create dozens of entities competing against each other. Such competition runs the risk of diluting the firm's focus on its primary task. After all, a generation of experts have emphasized that firms are better off focusing on their core competence than on diversifying into unrelated businesses.[22] Thus, the firm that embarks on internal markets must ensure that the competition is about alternate technologies that are central to the firm's mission and do not take the firm into completely unrelated fields.

For example, it makes eminent sense for Philips, a lighting company, to encourage competition among its employees for the next platform technology that will empower its lighting products, be it incandescence, fluorescence, light-emitting diodes (LED), or microwave electrodeless discharge (MED). These are all technologies with plausible futures in lighting. It does not make sense for Philips to initiate competition for engine technologies, which are at best peripheral to its mission. Similarly, the race for the next technology that will power the automobile engine of tomorrow is not yet decided. It makes sense for GM, an automobile company, to have measured investments and some degree of competition among teams for all of the rival technologies listed above. It does not make sense for GM to initiate internal competition for lighting technologies, which is peripheral to its mission.

Implementing Internal Markets

We can classify organizations by the extent to which they generate and select ideas or innovations. Using two levels, internal or external to the firm, on each of these two dimensions gives us four cells (see Table 6.1). The classic firm (for example, Apple) is one in which innovations are generated primarily by internal employees and then selected by internal managers.

Classic universities are those where ideas in the form of papers are generated internally but selected for publication by external journals. Publishers may be considered a form where innovations are generated externally by various authors but selected internally by a small group of acquisition editors. Finally, we come to

Table 6.1. Classification of Organizations by Degree of Internal Markets

Selection of Innovations	Generation of Innovations	
	Internal	**External**
Internal	Classic Firms e.g., Apple	Classic Publishers e.g., HarperCollins
External	Classic Universities e.g., Stanford	Innovation Hosts e.g., YouTube

Source: Adapted from Terwiesch and Ulrich, *Innovation Tournaments.*

innovation hosts, which serve merely as a platform where outsiders can generate innovations and other outsiders vote for their favorites. These platforms are highly dynamic, highly efficient, and very contemporary. Ideally, fostering internal markets means moving the organization from the top left cell to the bottom right cell. However, such a dramatic shift remains an aspiration that will be very difficult to implement in the short term, if at all. In most cases, firms can steadily increase internal markets by adopting one of several organizational forms as explained next.

A question the reader might ask is why should firms not emulate Apple, which used an internal-internal mode? Apple did so under the direction of Steve Jobs. His deep, intuitive understanding of consumers' future needs is highly unusual. If a firm does indeed have a Steve Jobs, then it could successfully employ the internal-internal mode. But for most firms with limited talent, moving to external-external mode ensures bringing the market within for productive generation and selection of ideas.

An important principle to consider is having separate processes for evaluating radical and incremental innovations. Incremental innovations are improvements in design or components within existing platform innovations. Radical innovations are the start of new platform technologies based on entirely new scientific principles (see Chapter 2). 3M makes it a point to keep the process for evaluating radical innovations separate from that for evaluating incremental innovations.[23] An entirely new team, not one wedded to and invested in the old technology, evaluates the radical or platform innovation. This way, the radical innovation is not viewed through the lens of the old technology. Doing otherwise will lead to watering down the radical innovation or entirely rejecting it (see Chapter 3).

Several organization forms can slowly introduce internal markets to an organization. These forms embody some aspect of an internal market, but they are sufficiently local that they do not require a radical change in organization structure. They are listed in the order of increasing commitment of resources, space, funds, and internal markets. As a result, they are increasingly costly in terms of employee tension, resource commitment, and management time. But at the same time, they are also increasingly productive in terms of stimulating, generating, or commercializing innovations.

Idea Fairs. Subu Goparaju, senior vice president at Infosys, said that the company receives a great number of ideas from employees. However, 90% of the ideas are not valuable, 9% of the ideas are okay, and less than 1% are great. The problem is identifying the 1% while, as he says, "The 99% need to be engaged."[24] As emphasized earlier in this chapter, generating a large number of ideas is a strength, not a weakness, as it increases the chance of finding one great idea. However, screening ideas is a challenge. The idea fair is one solution. The fair provides a mechanism to screen the 1%, while the chance to win the reward(s) for the winner(s) can motivate the 99%.

An idea fair is a periodic event where individuals or teams propose ideas to judges for seed funding. The fairs could take the form of research seminars, a day or week where all participants can display their ideas, or a website that has descriptions of each idea. A team of judges then selects ideas. The judges may be drawn from peers, senior managers in the organization, or experts from outside. Participants may be encouraged to vote on other ideas excluding their own. The judges may use such votes in arriving at their judgment. After a review process, managers may decide to support the best ideas with funds or release time for employees. The output would be a formal proposal for substantial funding.

For example, each year Google sets aside one week called Innovation Week. During that week, employees can pitch their ideas to win greater support and resources. As another example, in 2010, PwC initiated a competition where teams of employees all over the United States could compete with proposals for helping the firm grow by 25% in the next planning cycle. Judges for the competition were drawn primarily from within the organization. These are forms of internal markets for ideas that are relatively easy to initiate and pay off right from the start, although they provide only a starting point and not a finished innovation.

Research Contests. In this case, resources are made available for competing proposals by individuals or teams of employees. The proposals would have to show a body of completed work and an adequate market for the potential innovation. The reward would be funds, facilities, or talent to develop the innovation in a one- to three-year time frame. This form of internal competition requires more investment from the firm but also delivers more output than the idea fair.

For example, 3M runs a competition for seed funding for teams that often form between divisions and groups to work on new technologies and products. Both 3M and Google have a feature where an employee who uses his or her (15% or 20%) time for an innovation project can solicit coworkers to contribute their (15% or 20%) time to the his or her project. This is an excellent system for three reasons. First, it relies on the wisdom of the crowds. Employees are likely to donate their own time to someone else's project. Thus, employees vote with their feet for the project they think is most deserving. Second, it reduces the onus on management to evaluate hundreds of ideas and projects. Third, it puts the burden of proof on the employee to establish the credit worthiness of his or her own project by winning support from coworkers. Such support in the form of other employee's time increases the progress on the project.

195

Commercialization   Contests. Commercialization contests would be for completed research projects that have produced a prototype that is almost ready for commercialization. The team that has developed the innovation would then have the option to present the proposal for commercialization to various business units within the corporation. It's best to have a two-way competition among the prototypes for acceptance by a business unit and among business units for adoption of a prototype. The final decision could rest with experts within and outside the firms, based on past record and fit with the current business's portfolio. This is a serious form of internal market that requires considerable involvement and support from top management and business units. However, it provides an outlet for commercializing innovations that might otherwise stay on the shelves of the firm's laboratories. It addresses a persistent problem facing some firms with large R&D labs (such as Yahoo!, 3M, Microsoft). In the words of a former VP of Labs at HP, "Our problem is not generating innovations. Our problem is getting them out of the door."

Contest for Internal Start-Ups. Groups that have already developed and tested an innovation compete for a mandate from senior managers to commercialize the innovation by starting up a new business unit for this purpose. This form of internal market requires a huge commitment of talent, resources, and time from management. But it has the potential for substantial payoff if the commercialization is successful.

Competing Divisions or Business Units. Two or more divisions or business units may compete with each other for the same market with alternative technologies. We may think of the two divisions as two rival small firms within the organization. Each is attuned to the latest technologies in order to best serve consumers' emerging needs. For example, in the early decade of the home printer market, HP housed the inkjet technology and the laser technology, each in a rival division. Each division could promote the technology in competition with the other division. As it turned out, neither technology was universally superior to the other. This healthy competition ensured that both technologies got adequate support. They ended up serving different consumer segments while HP dominated the home printer market.

Autonomous Units. A firm can entrust autonomous groups within a corporation with a secret or semisecret mission to develop an innovation without interference from the parent corporation or division. A term sometimes used for such a unit is *skunk works*. The term probably originated with Lockheed Martin's Advanced Development Programs (ADP), which is responsible for some well-known aircraft design, including the U-2, SR-71 Blackbird, the F-117 Nighthawk, and the F-22 Raptor. Another good example is IBM's Boca Raton division in the early 1980s, which was entrusted with developing the PC. The parent corporation, heavily focused on the mainframe, was skeptical or opposed to any involvement with microcomputers. On the one hand, the Boca Raton division, on the other hand, given the resources, autonomy, and talent, developed and successfully marketed the IBM PC in one year. Of all forms of internal markets, autonomous units and competing divisions involve the greatest commitment of resources, talent, and management time. However, if they are skillfully managed, they can ensure the commercialization of potentially profitable innovations.

Divestiture. A divestiture is a group or division that is separated from the parent and given full autonomy to pursue a special product market. There are two major forms: spin-off and management buyout. The spin-off is publicly traded on the stock market and thus has public ownership. A management buyout is the purchase of a unit responsible for an innovation by current managers of the unit. In either case, the parent can retain an interest in the divestiture and an option to buy it back if it turns out to be highly successful. My coauthored research on the topic indicates that although spin-offs may lead to higher initial sales and profits, buyouts lead to higher sales and profits in the long term.[25] The probable reason is that the owner managers (of buyouts) are more interested in long-term payoffs than the agent managers (of spin-offs).

In the last three forms of these organizational structures, perhaps the hardest factor to deal with is the assignment of talent to the new venture. This talent is no longer available to the parent organization. Senior managers may be loath to part with talent, but the organization must keep in mind the greater good. Keeping talent involved in a divestiture in which the parent has a stake has a greater potential payoff, compared to the loss of talent departing in frustration over noncommercialization of their innovation. Moreover, highly entrepreneurial individuals are more likely to stay with a corporation when given the task of commercializing a challenging innovation than managing an existing product or service. For example, in the 1970s Xerox developed most of the innovations of the computer age in its famed labs, PARC, but commercialized only a couple. Due to this failure to commercialize, much of the talent in Xerox's labs left to start up their own ventures or to join firms that commercialized their innovations.

In the first four of these forms, the decision maker who decides who wins and who loses is typically within the organization. That is, a senior management team will decide who wins and proceeds to the next round or stage of development, and who loses and will have to terminate their effort. To better internalize markets, it's best to have external experts included in the decision team or at least make available to the decision team the opinion of experts. In the last of these forms, the decision maker is the market of consumers outside the firm. The market decides which product or technology is better and thus who wins. Letting external consumers decide is the most efficient form of internal markets but also the most costly in terms of investing funds, duplicating resources, and the emotional cost to employees. Thus, managing internal markets is critical for best results.

Managing Internal Markets

The success of internal markets depends primarily on managing this force for innovation. The success depends on determining how to incentivize internal markets, when to set up internal markets, and when to terminate them. Table 6.2 lists a large number of factors that dictate when to set up and when to terminate. The decision to terminate internal markets is relatively straightforward. When the group, division, or team has failed to develop a viable, commercializable, or successful new product, then it needs to be terminated. However, certain internal and market conditions provide strong reasons to set up internal markets.

Incentivizing Internal Markets

Internal markets could easily degenerate into destructive internal competition, in which competing groups withhold information from each other, undercut each other for resources, and work explicitly for the downfall of the competing group or division. Such internal competition was responsible for the downfall of Sony's MP3 player even though it was introduced before the iPod

Table 6.2. Criteria for Setting Up Internal Markets

Criterion	Favoring Internal Markets	Disfavoring Internal Markets
Business model uncertainty	Two or more business models are possible with uncertainty as to success	Industry has coalesced on one business model
Technological uncertainty	Two or more rival technological platforms with uncertainty as to success	Industry has coalesced on one technology
Emerging niche	Emerging niche threatens firm	No new products or market niches on horizon
New product threshold	Firm has a high profit threshold for new products	Firm has low profit threshold for new products
Organizational inertia	Firm is slow to accept new ideas and innovations	Firm is quick to embrace new ideas and innovations
Organizational focus	Firm is focused on protecting its current technology or business model	Firm can focus on multiple rival technologies
Market potential	Huge market potential for rival products or technologies	Market is mature or declining
Talent availability	Firm has adequate talent to support competing teams or divisions	Firm faces a talent crunch
Resources for duplication	Firm has adequate resources to support internal markets	Firm faces a financial crunch

(see Chapter 2). In this case, the self-destruction was motivated by requiring all business units to reach a consensus. This policy meant that the business unit responsible for the MP3 player was held captive to the goals of the movie and music businesses. The latter were afraid that success from an MP3 player would undercut royalties from sales of movies and music. Incentivizing internal markets is finding the sweet spot between the lack of productivity from no competition to self-destruction from hypercompetition.

The sweet spot results from properly distributing incentives among individuals, members, and teams. For example, the founder and CEO of Resources Global Professional, a consulting firm, set up a system where one-third of incentives are based on each of individual performance, team performance, and company performance. Another scheme would be to encourage competition between groups with the winner's innovation project selected for further development, but the monetary reward shared equally with all teams that participated. Still another scheme is to reserve a portion of the incentive to individuals or teams who contribute to other teams. Whatever the form of incentives, requiring consensus among competing teams generally works to undermine healthy competition, as happened at Sony.

As Chapter 5 argues, incentives are powerful means to motivate innovation. Properly designed, they can encourage productive competition and discourage self-destructive competition.

Setting Up Internal Markets

Here are some important conditions when a firm should seriously consider setting up internal markets.

First, internal markets are called for when multiple business models seem viable with uncertainty as to which one will prevail. For example, around the year 2000, Internet firms were unsure about what would be the best means of profiting from

201

the internet. Possible business models would be subscription-based portals (AOL), advertising-based portals (Yahoo!), search (Google) or network communities (Facebook). Microsoft itself launched MSN, which obtained revenues from banner ads. However, it squelched a search-based model that grew spontaneously within the firm for fear that it would cannibalize its banner ad business (see Chapter 2). This would have been a good situation for internal markets. Microsoft could have enabled search-based advertising as a separate business unit within the corporation.

Second, internal markets are called for when two or more rival technological platforms coexist with uncertainty as to which will prevail. For example, in the automobile business, several auto engine technologies vie to be the auto engine of the future: internal combustion engine, hybrid ICE and electric, hydrogen cell, methanol cell, liquid natural gas fuel engine, ethanol fuel engine, or lithium-ion battery. In the 1990s and early 2000s, GM made a bet on hydrogen and invested over a billion dollars on the hydrogen cell. A better strategy would have been to float two to four divisions, each supporting a different technology. Competition would have determined which one would succeed.

A third condition favoring internal markets is an emerging product or market that threatens a firm's existing product or market. The natural reaction of the firm is to buckle up and work harder on its existing product to make sure it does not lose its existing market. Such a strategy is rational. However, this is also a great condition to set up another division or business unit that explicitly caters to the new market without being encumbered with responsibilities for the current market. For example, when the digital camera market started to emerge, Kodak had a strong position. Yet its preoccupation and focus on the film market hindered its full involvement and development of the digital photography market. It lost leadership in the latter market to

Japanese firms. This would have been a good situation to set up an entirely new division that focused entirely on the digital market without any responsibilities or ties to the film market.

A fourth factor favoring internal markets is the presence of a high threshold for introducing innovations. Some firms are so large that they set up a high threshold for introducing new products. For example, one firm, with over $100 billion in sales, has a threshold for radically new products that requires a new product to generate $1 billion in sales in three years. For most such new products, this is close to an impossible goal to meet, especially if takeoff of new products averages six years. Yet for such a large firm, going after a large number of niche markets can become a distraction for management, which needs to focus on its primary business. In such a situation, the use of spin-offs or buyouts to commercialize new products should be seriously considered. The firm can take a stake or option in the spin-off or buyout to ensure it regains its initial investment. Moreover, should the innovation take off, the firm is in a preferential position to buy and integrate the divested unit.

CONCLUSION

This chapter describes why firms should set up internal markets to preempt competition from innovative start-ups and discusses different forms to achieve this.

- A firm exists because it has fine-tuned a means of producing and delivering a product or service to a segment of consumers far more effectively and efficiently than any other firm. That fine tuning ensures a stream of profits. Firms develop bureaucracies to protect this stream of profits. Bureaucracies are efficient at managing current resources. They are weak at developing innovations and may even kill off innovations.

- All over the world, millions of entrepreneurs are hungry for the profits from current incumbents. They are designing the next big innovation with the firm's customers in mind. Markets are strong where firms are weak. They channel resources to those entities that are most innovative. Markets weed out lumbering giants and foster innovative start-ups.

- Incumbents need to develop internal markets to keep innovation thriving within. Bringing the market inside the firm can help a firm stay ahead of this diverse, unseen, and worldwide competition. Such markets provide a forum for innovators to offer alternatives and share information, allowing managers to choose among alternatives and provide support for those selected.

- In general, letting more employees and outsiders participate in the generation and selection of innovations ensures a bottom-up rather than top-down approach. In so doing, the firm can benefit from the wisdom of the crowds.

- To ensure success, firms also need to watch out for and control negative effects of markets: cascades and bubbles, cutthroat competition, lack of cooperation, duplication, and outright failures.

- Particular forms of internal markets include idea fairs, research contests, commercialization contests, competing business units, autonomous units, and divestitures.

- The most important rule in implementing markets is to incentivize employees and teams to ensure the productive development and commercialization of innovations and the avoidance of negative consequences of markets.

The history of business shows that markets have frequently generated new entrants that have displaced mighty incumbents. Internalizing markets is a means of preempting the market in this game.

CHAPTER 7

Empowering Innovation Champions

Innovation has nothing to do with how many R&D dollars you have. When Apple came up with the Mac, IBM was spending at least 100 times more on R&D. It's not about money. It's about the people you have, how you're led, and how much you get it.

—STEVE JOBS, CO-FOUNDER AND LATE CEO OF APPLE[1]

AS JOBS SUGGESTS TALENT is critical for innovation. This chapter explains how to hire and empower product champions to enable them to be innovative. Empowering innovation champions means providing them with resources, autonomy, and incentives to invent, develop, and commercialize innovations. One of the biggest threats that firms face today is the loss of talent to start-ups, either those founded by their own talent or by others who steal their talent. Empowering innovation champions ensures that such start-ups occur within the firm rather than outside in the market.

Legendary exit of champions from incumbents include Nikola Tesla leaving Edison to develop AC with George Westinghouse (see Chapter 2); Gordon Moore, Robert Noyce, and six others leaving Shockley Semiconductor to start the Fairchild Semiconductor Division; Moore and Noyce subsequently leaving that company to start Intel; John Warnock leaving Xerox PARC to cofound Adobe when Xerox would not commercialize InterPress; Steve Wozniak leaving HP to start Apple. Wozniak had even offered HP the first personal computer he created. HP declined the offer. Recent examples include Tony Fadell leaving Philips and later joining Apple to develop the popular iPod (see story later in this chapter); Roger Newton, champion of the hugely profitable Lipitor, leaving Parke Davis to start Esperion, which Pfizer subsequently bought back for $1.3 billion (see story later in this chapter).

Indeed, the United States is a vibrant market for such start-ups precisely because of such mobility. Silicon Valley is an epitome of such mobility and innovation. The very success of the markets in the United States and Silicon Valley to enable innovation champions to found start-ups on their own pressures firms to empower innovators within rather than bleed them to the market.

Are innovation champions just lucky individuals? What are their characteristics? Can teams substitute for them? Should a firm have one at the top or many at the bottom? This chapter addresses these issues with examples.

Luck Versus Innovation Champions

Luck or "being in the right place at the right time" is one of the most commonly attributed reasons for the success of innovators. Examples abound. Ray Croc, a milkshake salesman who built McDonald's hamburger franchise, supposedly stumbled on the formula when he noticed high sales of milkshake machines from a fast-food store in Pomona. Bill Gates supposedly stumbled on the contract from IBM for the first operating system for the PC because the leading candidate, Gary Kildall, was out flying his plane. Steve Jobs supposedly stumbled on the idea for a graphical user interface (popularized as Windows) on a lucky visit to the Palo Alto Research Center, which had a working prototype. And Roger

Newton, who championed the development of the multibillion-dollar drug Lipitor and then cofounded and sold Esperion for $1.2 billion has been called "the luckiest man in the drug business."[2]

These anecdotes have fed the myth that luck is the root cause of innovators' success . One author puts luck down as one of the first laws of enduring innovation success.[3] Indeed, throughout history, belief in luck has been quite strong, leading people at various times to adopt lucky charms, wear bracelets, and make signs to get lucky. Knocking on wood, the number 13, a black cat, and walking under a leaning ladder are common signs of good or bad luck. Polls indicate that until even recently up to 75% of Americans considered themselves to be at least a little superstitious.[4] Luck seems to have "the power to transform the improbable into the possible, to make the difference between life and death, reward and ruin, happiness and despair."[5]

My coauthor Peter Golder and I did a deep study of many famous stories about the start of great innovations and the markets they fueled, including the four above. We tracked the origin of sixty-six markets by researching archives going back decades and, in some cases, over a hundred years. Our results are published in a couple of articles and a book.[6] We found that under scrutiny, luck fades as an explanation of innovation. Rather, innovators exhibit some distinct characteristics that explain their success and make them appear lucky: vision of future markets, distinction from the norm, persistence in the faces of odds, and willingness to take great risks. These traits enable champions to see great opportunity in ordinary events and capitalize on them to create innovations. In hindsight, without knowledge of the details of the events and the characteristics of champions, these events appear as lucky breaks. But on close scrutiny, it's the characteristics of champions that enable them to identify and create these lucky breaks. Luck is not the cause of success. It is actually the fruit of vision, uniqueness, persistence, and risk taking.

For example, the McDonald brothers were the founders of the hugely successful fast-food store in Pomona that was also selling a lot of milkshakes. The brothers lacked either the vision or the energy to expand the successful store. Ray Croc had those characteristics. When the owners refused, Ray Croc bought the store from them for $2 million and set out to build a national and then global franchise. Likewise, at PARC, the graphical user interface was available to Xerox for commercialization. Neither the firm nor any engineer at PARC did much with commercializing it. Steve Jobs, who was then deeply involved at Apple in building user-friendly products for consumers, did. Similarly, Gary Kildall, who had already had an operating system for personal computers, did not see the market when IBM came shopping for an operating system. Bill Gates who was intent on being at the cutting edge of the emerging personal computer revolution, did. The story later in this chapter will document how Roger Newton crossed numerous hurdles and labored long and hard to get Lipitor into trials and into market. He also built Esperion from scratch after leaving the firm that benefited from Lipitor. Luck has little to do with his success.

Characteristics of Champions

These examples suggest some characteristics of champions that distinguish them and make them appear lucky.

First, champions have a vision for the future mass market. They see what others around them do not. They are principally visionaries with a unique worldview. The vision of champions radically alters the current groupthink of the industry, thereby providing an innovative approach to addressing consumer demand. Envisioning the mass market is the most valuable characteristic of champions because it foresees how the market is evolving and identifies its need ahead of the competition. Croc, Gates, and Jobs envisioned huge future markets for fast food, personal computing, and easy computing that others of the time did not see, including those who had promising products.

Second, champions are mavericks and dissenters. They dissent from the norm and from experts at the time. Their vision is unique. Most people around them do not share their vision. However, this uniqueness, this tendency to disagree with the norm, is the reason that champions see opportunity where others do not. For example, Tata's idea to create a $2,500 small car a few years back was ridiculed by senior executives of the auto industry. Akio Morita's quest to develop a portable music player was repeatedly resisted by Sony's own engineers. Such resistance and ridicule is why innovation champions often leave the organization in which they planned to develop their innovation. For example, Newton's persistent effort to develop and commercialize Lipitor caused so much distress in Parke-Davis that he left the firm, even though the product was launched and became highly successful.

Third, champions have the conviction to persist against heavy odds. Often the champion must fight a lonely battle to persuade others about his or her vision. The market for the innovation may not exist, may be radically different from the current market, or its full potential is difficult to fathom. There may be numerous set-backs in the production, manufacture, or testing phases of product development. Entrenched interest within the firms may strongly resist the innovation. More important, the product might not have financing for a successful launch. All of these possibilities would easily restrain a budding idea. Champions have the motivation and passion to overcome these obstacles and persist with the vision they believe holds the promise of success. For example, King Gillette struggled for many years to come up with the technology to develop a safety razor with a disposable blade, when the technology at the time was for reusable knives for shaving.

Fourth, because of their vision of the innovation's future market, champions are willing to take risks to bring it to fruition. The resources, talent, and responsibility that they get reduce their aversion to risk. With the conviction that their new product will be a future success, champions are able to tolerate risk and instill this trait in their teams. For example, Fred Smith took enormous risks over almost a decade as he sought to build a national express mail delivery system from scratch. Jeff Bezos took great risks under tremendous pressure in choosing rapid growth over profits to build Amazon into an electronic retail powerhouse. Mark Zuckerberg took great risks in foregoing repeated lucrative offers to purchase his big innovation, Facebook. Chapter 3 describes these stories in detail.

These unusual characteristics enable innovation champions to transform ordinary events and ideas into extraordinary innovations. To those not knowledgeable of all the facts, the events and ideas seem like big lucky breaks that befell ordinary people.

Testing Luck

Psychologist Richard Wiseman did a long-term study to carefully test the validity of luck.[7] His findings further discredit the theory of luck and reinforce the theory of distinct characteristics for the success of innovators.

Wiseman placed advertisements in newspapers and magazines, asking people who considered themselves extraordinarily lucky or unlucky to contact him. He attracted four hundred volunteers over the years representing a variety of ages, backgrounds, and jobs.

He interviewed these volunteers, asked them to keep diaries, respond to questionnaires, answer intelligence tests, and participate in experiments. His findings showed that luck is not magical. People are not born lucky or unlucky. Nor is luck a random event. Rather, people's thoughts and behavior are primarily responsible for their self-styled good or bad luck. Just like our study reported above, luck is not the cause of success but the fruit of human cognitions and behavior.

Wiseman found that lucky people generate their own good luck through four principles. They notice chance opportunities, create self-fulfilling prophecies through positive expectations, make lucky decisions by relying on their own intuition, and transform bad luck into good through resilience. Interestingly, the first two of these characteristics are similar to the first one that emerged from my own coauthored research: vision of the mass market. The latter two of these characteristics are similar to the second one that emerged from my research: persistence against great odds. Wiseman's other findings expand what I call the characteristics innovation champions.

For example, Wiseman's experiments found that self-styled lucky people consistently encounter chance opportunities whereas self-styled unlucky ones do not. An experiment he conducted explains the difference. He asked all his participants to count how many photographs were in an issue of a newspaper. On average, lucky people took seconds to do so while unlucky ones took two minutes. The reason is the following. The second page of the newspaper had a half page message that stated, "Stop counting—there are 43 photographs in the newspaper." The unlucky people tended to miss it while the lucky people tended to catch it.

Further experiments showed that unlucky people missed chance opportunities because they are tense and anxious and too focused on specifics that they are searching for. Lucky people are relaxed and open and see beyond the specifics they are looking for. Lucky participants introduce change and variety in their lives. Unlucky participants are focused and repeat the same set of narrow behaviors. Other experiments revealed that lucky people consider themselves lucky when they encounter some mishap because it could have been worse. However, when unlucky people encounter the same mishap, they attribute it to just their own bad luck. Thus, lucky people tend to have a positive outlook in life and have high expectations of the future.

The overall message from Wiseman's tests of lucky and unlucky individuals is the same as that from our archival research of innovation champions. Champions are not born lucky and are not just fortunate, but have distinct characteristics that make them appear lucky.

Champions Versus Teams

The thinking among researchers has swung for and against champions. The current trend seems to favor teams and oppose champions. For example, one study suggests that champions do not directly affect the performance of new product development.[8] Other studies have praised the advantage of teams. The rationale for teams is that they represent collective wisdom, prune extreme ideas, and screen out erroneous thinking. However, precisely for these reasons, champions play a critically important role in the context of innovations.

First, good talent is scarce. Andy Ouderkirk, Corporate Scientist Carlton Member at 3M Corporation, reports on a fascinating finding from internal research at 3M.[9] The firm analyzed the productivity of scientists in terms of patents registered. The study was that the number of patents increased along the breadth of the knowledge of the scientist and more so along depth of the knowledge of the scientist. Breadth is knowledge across areas while depth is knowledge in one area. However, the greatest number of patents were for a few scientists who combined depth and breadth, whom the authors of the study called architects. Such scarce talent, which combines depth and breadth, would be prime candidates for innovation champions. Richard Friedrich, director of Cognition Based Analytics at HP Laboratories, encapsulates the challenge that a large corporation such as HP, with 350,000 employees, faces, "We bet on people, not products. . . . Most people are not innovators."[10] Thus the challenge is to identify and empower such talent as champions.

Second, once entrusted with responsibility, champions are motivated to work for the success of the task entrusted to them. The assignment of responsibility makes it difficult for the champion to hide or excuse him- or herself. Thus, as the leader, the champion will strive to assemble resources and talent to get the job done. He or she will also motivate and monitor the team in order to get the most out of them. However, this role does not come automatically with the appointment. Research by Professors Gina O'Connor and Christopher McDermott suggests that leaders need to evolve into the role of champions.[11]

Third, teams involve collective decision making. They tend to proceed on a majority vote. However, innovations, especially radical innovations, often are the intuition of a single individual. Opinions that are typically known or held widely or by a majority are unlikely to be novel or innovative. They are probably already part of the fabric of everyday life and everyday products. Innovations tend to arise from the insight of creative individuals. Often, the internal structure of an organization hinders such insight. In particular, a long review process can stifle enthusiasm, excessive critique can stymie creativity, and extensive evaluation can hurt timeliness. When a creative individual becomes an innovation champion, he or she can cut through such collective decision making and persuade a team or whole organization of his or her intuition.

213

Thus, on the one hand, there is great danger that a team may prune out the most promising, high-potential ideas because they are supported by a minority or one individual. On the other hand, champions can easily focus on radical innovations, which could get screened out by a majority vote of a team. The presence of a champion does not negate the role of teams. Rather, it provides the team with a clear and indisputable leader offering important benefits to the organization and the task at hand.

Fourth, the appointment of a champion clearly entrusts responsibility of a task to an individual. This assignment of responsibility makes it easier for senior management to reward or punish (judiciously, as we shall see later) good or bad performance, respectively. Responsibility is diffused when assigned to an entire team. Management often has difficulty tracking down who is responsible for innovation and for providing appropriate rewards to the individual.

Champions at the Top Versus the Bottom

A key issue when discussing champions is whether there should be one at the top or many around the whole organization. Akio Morita in Sony, Ratan Tata in Tata Motors, and Steve Jobs at Apple are examples of a champion (CEO) at the top, as the subsequent cases illustrate. However, more important is that a firm should tap its entire pool of employees to identify, incentivize, and develop distributed champions throughout the organization. The subsequent cases show that champions within the organization, such as Roger Newton and Tony Fadell can be equally impactful. In general, relying on champions throughout the organization is preferable to relying on only one at the top, for several reasons.

First, relying on the whole employee base ensures a much wider pool of potential champions. The risk of relying on one innovation champion at the top, such as the CEO of the organization, is huge. The firm puts all its future eggs in one basket. If the CEO is a repeated visionary, as Jobs was at Apple in the 2000s, the firm comes out a huge winner. But if the CEO turns out to be repeatedly wrong, the firm could well fail, as Apple very nearly did in 1985 when Jobs was fired from the company. Failures are common with innovations. Beforehand, it is difficult to predict who might be a good champion; tapping the whole employee pool is an excellent approach to reducing risk.

Second, one can consider the firm as a pool of talent and energy. This talent harbors a vast number of ideas, in primitive form, that could mature into successful innovations under the right conditions. The energy could provide the organization with fresh impetus as its growing bureaucracy slows it down. Why not tap into this talent pool for champions? A survey at the University of Southern California indicated that half the students were interested in starting their own businesses.[12] The student body at the university is about 37,000. Thus, there were 18,500 ideas (albeit many primitive ones) for entrepreneurship and innovation. Most organizations likewise have employees who might harbor ideas for innovation and entrepreneurship. Most of these ideas will be unproductive (see Chapter 5). But unless a firm generates them, it will not find the few that will be winners. There is certainly a role for the CEO of a firm to be the champion of innovation. But there is an even greater opportunity for tapping into the whole talent pool of a firm to nurture champions.

Third, starting with a large pool gives the firm leverage in sifting strong from weak champions. In evaluating talent, the mean of the talent pool is not so important. The variance in talent and the maximum performance is what matters. The reason is that the future of the firm is defined not so much by the mean performance of all employees but by the brilliance of a few who can generate new ideas and motivate and lead a team to translate them into new products and new markets.[13] The probability of identifying such outstanding talent increases with the variance in talent and the inclusion of top performers. Thus a firm is better off tapping the whole employee pool to identify champions.

Fourth, the leadership at the top has often been at the company for a long time and is immersed in a set way of thinking and executing. Employees throughout the organization are more likely to think of solutions beyond the routine and traditional. Especially when it comes to developing radical innovations, such out-of-the-box thinking is critical. Thus, it is better to tap the whole body of employees for talent that could be developed into champions. Google's Associate Product Manager program (discussed in the following section) is a good example of this approach. Alex Backer, founder and CEO of Ab Inventio, explains how he devolves power through the organization. "We give people autonomy because people do not like to be managed. Everyone can choose their own title."[14] Though Steve Jobs is a visionary champion in his own right, he believed in empowering talent within the firm and not micromanaging everything. As he says, "The people who are doing the work are the moving force behind the Macintosh. My job is to create a space for them, to clear out the rest of the organization and keep it at bay."[15]

The following stories reveal the role of champions in organizations and illustrate these principles at work.

Distributed Champions: Google's "Young Turks" Program

Google is frequently ranked among the world's most innovative companies. The firm started off in the early 2000s and surpassed older giants such as Yahoo! and Microsoft based on a simple but radical innovation in search. Since its founding, lots of competitors have been close on its heels, striving to develop a better search engine. Google has realized that to stay ahead of the competition, it needs to attract and retain the best talent in the market and train them to be unrelentingly innovative. That realization has being reinforced by the tremendous pressure of talent migration facing the company. On the one hand, competitors are often looking to pirate top employees. On the other hand, top employees themselves are interested in taking their ideas private and starting their own businesses. Google's realization led to the development of the Associate Product Manager (APM) program, a type of young turks program.

Google's Associate Product Manager program breaks the traditional promotion mold by identifying and mentoring champions early in their careers. The program rewards innovation, irrespective of age or seniority, by giving employees substantial leadership roles.[16] One participant said of the program, "We invest more into our APM program than any other company has ever invested into young employees."[17] Google tried hiring senior product managers from other companies such as Microsoft but abandoned that strategy because the hires could not adapt to the Google culture. Now the APM program picks the best and the brightest talent, usually fresh out of college, and allows them to head key projects within the company. Google helps candidates in the program cope with their vast responsibilities by providing each with a buddy, a mentor, and a management coach.[18]

Google APM Brian Rakowski, a Stanford graduate, was put in charge of Gmail and was given the responsibility of launching a big product. Rakowski was only 22 at the time.[19] Google APM Frances Haugen led a team that analyzed customer results for multibillion-dollar Google AdWords product, which places ads on search results. Haugen was also 22 years old at the time. Her staff of about twenty, included engineers and people twice her age.[20]

Prem Ramaswami was only 25 years old when he was put in charge of Google Checkout (an online-payment application).[21]

The ability to head a global project at such a young age is a big motivation for the highly talented.[22] Apart from the monetary benefits and the peer and industry-wide recognition, the program has helped engender a new class of entrepreneurs. Of the program's candidates that left Google, many have done so to start their own technology company. Another advantage of being a candidate in the program is its appeal to venture capital firms looking to fund new companies. Google pursues this program even though it may upset senior employees who are bypassed and APMs who might leave the program to start off on their own. Marissa Mayer, a former Google vice president, explains the rationale for the program, "That kind of restlessness," she says, "is the gene that Larry and Sergey look for. We get two to four good years, and if 20 percent stay with the company, that's a good rate. Even if they leave it's still good for us. I'm sure that someone in this group is going to start a company that I will buy some day."[23]

Thus Google invests a great deal to attract, train, and empower leaders, many of whom may leave the firm, in order to get the best ideas and innovations from them. What is unique and most valuable about the company is that these champions are distributed across the whole firm. Google does not subscribe to the philosophy of one super champion at the head of the company. This philosophy has many merits, as stated above. It also contrasts with some of the subsequent examples, especially with that of Apple.

Serial Champion: Roger Newton

Roger Newton's championing of Lipitor—the most profitable drug as of 2012—is a fascinating story. Newton joined Parke-Davis as a senior scientist after earning a PhD in nutrition from U.C. Davis. With fellow scientist Dick Maxwell, he established a drug discovery program, working toward treatments for atherosclerosis, the thickening of the artery wall due to buildup of plaque from "bad" cholesterol. The team focused on reducing quantities of low-density lipoproteins, or LDL, the bad cholesterol, and increasing quantities of high-density lipoproteins, or HDL, the good cholesterol.[24]

Among scientists in the atherosclerosis team, Newton's ability to envision potential where others see failure set him apart. This ability led to his eventual position as the project chair of a group working on a medication to reduce LDL levels. With the leadership of Bruce D. Roth, after several long years of hard work, the team synthesized five potential candidate compounds to proceed through clinical trials.[25]

The team's enthusiasm and persistence were put to the test as their compounds failed one after the other. The first two of the five compounds were found to be toxic. The third compound was absorbed by other organs, and the fourth was patented by a competitor.[26] However, Newton and Roth had a vision of what the market needed and an LDL pill that could fit that need. They continued research with this vision in sight. Their tenacity paid off. After long months of research, they identified a fifth compound (atorvastatin) that showed promise. Furthermore, the team discovered that the compound existed in mirror forms.[27] If the more potent form could be isolated, the drug could be very effective.

While the research department was enthusiastic about this latest compound, management and marketing became increasingly hesitant to endorse it because their four prior attempts had failed. Management wanted to stop production of atorvastatin. The marketing department reasoned that even if this compound passed clinical trials, it would be difficult to market against competition.

Four other statin drugs had already entered the market from companies with strong physician and patient relations. Management believed that Lipitor would be swept away by its competitors.[28] They proposed a new product that was certain, they believed, to attract more customers.

However, Newton said of those four failures, "I look at that not as failures. I look at that as learnings."[29] Newton's persuasive skills were put to the test at a Parke-Davis internal meeting. As the champion in support of Lipitor's entry into clinical trials, he faced an impatient and frustrated management team head-on. "When people wanted to walk away from it because it was the fifth statin, I'm the guy who got in the way and said, 'you can't do that.' . . . I put my proverbial neck in the guillotine,"[30] Newton recounts in a lecture. He effectively argued with management for his product to continue through clinical trials. Roger pleaded for what he believed was "the right thing to do."[31] As Michael Pape, a collaborator on Lipitor and cofounder of Esperion, put it, "You have to have someone who can communicate the data. . . . Roger was persistent and aggressive."[32] Newton reassured management that the product would do anything but fail. His team's drive and passion played a strong factor in getting this fifth compound accepted and into production.[33] One reporter describes his achievement in these words, "His persistence and courage . . . saved the atorvastatin program from the drug development dustbin."[34]

The fruits of Newton's labor were enormous, with sales surpassing $1 billion in the first year. Eventually it became one of the biggest blockbuster drugs on the market with a peak of $12.9 billion in sales in 2007.[35] Newton himself credits Pfizer with cleverly marketing the drug. However, his core contribution in championing research and clinical trials for the drug is also clear.

Unfortunately, the force with which Newton fought for Lipitor's case caused him to lose favor with management. At

Parke-Davis, Newton worked more as an entrepreneur than a traditional manager who implemented strategies of his superiors. As David Scheer, a cofounder of Newton's company, Esperion, recalls, "[Newton] had wanted to segue into a place where he didn't have constraints, a position where he had more empowerment and encouragement."[36] This created conflicts with management. As Lipitor grew in popularity, Newton's career declined. He was removed from his administrative position, his influence diminished, and his research group was disbanded. In 2000, Pfizer took over Warner Lambert, of which Parke-Davis was a subsidy, in order to gain complete control of Lipitor. By then, however, Newton, and several members of Lipitor's research team had left Parke-Davis. Newton charitably describes his treatment, thus, "I was involved in a re-organization. I couldn't do the science that I wanted to do. I couldn't pursue what I was really interested in"[37]

Newton's entrepreneurial streak kicked in and he and fellow doctors from the Lipitor team set out for Ann Arbor, Michigan, where they cofounded Esperion, a pharmaceutical company. Esperion, like Newton's previous department, worked primarily in the atherosclerosis field and provided Newton with both the knowledge and materials to pursue products without managerial constraints. The company blossomed and in less than two years was ready with its first product for clinical trials. In a small trial, the team's latest discovery, a big protein that had to be injected through an IV line, seemed to clear artery plaque.[38] Eager to cash in on Esperion's discovery and in an effort to protect their $1 billion investment on another HDL-raising drug, Pfizer acquired Esperion for $1.3 billion as a semi-independent organization.[39]

While certain Esperion-invented drugs appeared to have promise, they never advanced into clinical trials because of problems with the manufacturing design. Pfizer's HDL pill, Torcetrapib, increased mortality in a big clinical trial, causing more fiscal problems for the company. As a result, several Pfizer plants, including the Esperion facility, were scheduled for shut down. Again, Newton refused to just sit back. In 2008, he secured sufficient venture capital to restart Esperion. Says Newton of this venture, "I have a vision of wanting to continue the work we started with the first Esperion."[40] As a newly opened company, they hope to put one of their first products, ETC. 1002, through clinical trials.[41]

Lipitor is, even today, the most profitable drug ever on the market.[42] But it represents much more. It began as part of Newton's dream to make a difference in the world. Because he was persistent, passionate, and had a vision of the market, the dream became a prototype and, after passing clinical trials, had an impact on millions of lives. Of working in pharmaceutical research, Newton says, "This is not something for the weak of spirit or someone who is not willing to persist."[43]

Championing Mass Market of the Future: Tata Nano

Ratan Tata's revolutionary people's car, the Nano, exemplifies the importance of a champion in envisioning the market for new products. In 2003, at age 65, Ratan Tata was the chairman of the Tata Group of Industries, one of the largest and most respected Indian conglomerates with subsidiaries in software, hotels, steel, cable, wireless, and automotive. He was not the founder but the great-grandson of the founder of the Tata conglomerate. Tata Motors was the largest and leading automotive firm in India. They were the leader in commercial vehicles, fifth in the world in the production of medium and heavy trucks and the second largest heavy bus manufacturer.[44] However, up until the release of the Nano, Tata Motors was a relatively new player to the passenger car market while the market for extremely low-priced cars (below $5,000) was unheard of.

Ratan Tata said he always had "some sort of unconscious urge to do something for the people of India and transport had been an area of interest."[45] Tata dreamt up the idea for a people's car after viewing the unsafe driving conditions prevalent on Indian streets. "I observed families riding on two-wheelers—the father driving the scooter, his young kid standing in front of him, his wife seated behind him holding a little baby. It led me to wonder whether one could conceive of a safe, affordable, all-weather form of transport for such a family."[46] In India, middle and lower-middle class families choose to transport their families on two-wheelers because, on the one hand, they cannot afford automobiles that cost $5,000 and above. On the other hand, they could afford two-wheelers because of their low cost (under $2,500).

Tata recounts that he never started with the mission of building a $2,500 (Rs 100,000) car. He says:

> I was interviewed by the [British newspaper] *Financial Times* at the Geneva Motor Show and I talked about this future product as a low-cost car. I was asked how much it would cost and I said about Rs1 lakh (100,000). The next day the *Financial Times* had a headline to the effect that the Tatas are to produce a Rs 100,000 car. My immediate reaction was to issue a rebuttal, to clarify that that was not exactly what I had said. Then I thought, I did say it would be around that figure, so why don't we just take that as a target. When I came back our people were aghast, but we had our goal.[47]

When Ratan Tata first announced the price of the car, critics ridiculed the possibility of successfully launching a vehicle priced at only $2,500. They argued that regulators would not allow such a stripped-down car on the streets, that consumers would not want to buy it, and that if the vehicle did actually hit the market it would generate slim profits, if any. When the General Motors chief for Asia, Nick Reilly, heard of the vehicle he scoffed at it, saying that to succeed "it has to be more attractive than a *used car* that sells for the same price."[48] Other critics expressed the opinion that the finished product would simply be a four-wheeled auto-rickshaw. Auto-rickshaws are three-wheeler taxis, common in most Indian cities. They have a canvas roof and open sides and are noisy, unsteady, and very polluting. Auto-rickshaws can transport two passengers in the back seat, but often transport more people plus their baggage.

Tata had to endure many failures in the fabrication of his vision. Indeed, Tata's initial dream was only a set of two-wheelers joined together. In 2003, Tata commissioned an engineering team, led by 32-year-old Girish Wagh, to begin designing the new "people's car," with three requirements for the new car: it should be high performance (regarding fuel efficiency and acceleration), adhere to Indian vehicular regulations, and most important be low cost.[49] The first attempt by Wagh's team was a dismal failure. The vehicle conformed exactly to what the critics believed it would be. In an attempt to cut costs the prototype had bars on the side instead of doors, had plastic flaps to keep out the monsoon rains, and looked much more like a rickshaw than a car. An attempt to include a larger engine to boost power by 20% still failed. Even Wagh admitted, "It was an embarrassment."[50]

At that point Tata made a shrewd observation. Although at first the car was envisioned as a rural mode of transport with no doors or windows but roll-down curtains, as the project progressed Tata realized that there was a huge mass market for a car built, "like everyone expects a car to be."[51] Even while stressing the needs to cut costs on parts as low as 50 cents, Tata was also conscious that there should be no quality stigma attached to buying the Nano. "Nobody wants a car that is less than everybody else's car,"[52] Tata said.

But building the Tata Nano to meet that cost budget was a huge challenge. Luxuries were excluded from the design to meet the low price target. The Nano had no radio, power steering, power windows, air conditioning, or even airbags. To further reduce costs, engineers reduced the weight of the car, cutting material costs. Part sourcing was conducted through Internet auctions. Parts, dashboards, panels and frames all snap together, reducing labor and eliminating nuts and bolts. Tata himself vetoed the design of the traditional windshield wipers for one with a single wiper instead of two, giving the car a cleaner look and further cutting costs. But even then progress toward manufacturing the car to sell for $2,500 was slowed by the rising price of raw materials. As the possibility of fabricating this car dwindled, Tata stubbornly stood by his vision. "I hope it will be seen as the car . . . which changes the manner in which people in rural and semi-urban India will travel," said Tata. "It will be a profitable venture for the company."[53]

The vision of a $2,500 car for the masses drove the entire design of the Nano. The Nano took five years of tedious designing to meet the vision that Tata had for the Indian market. Finally, on January 10, 2008, Ratan Tata delivered on his vision when he displayed the Tata Nano at the biennial Auto Expo 2008 in New Delhi, India. At a revolutionary $2,500, the Nano will cost about as little as the optional DVD player in a Lexus LX 470 SUV1. The Nano is less than half the cost of its closest competitor, the Maruti 800. Even a one- or two-year-old secondhand Maruti 800 sells for about $5,000. The Nano's price is even more attractive when compared to some of the high-end two-wheel scooters and motorbikes that sell in India for about $2,000. The Nano's exhibit was the biggest attraction at the 2008 Auto Expo. The display aroused great excitement among consumers in India, tremendous media attention worldwide, and strong criticism from environmentalists and green advocates. Auto dealers and Tata offices were besieged with inquiries from eager consumers in India, who were quite disappointed that they could not drive off with one right away.

As I explained in the *San Francisco Chronicle*,[54] critics may dismiss the Nano as a small, very basic, very poor man's car that causes a mere ripple on the world market. However, the Nano is a radical innovation that can revolutionize automobile manufacturing. Why so? The Nano incorporates three innovations which together make it quite amazing. First, the Nano uses a modular design that enables a knowledgeable mechanic to assemble the car in a suitable workshop. Thus, Tata can outsource assembly to independent workshops that can then assemble the car on buyers' orders. Second, the low cost of the Nano comes not only from its exclusion of frills and luxuries but its inclusion of numerous lighter components from simple door handles and bulbs to the transmission and engine components. The lighter vehicle enables a less polluting, more energy-efficient engine, just when fuel costs are soaring. Third, the Nano's novel design uses a much smaller wheelbase yet allows for 15% more space. These innovations enabled Tata to introduce the Nano at a base price of $2,500. The easily dismissed price point could well represent the most radical innovation of the Nano. Tata Nano meets Euro IV safety and pollution standards. Tata intends to market the product internationally in a couple of years. Competing manufacturers have no immediate answer and could only review their plans for launch of rival brands years in the future. Even then, their prices would not match that of the Nano.

Although it is the product of vast number of engineers and laborers working devotedly to bring it to fruition, the Tata Nano in many respects represents the realization of the vision of its champion, Ratan Tata. Despite the doubts of meeting both the time line and price goal, Ratan Tata remained unfazed and finally delivered on his vision. He achieved what a large corporation, much less a conglomerate, would find hard to achieve: envisioning an unusually low price point to appeal to the mass market and delivering a radical innovation at that price point. As he put it simply, "A promise is a promise."[55]

Championing a Music Revolution: Apple iPod

The Apple iPod was a highly successful product by itself. However, its real importance to Apple is that it became a platform and template for a series of innovations, including iTunes, the Apple store, iPhone, iPad, and the App Store.

Today the iPod and iTunes are so closely associated with Apple that it is hard to remember that Apple wasn't always a music company. Yet Apple started out as a computer company that pioneered the age of user-friendly personal computers. Originally, it had nothing to do with music or with mobile music gadgets. The firm that created mobile music was Sony, with the introduction of the Walkman. Also, Sony had an MP3 Player before Apple did. How then does Apple now own 75% of the mobile music market, while Sony is struggling? Before Apple marketed the iPod, Sony was five times the size of Apple in market capitalization. After the iPod became a success, Apple was double the size of Sony in market capitalization. How did Apple become a mobile music company? How and why did Sony lose its grip on the mobile music market? The answer to the first question probably lies in the vision and leadership of Steve Jobs and his empowerment of another champion, Tony Fadell.[56] Chapter 2 provided the answer to the second question.

One of the problems in the design of new products is the large number of decisions that have to be made about various attributes at many levels. For example, attributes on a mobile music player include size of player, thickness of player, number of buttons, shape of buttons, functions of buttons, capacity of player, quality of sound, access to library of songs, ability to add songs, and so on. Designers resolve these problems by surveying consumers for their preferences or by running experiments in which prototypes are presented to consumers for their evaluation. However, the problems becomes complex when consumers are unaware of or can barely envisage the new product. In such situations, the vision and passion of a champion can give designers clear directives as to what attributes to emphasize and what levels on those attributes to target.

Steve Jobs and Tony Fadell represent types of champions who achieved this with the Apple iPod. Their achievement is particularly commendable given that Apple was not a music company, whereas music companies like Philips and Sony had vast experience and resources in music. Jobs's passion was for an easy-to-use mobile music player. Fadell's passion was for the very concept of a digital mobile music player. Further, as the subsequent story illustrates, both Jobs and Fadell showed a remarkable vision of what such a player should be, when existing players were not doing well and Sony and Philips did not seem passionate about one.

The origin of the iPod reveals a fascinating story of how champions can bring their passion to shape innovations in ongoing corporations. The iPod seems to have originated from a fusion of early ideas developed by Tony Fadell and ideas developed at Apple. Fadell was then an independent contractor and an innovator in digital technologies. He held senior technology positions at General Magic and subsequently at Philips. He started at Philips in 1995 as chief technology officer, responsible for the mobile computing group that developed a number of Windows CE–based handheld gadgets. He rose to become vice president of Strategy and Ventures at Philips. It was probably while working at Philips that Fadell envisioned designing and marketing a small hard-disk-based MP3 player with a complementary music service.[56] That Philips did not recognize his talent and let go one of the architects of the iPod is a sad example of mismanaging champions.

In early 2001 Fadell left Philips and started his own company, Fuse, to develop a mobile music player. Fuse failed to get a second round of funding and had to shut down. Fadell approached several companies with his idea for a mobile music player including Sony, Philips, and RealNetworks.[57] Most of the companies were not interested but RealNetworks showed some interest. He joined RealNetworks to develop this product but quit only six weeks later over an argument about his moving to Seattle.

It was then that Fadell and Apple connected. Apple was looking for a champion to lead a digital music player project and Fadell was looking for an interested firm with resources. Apple initially gave Fadell an eight-week contract to design a product for Apple.[58] Satisfied with his work, Apple hired Fadell and gave him a team to work on a portable MP3 player that ultimately became the iPod. As is typical of Apple, the project was veiled in secrecy.

Soon after being hired by Apple, Fadell approached PortalPlayer, a company that was already working on a couple of reference designs for an MP3 player.[59] Ben Knauss was a senior manager at PortalPlayer. In one of his first meetings with PortalPlayer, Fadell supposedly said, "This is the project that's going to remold Apple and 10 years from now, it's going to be a music business, not a computer business."[60] At the time, PortalPlayer had 12 suppliers designing MP3 players based on the company's designs.[61] However, PortalPlayer decided to contract only with Apple. PortalPlayer's designs for MP3 players were primitive. "It was fairly ugly," said Ben Knauss, then a senior manager at Por-talPlayer. "It looked like an FM radio with a bunch of buttons." The interface "was typical of an interface done by hardware guys."[62] But Fadell's vision of the final product allowed him to realize the potential of the design. As Knauss put it, "Tony figured the product was there."[63]

No sooner than the project began at Apple, Steve Jobs became involved. "The interesting thing about the iPod was that since it started, it had 100 percent of Steve Jobs' time," said Knauss. "Not many projects get that. He was heavily involved in every single aspect of the project."[64] Jobs increased his meeting with the team from once every two to three weeks to daily. "They'd have meetings and Steve would be horribly offended he couldn't get to the song he wanted in less than three pushes of a button," Knauss said. "We'd get orders: 'Steve doesn't think it's loud enough, the sharps aren't sharp enough, or the menu's not coming up fast enough.' Every day there were comments from Steve saying where it needed to be."[65]

In its ease of use, the iPod bears the stamp of Jobs, who was unrelenting in his drive to simplify the look and feel of gadgets and rid them of buttons.[66] It was Jobs's vision of the market that allowed him to foresee the need of an "intuitive" design. The rotary button on the iPod makes dialing a song easy and epitomizes its ease of use. "Most people make the mistake of thinking design is what it looks like," said Jobs. "People think it's this veneer—that the designers are handed this box and told, 'Make it look good!' That's not what we think design is. It's not just what it looks like and feels like. Design is how it works."[67]

As the iPod project neared completion, it was almost killed because of poor battery life. The problem was fixed and the iPod was launched successfully. Fadell was promoted to vice president of engineering for Apple's iPod Division and is credited with supervising development of the first two generations of the iPod.

Jobs' involvement in the iPod bears similarity to Tata's involvement with the Nano. Each was not literally involved in the day-to-day operations. However, their broad directives deeply influenced day-to-day development of the respective products. In the case of the Nano, it was Tata's setting the ridiculously low $2,500 price that shaped every innovation and the whole stream of development. In the case of the iPod, it was Jobs' insistence on an ultra-simple intuitive design that shaped the development of the final product. As his biographer summed it up, "Not since the original Mac had a clarity of vision so propelled a company into the future."[68]

Mobilizing an Organization for Innovation: Sony Walkman

One of the drawbacks of successful corporations is that they have a large bureaucracy. Bureaucracies hinder timely innovations because of their complex rules, slow decision making, and groupthink. A champion can cut through this bureaucracy to drive a new product to market in a timely manner. Sony's development and marketing of the Walkman is a case in point.[69] Because the Walkman is the creator of the market that the iPod now dominates, the story is a great complement to that of the iPod. It also demonstrates what Sony had at the time of the Walkman and probably lacked by the time of the iPod.

Ironically, the Walkman arose from a failed innovation, the Pressman. It was championed by two of Sony's cofounders, Chairman Akio Morita and honorary Chairman Masaru Ibuka. In 1978,

Mitsuro Ida and a team of engineers at Sony designed a compact (5.25″ × 3.46″ × 1.14″) stereo tape player. However, the small size left no place for a recording device. At that time, a player without a recording device was not of much use. As such, the Pressman was a failure. The engineers focused intently on how to fit a recording device into the gadget.

However, when the gadget caught Ibuka's eye, it triggered another vision. He recalled an entirely independent effort elsewhere in Sony where engineers were trying to develop lightweight headphones. At that time headphones were large, heavy gadgets weighing almost a pound, which audiophiles used to listen to music from their stereo systems.[70] Lightweight, compact headphones were unknown. Ibuka realized that linking lightweight headphones to the Pressman would create a player that could produce good-quality music, but also one that was portable. The key idea of the Walkman was born.

However, at the time "in the world of tape recorders, Ibuka's idea was heresy. He was mixing up functions. Headphones traditionally were supposed to extend the usefulness of tape recorders, not be essential to their success."[71] Moreover, design groups within Sony were quite focused on their individual tasks. For example, the headphone and tape recorder groups did not talk to each other. Thus, Ibuka's vision also connected two design groups working in isolation. But the response of the two groups did not ignite enthusiasm for the product; rather, they met the idea with polite indifference. They felt that a player with no recording function and no speakers would be a failure. It would lack the two important abilities, music recording and playback for others' listening pleasure. So his idea got no support from any of the engineers at Sony.

Ibuka went to his thirty-year partner and cofounder, Akio Morita, who loved new gadgets and was receptive to new ideas, even questionable ones. Morita decided they should build and try a prototype, especially since the separate ingredients (player and headphones) were available. The two loved the results of the experiment—the quality and convenience of music while on the go. The product gave them an experience of music neither had ever enjoyed before.

Morita decided immediately to lean on the tape recorder division to develop the gadget. In so doing, he shocked the division, because the product appeared so irrational. However, though he did not dictate the course of action, he made clear to the division that this was his pet project and he was really interested in its success. The division proceeded with development. The actual responsibility for building the gadget was given to an engineer, Yasuo Kuroki, under the supervision of Kozo Ohsone, the general manager of the division. By early 1979, they had some prototypes that had a breakeven price of about $249 (¥50,000). However, the price that may appeal to consumers was thought to be $170. The marketing people thought the product was "dumb," too expensive, and lacked recording ability.[72]

At a meeting with engineers to resolve the conflict, neither side gave in. The engineers refused to see the logic of the product while Morita remained convinced the product would appeal to teenagers. His passion for the product grew from his observation that young people wanted their music with them wherever they went. At a subsequent meeting to haggle over the price, the engineers finally conceded that they could produce a product for $200. With that small concession, Morita pushed for a price of $165 and a launch date four months away—a speedy delivery time that might well look absurd to a normal employee in the division.

Morita set a target of 60,000 units for the first run. Kuroki thought that target was too high. He was more comfortable with a target of 30,000 units. Not only did he judge the smaller number to be more reasonable but it implied lower losses—because costs seemed to exceed the list price per unit. So he made a deal with Ohsone, without the knowledge of Morita. They would order parts for 60,000 units but produce and inventory only 30,000 units.

The product was launched in July, 1979, with a very limited marketing budget but lots of samples to the press and potential innovators. The press greeted the new product with great excitement. But the target group, teenagers, was lukewarm. Then in August, sales began to pick up. By the first week of September, the product was a hit, and the stock of 30,000 units ran out. Morita wondered why the inventory had run out at the low number, when he had set a target of 60,000 units. He was furious to learn of the lower production level.

The Walkman was soon launched in the United States as the Soundabout and the United Kingdom as the Stowaway, because Sony marketers considered the Japanese name, Walkman, to be funny. However, tourists brought the product from Japan to both countries as the Walkman. And that name stuck. Sony went on to develop a better model, the Walkman II, to overcome limitations of the first product and keep ahead of competitors. When the Walkman II was launched, that product became a huge success. By the end of 1998, Sony had sold about 250 million units worldwide.

Morita got one thing wrong about the market. The initial buyers were not teenagers but yuppies. Perhaps the price was one that made it affordable to the latter group. But in most other aspects, Morita's vision of what the market wanted and at what price point was right on target. Morita's passion for the product resembles that of Jobs for the iPod. His setting of an unrealistically low price seems similar to that of Tata with the Nano.

Steps in Empowering Champions

These examples show the importance of champions in developing and commercializing innovations. Empowering champions in a firm requires some major steps.

First, the firm needs to define a clear product-market domain in which an innovation needs to be developed. For Apple in 2001, it was a digital music player; for Sony in 1979, a mobile music player; for Tata in 2003, an ultra-cheap car. For radical or disruptive innovations, this space could be one in which the firm currently has no product at all, as in the preceding examples. Carving out this space ensures minimal interference from the bureaucracy of the current organization, which could become an impediment as illustrated in Chapter 2 on cannibalization.

Second, the firm needs to identify champions. It should look both to senior talent with experienced records as champions and to young talent with ideas and energy for championing. Most important, the organization should make a concerted effort to identify and grow champions from the talent within. Google's Associate Product Manager program is one example.

Third, the firm needs to empower a champion with clear responsibility, adequate resources, and talent to develop the innovation. For the iPod, Tony Fadell played that role. For the Walkman, Kuroki played that role. For Lipitor, Roger Newton played that role. In addition, Chapters 5 and 6 show how incentives for enterprise and internal competition can be designed to motivate champions to be productive.

Fourth, the firm or champion could provide some broad parameters of performance for what the finished product should look like. Price often is an important parameter in this set. But quality, performance, or convenience are equally critical parameters, as some of the other examples illustrate. For example, Apple cofounder Steve

Wozniak said of his coconspirator Steve Jobs's fanatical dedication to the quality of Apple's innovations, "That's [the] way he operated throughout his entire tenure at Apple . . . every product from Apple spoke like it was Steve Jobs. . . . [Jobs was] not going to put out just some great stuff. It's got to be insanely great."[73]

CONCLUSION

This chapter explains the following important principles in empowering champions of innovation:

- The success of innovation champions appears to but does not really arise from luck. It really arises from champions' distinct characteristics.
- The key characteristics of innovation champions are vision of the mass market, dissension from the norm, persistence in the face of odds, and embracing risk.
- Innovation champions tend to conflict with bureaucracy due to these very characteristics.
- Unsupported innovation champions will leave an organization, taking with them promising ideas and innovations.
- Although CEOs have a role to play in championing innovations, a firm is best off trying to empower champions across the whole pool of its employees.
- Innovation champions can be developed within a firm by proper structuring of responsibility, goals, talent, and resources. In addition, incentives and competition can be structured to motivate and empower innovation champions.

CHAPTER 8

Culture Versus Alternate Theories

Arguments and Evidence

Culture isn't just one of the drivers. It is *the* driver of the innovation of firms.

THE PRIMARY THESIS OF this book is that the culture of a firm drives its innovativeness, or the degree to which it introduces radical innovations. Chapter 1 gives a synopsis of the meaning of culture and subsequent chapters detail each component of culture. Critics may argue that the examples in each chapter have been cherry-picked to support that particular example of culture. Such critics may want to see broad cross-sectional evidence in support of culture as the primary driver of innovativeness. This chapter provides such evidence.

The need for evidence is especially important because scholars across a variety of disciplines have proposed alternate theories or explanations for the innovativeness of firms. Few studies have scientifically compared all these competing theories to ascertain which one is most consistent with the evidence. This chapter also serves that goal.

Over the last twenty years, my coauthors and I have formally tested various alternate explanations for innovativeness and published our results in a series of peer-reviewed articles.[1] The

237

important feature about these studies is that they are not based on cherry-picked examples but on an objective sampling of markets and firms. The studies that we have assembled provide strong evidence that the internal culture of the firm trumps every alternate theory for what could be the driver of a firm's innovativeness. This chapter classifies and reviews each alternate theory and presents the evidence we have collected on each.

The many alternate theories for firm innovativeness can be grouped into either micro-theories that operate primarily at the market level or macro-theories that operate primarily at the global or country level.

Micro-Theories

Among the explanations for firm innovativeness, four theories or effects have become popular, partly due to books or articles espousing them: Wall Street effect, the size effect, disruptive technology effect, and S-curve effect. This section briefly describes these theories and then presents contrary evidence from one of my large cross-sectional coauthored studies.

Wall Street Effect

When I was presenting the thesis of this book at a meeting, a senior manager from a large multinational corporation stood up and said, "It's not the incumbent's curse, it's the Wall Street Curse." He went on to explain that the key reason that publicly traded incumbents today are not innovative is because senior executives work very hard to shore up the stock price on Wall Street by meeting the numbers. The numbers here are sales and earnings forecasts. He went on to state, "No one got fired for meeting the numbers." We all know that many CEOs got fired for sustained or sharp declines in sales, profits, and especially market capitalization.

Can managers boost their firms' stock prices by adopting short-term measures? What are these measures? Do they take away from innovation? There are at least two ways that firms can boost earnings through so-called short-term measures. First, managers can cut costs in administration, manufacturing, marketing, and R&D. Second, managers can lay off employees, especially in functions not essential to immediate sales and marketing, such as R&D. Both these measures may lead to higher profits, earnings, and stock prices, at least in the short term. To the extent that these cuts in costs or laying off employees affect R&D or any innovation activity, it will reduce the flow of future innovations despite increasing short-term profits, earnings, and possibly stock price. If indeed such measures increase short-term stock price at the cost of long-term growth and market cap, then the measures would be myopic. At least one study shows that such myopic practices do exist, especially in recessions.[2]

The Wall Street Curse boils down to this phenomenon: pressure from investors on Wall Street causes managers to cut investments in innovation to boost current earnings and stock prices, at the cost of future innovation, growth, and long-term market cap.

Is this really true? How does the stock market respond to announcements about investments and progress in R&D and innovation? Does the market really respond negatively to such investments?

To answer this question, Professor Ashish Sood of Emory University and I analyzed 5,481 announcements made by sixty-nine firms in five markets between 1977 and 2006.[3] These announcement related to various stages of the innovation process, beginning as early as opening a lab or starting a research project, through the developments of prototypes and patents, until the launch of a product and its winning awards. The method used for the analysis depends on market returns to announcements calculated via an event analysis. Our analysis controlled for a large number of other explanatory variables, especially market factors that are known to affect returns (market movements, small versus large firm effect, growth versus value stocks, and momentum). What we found came as a big surprise and runs counter to the Wall Street Curse. In particular, five findings are highly pertinent to this discussion.

1. On average the stock market responds positively (not negatively) to announcements about innovation and R&D, including those made at the start of innovation projects, such as opening a lab.
2. The returns to announcements about innovation projects are positive even though they are made on average of about 4.5 years before the actual launch of a new product emerging from the project.
3. Negative events, such as canceling a research project or cutting funding for research, result in negative returns.
4. The negative returns for negative announcements are steeper in absolute values than the positive returns for the corresponding positive announcements.
5. In a few cases for which we had cost or investment data, total returns to the research effort were about *three times* the value of the funds invested in the research effort. For example, between 1999 and 2008, HP spent $34 billion on R&D but earned $108 billion on returns from this investment.

These results show that the stock market is not as oriented toward the short term as it is often criticized to be. If one analyzes the data carefully, the market does respond positively to long-term innovation and growth. The Wall Street Curse is a scapegoat for failure to make the tough decisions that need to be made when investing in long-term research projects for innovation. The root cause of the problem is the incumbent's curse laid out in this book.

Size Effect

The size effect comes from the theory of creative destruction ascribed to Joseph Schumpeter.[4] The central thesis of this theory is that radical innovations destroy old ones but create new markets that increase consumer welfare. For example, the automobile industry destroyed horse carriages, the personal computer and printer destroyed typewriters, and MP3 players destroyed mobile tape players. While there was much pain with the demise of an old market, the welfare of all consumers improved with the rise of the new technology. The important question the theory addresses is: who introduces the radical innovations? Schumpeter and his followers assume that all such radical innovations are introduced by small firms and that the destruction of the old industry invariably involves the failure of large firms.

My coauthor Rajesh Chandy of the London Business School and I tested this hypothesis. Our results were published in a peer-reviewed scientific journal.[5] We decided to focus on two broad categories of products—office products and consumer durables—because they are the most often studied in this area, enabling us to compare findings with prior studies. Within these two markets, we sampled *all* major innovations over the prior 140 years. Our criterion for major innovation was whether the innovation led to a new market that generated over one million dollars in revenues. Three experts classified these innovations on a 9-point scale of radicalness. We defined radicalness based on how much the innovation used an entirely new technology and provided substantially new benefits to consumers compared to the product it replaced.

241

The primary research question of our study was whether radical innovations came from large firms or small firms. Contrary to Schumpeter's belief, we found that the number of radical innovations from large firms (42%) was only a little lower than those from small and medium firms (48%). Moreover, in a multiple regression model, the size of a firm was not a significant determinant of the radicalness of an innovation. Further, an analysis across time explains how the small firm theory may have originated (see Figure 8.1). Prior to World War II, 83% of radical innovations were from small and medium firms and only 17% were from large firms. After World War II, that distribution shifts dramatically: 74% of radical innovations are from large firms and only 26% are from small and medium firms. Thus, Schumpeter's theory and those of others who followed him were likely based on evidence prior to

Figure 8.1. Size of Firms Introducing Radical Innovations by Time Period

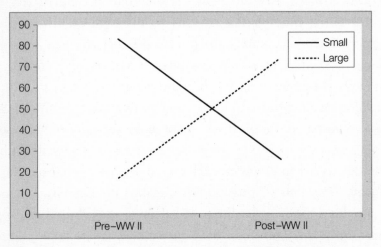

Source: Adapted from Chandy, Rajesh and Gerard J. Tellis, "The Incumbent's Curse? Incumbency, Size and Radical Product Innovation," *Journal of Marketing*, 64, no. 3 (July 2000): 1–17.

World War II. The situation today has changed dramatically, as Figure 8.1 shows.

That a large number of all radical innovations now come from large firms implies that many large firms are innovative. But small and medium firms still produce a nontrivial number of radical innovations, implying that in those markets, some large firms fail to come up with the radical innovation. So the question remains: why are some large firms innovative and others not? Our answer is that it is not size per se that matters but the culture of the firm.

A good example is the case of IBM. In the 1970s, IBM was the leading manufacturer of mainframe computers. Prior to the birth of desktop computing, IBM mainframes dominated the computer market. True to Schumpeter's small firm thesis, a small start-up in New Mexico called MITS introduced the first desktop computer called Altair. The Altair was primitive and stayed a hobbyist's toy until Apple introduced the Apple I and popularized personal computing. It was only in 1980 that IBM decided to enter the market. Why the delay? Prior to its entry, IBM's internal culture was centered on mainframes. Longtime IBM insiders either saw no value in desktop computing or feared it would cannibalize the huge profits from the mainframe business. So the mainframers stalled or killed every effort at introducing a desktop computer.

But IBM did ultimately introduce a highly successful personal computer in 1981, the IBM PC. To overcome the culture within, IBM set up a skunk works[6] at Boca Raton, Florida, completely independent of headquarters, with the mandate of introducing a personal computer in one year. It even kept the division secret from mainframers at IBM to prevent any effort to cripple the project. Thus, it was the creation of an autonomous unit, free from the stifling culture of the mother ship, which enabled IBM to overcome its own noninnovative culture. In this case, the large firm failed to innovate before 1980 but still did in 1981. The difference was the culture within and the efforts used to overcome it, not the size of the firm per se.

In the early 1990s, IBM was on the verge of implosion with the rise of rivals Microsoft and Intel, and the decline of its personal computing and mainframe businesses. At that point, the firm hired Louis Gerstner Jr., CEO of RJR Nabisco. In a period of nine years, Gerstner orchestrated a radical change in IBM, transforming it from a hardware company focused on patents to a services company focused on complete IT solutions for business clients. IBM became once again a highly innovative company. One could argue that Gerstner did not change very much. After his retirement, at a major conference in Los Angeles, when asked what he changed at IBM, he answered with one word, "culture." Chapter 5 describes this amazing transformation.

This book does not dispute creative destruction per se. It instead refutes a major premise of that theory that innovations that cause such destruction come exclusively from small firms rather than large firms. Our research suggests that not size but culture (as described in prior chapters) drives a firm's innovations.

Disruptive Technology Effect

Professor Clay Christensen of Harvard University put forth the theory of disruptive technology in a top-selling business book.[7] The essence of the theory is that leading firms in a market invest in the currently dominant technology even when its performance, as measured on the primary dimension of performance, exceeds the needs of the mass market or majority of consumers. During this time, a new (disruptive) technology emerges on the horizon. The new technology is superior to the dominant technology on some secondary dimension that appeals only to a niche market and not to the mass market, and so the market leaders ignore or belittle the new technology. Initially the new technology's performance is inferior to that of the dominant technology and below the needs of the mass market on the primary dimension of performance. For this reason, the mass market does not embrace the new technology. However, the new technology continues to improve in performance on the primary dimension until it meets the needs of the mass market. Then, because it is also superior on the secondary dimensions of performance, it represents a better buy for the mass market than the dominant technology. At that point, the new technology disrupts the dominant technology.

Which firm introduces the new technology? Christensen's answer reflects a key finding of the theory: "The firms that led the industry in every instance of developing and adopting disruptive technologies were entrants to the industry, not its incumbent leaders."[8] According to this result, all incumbent leaders cling to the old technology while all new disruptive technologies are introduced by new entrants to the market.

One problem with this theory is that it does not contain a precise, unambiguous definition of "disruptive technology" prior to and independent of disruption. What exactly is a disruptive technology *before it disrupts?* How does an analyst identify it? In the absence of such a definition, there is the danger of defining the disruptive technology after the event. That is, after some new technology disrupts incumbents, it will be classified as disruptive. In that case, the theory becomes circular and has no predictive value.

Professor Ashish Sood and I carried out a study to test this theory and imbue the concept of disruptive technology with meaning. Our study, published in a peer-reviewed scientific journal,[9] is based on thirty-six technologies across seven markets. We took pains to sample *all* technologies in each market, both those technologies that disrupted and those that did not, those that were new and those that were old. For each market, we sampled a time period ranging from 53 to 127 years. Overall, the data took several years to collect and involved a team of research assistants. We defined a technology on scientific principles independently of disruption. In particular, we defined those new technologies that are initially inferior to the dominant technology on the primary dimension of performance as "potentially disruptive."[10]

What are the results of this study? There is no doubt that new technologies arise with increasing frequency and that they destroy entire markets. Consistent with the theory, we too find that new technologies initially appeal to niche segments but later with improvement, they appeal to the mass market. However, our study refutes the two most important tenets of the theory of disruptive technology. First, incumbents in a market introduce potentially disruptive technologies *more frequently* (53%) than new entrants (47%). Second, and more important, incumbents are significantly *more likely* to cause disruption in a market than entrants.

Thus, contrary to Christensen's theory, disruption is not the prerogative of new entrants. We find that some incumbents are disrupted by new entrants, while other incumbents themselves introduce disruptive technologies. In other words, some incumbents are innovative and others are not. What is the reason for this difference? The thesis of this book is that the internal culture of the firm determines whether it will be innovative or not, not its status as an incumbent or the arrival of some external technology. Firms that have an innovative culture are able to develop, embrace, and deploy disruptive innovations. Firms that do not have such a culture cling to their old technologies and are disrupted.

For example, in the market of photography, digital photography has disrupted analog photography. Kodak was the dominant player in analog photography since its founding by George Eastman over a hundred years ago. The uninformed might suspect that some new entrant researched and introduced digital photography. However, surprisingly, the firm that developed the most technologies and that has the most patents in the digital photography market is Kodak. Yet Kodak did not become the unquestioned leader of digital photography. The reason is not because it ignored the new technology or failed to invest in it or failed to develop it as the theory of disruptive technology would suggest. The reason is Kodak's fear of cannibalizing its established film business based on the analog technology. Chapter 2 explains in greater detail the pervasive culture that critically inhibited Kodak despite efforts by its CEO.

There are some valuable insights in the theory of disruptive technology. However, the danger in this theory is to attribute failure primarily to an external technology. The real cause of success or failure is within: the culture of the firm.

S-Curve Effect

The S-curve effect or theory was put forth by Richard Foster, a former director and senior partner of McKinsey & Company.[11] The basic premise of the theory is that the evolution of the performance of a technology on a primary dimension of performance follows the shape of an S-curve. The S-curve emerges because the new technology's performance initially is flat due to technological hurdles, then improves rapidly as researchers overcome these hurdles, and finally flattens out in maturity as it reaches the limits of growth. A new technology emerges above the starting point but below the current level of the dominant technology when the latter is still in its ascendancy.

The theory asserts that all incumbents concentrate on the old technology and ignore the new one. In contrast, new entrants support and advance the performance of the new technology. However, by the time the dominant technology reaches its peak, the new technology hits its growth phase. The latter then surpasses the old dominant technology in performance and becomes the dominant technology. At that point, incumbents make a last effort to improve the old technology. They strive to push the limits of the old technology and may squeeze out a little performance from it, but the amount is too little to compete with the fast-growing new technology. As Foster states, "If you are at the limit, no matter how hard you try, you cannot make progress."[12] The incumbents then fail with the old technology, while the entrants who supported the new technology become the market leaders. As Foster states, "These [technology] patterns suggested that in most cases it is companies with new ideas and approaches, not entrenched large ones that collectively have the advantage—the attacker's advantage."[13]

The problem with this theory is that it suggests a path of technological evolution that is too stylized to hold for every technology in every market. Moreover, the theory is based on selective cases and not on an exhaustive list of all technologies in a market. By using selective examples, the author runs the risk of cherry-picking examples to suit the theory.

Professor Ashish Sood of Emory and I tested this theory with data similar to that collected in our study reported earlier.[14] We sampled every technology in six markets. By selecting every technology, we ensured that we did not cherry-pick examples to support or reject a certain position. We published this study in two articles: one in a peer-reviewed scientific journal and the other in a working paper of the Marketing Science Institute.[15]

Our study led to five results that were all contrary to Foster's S-curve of technological evolution (see Figures 2.3 and 8.2): (1) Technological performance does not evolve in the shape of smooth S-curves. Rather it evolves in a series of step functions; (2) sometimes, the evolution may show a spurt in performance even after a long period of dormancy; (3) new technologies emerge at random intervals, sometimes above and at other times below the performance of the dominant technology; (4) the performance

Figure 8.2. Technology Evolution in Printers

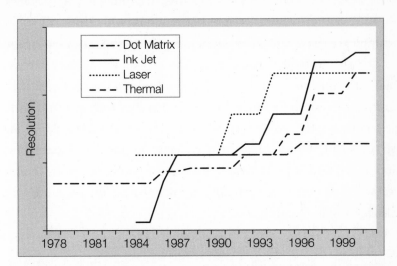

Source: Adapted from Sood, Ashish and Gerard J. Tellis (2005), "Technological Evolution and Radical Innovations," *Journal of Marketing*, 69, 3 (July), 152–168.

paths of technologies cross not only once, but multiple times; and (5) most important, an approximately equal number of new technologies come from entrants and from incumbents. Thus, contrary to Foster's view, new technologies are not the prerogative of new entrants. Why are many incumbents innovative while others are not? The underlying driver is culture. Those that have the necessary culture (described in the first chapter and elaborated in subsequent chapters) stay at the cutting edge of technological advances with radical innovations. Those that lack that culture fail to innovate and decline in market share or die out.

For example, Figure 8.2 shows that the technological paths of inkjet printing and laser printing crossed many times. Any firm that abandoned one of these technologies when surpassed by a rival would have lost a great opportunity.

Indeed, HP became the dominant player in printing because it backed both technologies. It established a culture of internal markets that allowed two competing divisions to each develop and market one of these competing technologies. Chapter 6 explains the principles of internal markets with this and other examples to show how a firm stays at the cutting edge of innovation.

Thus, although technologies do evolve in distinct curves, they are not single S-shaped but multiple-step functions. The danger in assuming a single S-curve is that managers may abandon a promising technology at the first indication of a flattening of the technology's performance. Most important, incumbents are not doomed to fail simply because they are incumbents. Rather, incumbents can remain dominant by building a culture for unrelenting innovation.

Macro-Theories

During the course of my many presentations to and discussion with executives, individuals have proposed rival explanations to the theory of culture that I have emphasized in this book. Oftentimes these rival explanations have been raised quite simply as plausible alternates: "Oh, that is typical of such and such (culture, country, religion, or climate)." Interestingly, these rival explanations are not merely those of lay people. Scholars over the decades have proposed several macro explanations for innovativeness. In this section, I summarize some of these theories in a nutshell even though entire treatises and books have been written and continue to be written in support of them. I then argue why culture is a better explanation of innovativeness than any of these rivals. Finally, I describe a study we conducted to test all these theories versus a theory of culture. When reviewing these theories, readers may see the limitations or fallacies in the arguments. Yet I include these theories to be complete in my review of other explanations and to establish the preeminence of culture as an explanation for a firm's innovativeness. I focus on the following alternative theories: religion, climate, geography, patenting, and education

Macro-Theories in a Nutshell

The explanation for *religion* rests on the argument that certain religions focus on inward bliss (Buddhism), abstinence (Hinduism), or rewards of the afterlife (Catholicism), whereas others focus on development and advancement of the internal self or external world (Judaism and Protestantism).[16] The latter religions motivate followers to build products, firms, or markets and adopt or commercialize innovations. Followers of the former three are less motivated to do so. Perhaps the best known proponent of this theory is Max Weber, who coined the phrase, "the Protestant work ethic."[17] Popular examples given in support of this theory are the greater economic progress and innovativeness of Northern Europe (predominantly Protestant) versus Southern Europe (predominantly Catholic) and the dominance of the West over the East in the last five centuries.

The explanation for *climate* rests on the argument that warm climates are not as conducive to work, industriousness, and innovativeness as are cool climates. In particular, hot climates lead people to minimize energy expenditure so as not to generate further heat from work, whereas cool climates lead people to work with greater frequency and effort in order to generate heat and keep themselves warm. Another explanation for climate is that warm climates are more abundant in natural, animal, and plant life, allowing inhabitants an easier lifestyle with less motivation for work. On the contrary, cold climates are more hostile, require long-term planning, and motivate people to work.[18] Both claims hold that innovativeness flourishes where there is a greater drive for and output of work. The evidence offered in support of this theory is the greater economic development in the last 500 years of Northern Europe over Southern Europe, North America over Central and South America, and Europe (predominately cool) over Asia (predominantly warm).[19]

The explanation for *geography* takes various forms. One of these, best put forward by Jared Diamond, is that certain geographic regions were well endowed with critical natural resources (primarily wild domesticable cereals and animals) and with good trade routes to neighboring regions. These then began to progress through a positive self-sustaining cycle of innovation and economic wealth. Diamond's primary evidence is the success of Mesopotamia, then Mediterranean countries, and then Western Europe over Africa, Australia, and North and South America, especially up to the sixteenth century.[20]

The explanation for *patenting* rests on the argument that a patent enables the recipient to reap monopoly profits from its commercialization for a period of time. This motivates the recipient to develop and commercialize innovations.[21] The need for such motivation increases with the cost, effort, and time required to develop and commercialize innovations. Intellectual property protection is a term used to cover protection by patents, copyrights, and branding, all of which could be related to the advancement of innovations. Evidence for patents as a driver of innovation has been used to explain why in the sixteenth to twentieth centuries more innovations were developed and commercialized in Western Europe over China and India. Though China and India were more advanced than Western Europe prior to the sixteenth century, the Europeans developed a more formal patenting system from about the fifteenth century than what existed in China and India.[22]

The explanation for *education* states that inventing requires at least some technical knowledge best attained through a strong education system. This factor is especially important for innovations in science and engineering.[23] During the twentieth century, the United States developed the most extensive, deep, and sophisticated education system in the world—especially at the postsecondary level. Some authors use that explanation to explain its come-from-behind advance over Europe to become a global superpower in the twentieth century with the highest number of innovations across most fields.

Refutation of Macro-Theories

Most of these macro-theories are based on observations of a narrow set of countries or across a narrow time period. One can refute these theories by giving examples of firms that have performed well on innovations outside of these sets of countries or time periods. The issue pertinent to us is whether these theories hold in the twenty-first century, with its radically different economic, political, and environmental conditions. Rather than proceed with theoretical arguments, I will present notable examples that run contrary to the theories presented above.

Good examples to refute the theory of religion are Japan, India, and the United States. Since the 1960s, Japan's economy developed rapidly to achieve high levels of innovation, at least in some fields (for example, automobiles, miniaturization, and robotics). Protestantism is not the dominant faith in Japan; Buddhism is. That Buddhism shuns materialism and strives for internal bliss has not hindered Japan from making great material progress. India is another good example. Prior to 1992, India's economic backwardness could be attributed to the Hindu philosophy that advocates renunciation of material goods and pleasures and reconciliation with one's karma or destiny. Indeed, the slow rate of growth in India from 1947 to 1992 was referred to derogatively as the "Hindu rate of growth." However, India was a prosperous country in several

253

time periods prior to the sixteenth century despite prevalent Hinduism. It was so wealthy that it became the destiny of numerous invaders and plunderers in prior centuries. Also, with economic liberalization in 1992, the economy grew rapidly and spawned numerous highly innovative firms.[24] The country is predicted to be one of the top three economic powers by 2050.[25] Clearly, Hinduism, the prevalence of which has remained approximately constant during this time period, cannot explain these dramatic changes in progress and prosperity. Further, the theory of religion cannot explain why the United States grew to be so much more innovative than Northern Europe in the twentieth century though both of them are predominantly Protestant. These examples of Japan, India, and the United States show that the theory of religion does not hold beyond a narrow set of countries (for example, Western Europe) over a relatively small time period (for example, the fifteenth to the nineteenth century).

Good examples to refute the theory of climate are Singapore, India, Greece, and Italy. Singapore is a country with a hot, humid climate. Yet in a period of forty years since 1962, the people of Singapore transformed a backward swamp into a highly developed country with the potential to develop innovations of its own. India has had a predominantly warm climate throughout the last three thousand years. However, as stated earlier, its economy changed dramatically during that time period. India was a wealthy country prior to the sixteenth century, wealthier than most, if not all, European countries. During much of the twentieth century until 1992, India was a poor, backward country with few innovations about which to boast. It developed rapidly due to economic liberalization in 1992 and produced impressive innovations. Yet, India's climate has not changed as dramatically as its economy has in the last two thousand years. Greece and Italy lag behind northwestern Europe in economic progress today, but around two thousand years ago, they were the very epicenters of economic progress and innovation in Europe—Greece during the glory days of Athens as a city-state, and Italy during the Roman Empire. Again, over the last twenty-five hundred years, the climate of Europe has not changed dramatically, though the fortune of these countries has. Thus, climate is a poor explanation of economic wealth and innovativeness.

Geography may have played an important part in the development of countries and regions at one time, but not any longer. With means of rapid transportation across the world and the growth of the Internet, people even in remote areas are now well connected with the world community. Thus, the isolation of communities, which hindered progress and innovation in the past, is no longer a hurdle.[26] The best example to refute the theory of geography is China. Until about 1421, it was the most advanced economy in the world with numerous innovations of the time.[27] Then it entered a long period of economic decline and stagnation. Beginning in 1978, it entered into a new period of rapid economic progress and innovation that lifted billions out of poverty.[28] China currently has the fastest growth rate of any major economy, has the second largest economy in the world, and is slated to become the largest economy by 2050.[29] Most important, it has developed innovations in many areas, albeit with complaints that these innovations may have been copied from the West. Throughout these dramatic changes in economic performance, China's geography did not alter much. What did change is its organization. Indeed, the culture for innovation, especially for firms within the country, changed the most. That better explains the rise, fall, and rise again of the Chinese economy.

The theories for intellectual property protection and education are valid. Although intellectual property protection and education are necessary for innovation, they alone are not sufficient. Most major economies of the world today have a minimum set of laws protecting intellectual property and have institutions that provide education at least for some portion of the population. Yet the innovativeness of firms within these countries varies dramatically. For example, the United States has an excellent system of intellectual property protection and university education. Yet within the United States, one-time strong and dominant firms declined and fell because of a failure to develop, embrace, or commercialize innovations, as the examples in Chapter 1 and subsequent chapters show. Indeed, in every country, one can find firms that are highly innovative and others that are not. What explains these differences? I explain these differences with the culture of the firm. And a culture that lends itself to innovation transcends the patent and education system within any country.

In 2003, Rajesh Chandy of the London Business School and Jaideep Prabhu of Cambridge University and I undertook a study to test the theory of culture against other micro- and macro-theories as a causative explanation for a firm's innovativeness. We published this study in 2009 in a peer-reviewed scientific journal.[30] What made this study challenging is that we targeted over four thousand firms across seventeen countries (see Table 8.1). Over 770 of these firms responded, representing a relatively good response rate of 20%.

For the survey, we developed a questionnaire that measured characteristics of the responding firm, including religion, geography, climate, patenting, and education. We also measured the innovativeness and culture of the firm. For these latter variables, we used standard published scales that were developed and adjusted through prior studies. These scales consisted of an average of three items for innovativeness and each component of culture. We worded multiple items with opposing positive or negative valenced terms, such that respondents with a particular response would have to switch between the right and the left end of the scale.[31] So doing

Table 8.1. Countries and Firms Sampled

Country	Sample	Responses
Australia	128	35
Canada	154	25
China	183	31
France	242	39
Germany	315	81
Hong Kong	167	15
India	139	28
Italy	99	32
Japan	409	57
Korea	333	87
Netherlands	62	17
Singapore	176	24
Sweden	113	26
Switzerland	80	23
Taiwan	243	83
UK	383	67
USA	848	102
TOTAL	**4,074**	**772**

Source: Adapted from Tellis, Gerard J., Jaideep Prabhu, and Rajesh Chandy (2009), "Innovations of Firms Across Nations: The Pre-Eminence of Internal Firm Culture," *Journal of Marketing*, 73, 1 (January), 3–23.

allowed us to discriminate between respondents' bad, thoughtless responses (that answer the same way across items irrespective of their valence) and good, thoughtful responses (that change with the valence of the items). In short, using multiple oppositely valenced items enables a researcher to distinguish between internally consistent and inconsistent responses. In addition, we collected market data on an exhaustive list of about two hundred variables for each firm, including economic conditions, R&D investments, stock market performance, and so forth.

257

Figure 8.3. Effects of Alternate Variables on Innovativeness of Firms.

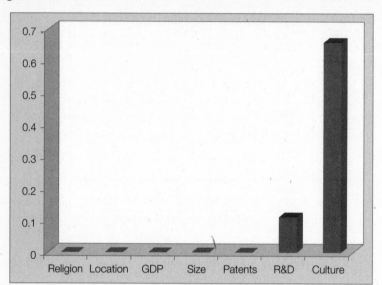

Note: Non-significant effects are portrayed as 0. Religion is measured as belonging to one of several religions including Catholic, Protestant, Hindu-Sikh, Buddhists, or Other. Patents are measured as citation weighted patents. Location is measured as latitude of the capital of the country from the equator. R&D is measured as percentage of all employees in R&D. Innovativeness is measured by a three-item Likert scale. Size is measured as sales volume. The effect of culture is the sum of the effects of five dimensions of culture that were significant, each measured by a three-item Likert scale: willingness to cannibalize current products, tolerance for risk, focus on future, incentives for enterprise, and empowerment of champions. Internal competition was not significant.

The study has two dependent variables: the firm's innovativeness and its stock market performance. The study has two important findings, one from each of these dependent variables. First, innovation is an important driver of financial performance. Second, the culture of the firm is the most important driver of the innovativeness of the firm (see Figure 8.3). In particular, five key components of culture turned out to be significant drivers of the innovativeness of the firm (all described in prior chapters except internal markets). Besides culture, the only other important variable that affected firm innovativeness is R&D by sales. In addition, none of the other drivers of

Table 8.2. Productivity of Patents in Sony and Apple in 2006

Firm	Market Cap	Patents
Sony	$40 billion	1,447
Apple	$45 billion	103

innovativeness posited by the various competing theories reviewed earlier were significant drivers of innovation.

When we presented our results at various conferences, audiences were especially surprised that patents did not turn out to be a significant driver of innovativeness. For decades, and in most economic theories, patents have been identified as an important output of innovation of a firm. However, our thesis is that patents may be a good measure of creativity but not of commercialized innovations. That is, having merely a large number of patents does not ensure that a firm is innovative. Table 8.2 shows this point dramatically.

For example, about the time the iPod was introduced, Sony had ten times as many patents as Apple. That huge body of patents did not help Sony much. As Chapter 2 detailed, before the launch of the iPod, Sony was five times the size of Apple in terms of market capitalization. However, once the iPod took off, Apple became twice the size of Sony (Figure 2.4). Thus patents represent a measure of inventiveness but not of commercialized innovations.

Indeed, a heavy emphasis on patenting may create an inward-looking culture of creativity. According to Louis Gerstner, former CEO of IBM, this is the mentality that ailed IBM when he took over.[32] However, market success depends on an outward-oriented culture of successfully commercializing radical innovations for future mass markets. Like patents, religion, geography, climate, patenting, and education have no explanatory power on the innovativeness of these 772 firms across seventeen countries (Figure 8.3). The survey instrument from this study can be used by firms to gauge their own innovativeness and benchmark their firm's culture and performance against the over 772 firms in our database.

CONCLUSION

Scholars from many disciplines have postulated several theories, both micro and macro, for the drivers of innovativeness of countries and firms within countries. This chapter reviews a number of these theories. Among micro-theories are the Wall Street effect, the size effect, the disruptive technology effect, and the S-curve effect. Among macro-theories are religion, climate, geography, patenting, and education. This chapter argues that the culture of the firm is a better explanation for a firm's innovativeness than these other theories. The chapter also describes four large, formal studies that present relatively objective evidence that none of these other theories constitute a compelling and complete explanation for the innovativeness of firms in contemporary markets. In particular, the fourth study shows that culture trumps every other variable as an explanation for innovativeness.

To show that the examples in the text are not cherry-picked, this chapter provides formal evidence in support of the theory of culture. The evidence is based on a series of studies involving massive data collection that were subjected to rigorous peer review. Most important, the studies are all based on systematic or random sampling—but not selective sampling—of firms, markets, or innovations.

Although firms cannot completely control Wall Street or their incumbency, size, country of operation, climate of operation, religion of employees, or technological evolution, they can control their culture. I define firm culture with three important traits: willingness to cannibalize successful products, embracing risk, and focusing on the future. Altering cultural traits is difficult. But traits are influenced by practices. Three important practices for innovation are: creating incentives for enterprise, establishing internal markets, and empowering innovation champions. A firm's leaders have the power and opportunity to change practices and thus shape its culture for innovation. The prior chapters explain each of these components of culture with case histories of successful innovation or missed opportunity

My explanation of culture births hope.

NOTES

Chapter 1

1. Golder, Peter N., Julie Irwin, and Debanjan Mitra, "Do Economic Conditions Affect Long-Term Brand Leadership Persistence?" Presentation at the Conference of Theory and Practice of Marketing, Harvard Business School, May 5, 2012.
2. Golder, Peter N. and Gerard J. Tellis, "Pioneering Advantage: Marketing Logic or Marketing Legend," *Journal of Marketing Research*, 30, no. 2 (1993): 158–170; Tellis, Gerard J. and Peter Golder, *Will and Vision: How Latecomers Grow to Dominate Markets* (New York: McGraw Hill, 2001).
3. A radical innovation is a new product, service, process, or business model that is based on a new scientific principle and provides substantially superior consumer benefits than was possible with the prior scientific principle in use. Chapter 2 describes this concept in depth.
4. Chandy, Rajesh and Gerard J. Tellis, "The Incumbent's Curse? Incumbency, Size and Radical Product Innovation," *Journal of Marketing*, 64, no. 3 (July 2000): 1–17; Chandy, Rajesh and Gerard J. Tellis, "Organizing For Radical Product Innovation," *Journal of Marketing Research*, 35 (November 1998): 474–487.
5. Gerstner, Lou, *Who Says Elephants Can't Dance?* (New York: HarperCollins, 2002), 185.
6. Apple's iPod was first and foremost a highly user-friendly product. One of the secrets to its success was that Apple achieved this great user-friendliness even though they included strong digital rights maintenance (DRM) to prevent illegal copying of songs, in order to gain access to songs from music companies.

263

7. "Larry Page and Eric Schmidt Hold Court at Google Zeitgeist," *TechCrunch*. September 27, 2011, http://techcrunch.com/2011/09/27/page-schmidt-zeitgeist-video/

8. "Larry Page and Eric Schmidt Hold Court," *TechCrunch*.

9. See summary at end of this chapter and details in chapter 8 .

10. Gerstner, *Who Says Elephants Can't Dance?*, 182.

11. Ibid.

12. Jaruzelski, Barry and John Loehr, "The Global Innovation 1000," *Strategy+Business*, Booz & Company, 65 (Winter 2010).

13. Tellis, Gerard J., Jaideep Prabhu, and Rajesh Chandy (2009), "Innovation of Firms Across Nations: The Pre-Eminence of Internal Firm Culture," *Journal of Marketing*, 73, no. 1 (January 2009): 3–23.

14. Dvorak, Phred, "Bad Luck Swamped Successes During Stringer's Sony Tenure," *Wall Street Journal* (February 2, 2012): A10.

15. See Chapter 2.

16. O'Connor, Gina Colarelli and Christopher M. McDermott (2004), "The Human Side of Radical Innovation," *Journal of Engineering Technology Management*, 21: 11–30.

17. Troianovski, Anton and Sven Grundberg, "Nokia's Bad Call on Smartphones," *Wall Street Journal* (July 18, 2012). Retrieved July 23, 2012, from http://online.wsj.com/article/SB10001424052702304388004577531002591315494.html

18. The awards include the William F. O'Dell Award for best paper from the *Journal of Marketing Research*, the Harold H. Maynard award for best paper from the *Journal of Marketing*, the Frank M. Bass award for best dissertation based article in *Marketing Science*, the Long Term Impact Award for the article with biggest impact over ten years in *Marketing Science*.

19. Golder and Tellis, "Pioneering Advantage"; Tellis and Golder, *Will and Vision*.

20. Chandy and Tellis, "The Incumbent's Curse?"

21. Chandy, "Organizing For Radical Product Innovation."

22. Tellis, Prabhu, and Chandy, "Innovation of Firms Across Nations."

23. Sood, Ashish and Gerard J. Tellis, "Technological Evolution and Radical Innovations," *Journal of Marketing*, 69, no. 3 (July, 2005): 152–168.

24. Sood, Ashish and Gerard J. Tellis, "Demystifying Disruptions: A New Model for Understanding and Predicting Disruptive Technologies," *Marketing Science*, 30, no. 2 (March-April, 2011): 339–354.

25. Sood, Ashish and Gerard J. Tellis, "Do Innovations Really Pay Off? Total Stock Market Returns to Innovation," *Marketing Science*, 28, no. 3 (May-June, 2009): 442–456.

26. Chandrasekaran, Deepa and Gerard J. Tellis, "The Global Takeoff of New Products: Culture, Wealth, or Vanishing Differences," *Marketing Science*,

27, no. 5 (September-October 2008): 844–860; Tellis, Gerard J., Stefan Stremersch, and Eden Yin, "The International Takeoff of New Products: Economics, Culture and Country Innovativeness," *Marketing Science*, 22, no. 2 (Spring, 2003): 161–187; Golder, Peter N. and Gerard J. Tellis, "Will It Ever Fly? Modeling the Takeoff of New Consumer Durables," *Marketing Science*, 16, no. 3 (1997): 256–270.

Chapter 2

1. Khanna, Tarun, Jaeyong Song, and Kyungmook Lee, "The Paradox of Samsung's Rise," *Harvard Business Review*, 89, no. 7/8 (July/August, 2011): 142–147.
2. Fan, Shay, "The Slate: A History of Innovation," *The Next Bench Blog*, 2010, http://h20435.www2.hp.com/t5/The-Next-Bench-Blog/The-Slate-A-History-of-Innovation/ba-p/52657
3. Ghemawat, P., "Market Incumbency and Technological Inertia," *Marketing Science*, 10, no. 2 (1991): 161–171; Kamien, M. I. and N. L. Schwartz, *Market Structure and Innovation* (Cambridge, MA: Cambridge University Press, 1982); Reinganum, J. F., "On the Diffusion of New Technology: A Game Theoretic Approach," *Review of Economic Studies*, 153 (1981): 395–406. However, a few economists have designed models to show the optimality of cannibalization: Nault, Barrie R. and Mark B. Vandenbosch, "Eating Your Own Lunch: Protection Through Preemption," *Organizational Science*, 7, no. 3 (May-June, 1996): 342–358.
4. Hill, Andrew, "The Architecture of a Company Being Built from Within," *Financial Times* (April 14, 2011): 16.
5. Ibid.
6. Based on data collected by the author and Deepa Chandrasekaran of Lehigh University.
7. Sood, Ashish and Gerard J. Tellis, "Technological Evolution and Radical Innovations," *Journal of Marketing*, 69, no. 3 (July, 2005): 152–168.
8. Oliver, Christian, "Fast Follower Leads the Way," *Financial Times* (March 20, 2012). http://www.ft.com/intl/cms/s/0/7b622220–6e57–11e1-b98d-00144feab49a.html#axzz20GC2mStm
9. Sood, Ashish and Gerard J. Tellis, "Do Innovations Really Pay Off?" *Marketing Science*, 28, no. 3 (May-June, 2009): 442–456; Borah, Abhishek and Gerard J. Tellis, "To Make or Not to Make: Stock Market Returns to Make Versus Buy Innovations," working paper, USC Marshall School of Business (2012).
10. Borah and Tellis, "To Make or Not to Make."
11. Tellis, Gerard J. and Ashish Sood, "A New Framework to Help Firms Select among Competing Technologies," *Visions*, PDMA, Vol. XXXIV, No. 3, 18–23, Oct. 2010.

12. Ibid.
13. This case is based on investigative reporting in Guth, Robert A. "Microsoft's Bid to Beat Google Builds on a History of Misses," *Wall Street Journal* (January 16, 2009): A1, A6.
14. "Microsoft's Bid to Beat Google Builds on a History of Misses."
15. Ibid.
16. Kunii, Irene M., Cliff Edwards, and Jay Greene, "Can Sony Regain the Magic?" *BusinessWeek Online* (March 11, 2002). http://www.businessweek .com/stories/2002–03–10/can-sony-regain-the-magic
17. Rose, Frank, "The Civil War Inside Sony," *Wired Magazine* (February 11, 2003). http://www.wired.com/wired/archive/11.02/sony.html
18. Ibid.
19. Ibid.
20. Ibid.
21. Ibid.
22. Isaacson, Walter, *Steve Jobs* (Kindle ed.) (New York: Simon & Schuster, 2011), 388.
23. Swasy, Alecia, *Changing Focus: Kodak and the Battle to Save a Great American Company* (New York: Crown Business, 1997), 21.
24. Rediff Interview, "Innovation Best Comes from People Who Know Nothing About the Topic," *Rediff India Abroad* (2006). http://www.rediff.com/ money/2006/aug/07kodak.htm.
25. Lucas, Henry C. and Jie Mein Goh, "Disruptive Technology: How Kodak Missed the Digital Photography Revolution," *Journal of Strategic Information Systems*, 18 (2009), 46–55.
26. Rediff Interview, "Innovation Best Comes from People Who Know Nothing About the Topic."
27. Ibid.
28. Lucas and Goh, "Disruptive Technology."
29. Swasy, *Changing Focus*, 30.
30. Smith, Geoffrey, William C. Symonds, Peter Burrows, Ellen Neuborne, and Paul C. Judge, "Can George Fisher Fix Kodak?" *Business Week* (October 9, 1997).
31. Smith et al., "Can George Fisher Fix Kodak?"
32. Tellis, Gerard J. and Peter Golder (2001), *Will and Vision: How Latecomers Grow to Dominate Markets*, New York: McGraw-Hill.
33. Ingrassia, "Gillette Holds Its Edge," 1.
34. Glazer, Emily, "Shaving's True Cost? It's All a Matter of Blade Life," *Wall Street Journal* (April 12, 2012): B8.
35. Ingrassia, "Gillette Holds Its Edge," 1.
36. Ibid.
37. Fan, "The Slate: A History of Innovation."

38. Wikipedia, "HP Slate 500." Retrieved August 17, 2011, from http://en .wikipedia.org/wiki/HP_Slate_500

39. Sherr, Ian, "Tablet War Is an Apple Rout," *Wall Street Journal* (August 12, 2011): B1–B2.

40. Worthen, Ben, "HP Needed to Evolve, CEO Says," *Wall Street Journal* (August 23, 2011): B1–B2.

41. Nault and Vandenbosch, "Eating Your Own Lunch: Protection Through Preemption."

42. Deutschman, A., "The Managing Wisdom of High-Tech Superstars," *Fortune* 130, 8 (October 17, 1994): 197–206.

Chapter 3

1. Sharer, Kevin, "Innovation at Amgen," Dean's Business Breakfast, at USC Marshall School of Business, February 8, 2005.

2. Timmerman, Luke, "Amgen CEO Kevin Sharer's Report Card," *Xconomy* (2011). http://www.xconomy.com/national/2011/12/19/amgen-ceo-kevin-sharers-report-card-c/

3. Terwiesch, Christian and Karl T. Ulrich, *Innovation Tournaments* (Boston: Harvard Business School Press, 2009). http://www.innovation tournaments.com/files/InnoTourn-BookExcerpt.pdf

4. For example, Crawford, C. Merle, "Marketing Research and the New Product Failure Rate," *Journal of Marketing*, 41, no. 2 (April 1977); Barczak, Gloria, Abbie Griffin, and Kenneth B. Kahn, "Perspective: Trends and Drivers of Success in NPD Practices: Results of the 2003 PDMA Best Practices Study," *Journal of Product Innovation Management*, 26 (2009): 2–23.

5. Barczak, Griffin, and Kahn, "Perspective: Trends and Drivers."

6. Chandrasekaran, Deepa and Gerard J. Tellis, "The Global Takeoff of New Products: Culture, Wealth, or Vanishing Differences," *Marketing Science*, 27, no. 5 (September-October, 2008): 844–860. Tellis, Gerard J., Stefan Stremersch, and Eden Yin, "The International Takeoff of New Products: Economics, Culture and Country Innovativeness," *Marketing Science*, 22, 2 (Spring, 2003): 161–187. Golder, Peter N. and Gerard J. Tellis, "Will It Ever Fly? Modeling the Takeoff of New Consumer Durables," *Marketing Science*, 16, no. 3 (1997): 256–270.

7. McGrath, Rita Gunther, "Falling Forward: Real Options Reasoning and Entrepreneurial Failure," *The Academy of Management Review*, 24, no. 1 (January 1999): 13.

8. Tezuka, H., "Success as the Cause of Failure," *Sloan Management Review*, 38, no. 2 (1997): 83–89.

9. March, J. G. and Z. Shapira, "Managerial Perspectives on Risk Taking," *Management Science*, 33 (1987): 1404–1418.

10. Dagmar, King, "Risk Taking Good for Business, CEO Says," *USC News* (August 2008). Retrieved July 20, 2012, from http://www.usc.edu/uscnews/stories/12050.html

11. Watson, Thomas J. Jr., *A Business and Its Beliefs: The Ideas That Helped Build IBM* (New York: McGraw-Hill, 2003).

12. Kahneman, Daniel and Amos Tversky, "Prospect Theory: An Analysis of Decision under Risk," *Econometrica*, 47, no. 2 (March 1979): 263–292.

13. Baumgartner, Jeffrey, "Prospect Theory, Risk and Innovation," *Innovation Tools* (June 10, 2009). http://www.innovationtools.com/Articles/EnterpriseDetails.asp?a=440.

14. Goparaju, Subu, "Culture of Innovation at Infosys," Advisory Board Meeting, USC Marshall Center for Global Innovation, May, 2012.

15. Swasy, Alicia, *Changing Focus: Kodak and the Battle to Save a Great American Company* (New York: Random House, 1997), 18.

16. Jobs, Steve, "You've Got to Find What You Love," Graduating Address at Stanford University. Palo Alto, California, June 12, 2005.

17. Denrell, Jerker and James G. March, "Adaptation as Information Restriction: The Hot Stove Effect," *Organization Science*, 12, no. 5 (September-October, 2001): 523–538.

18. Twain, Mark, *Following the Equator: A Journey Around the World*, (Hartford, CT: American Publishing, 1897).

19. Ariely, Dan, *The Upside of Irrationality* (New York: HarperCollins, 2010).

20. Jordan, Michael, "Failure." *Nike Air Commercial*. Retrieved July 17, 2012, from http://www.youtube.com/watch?v=m-EMOb3ATJ0

21. Petroski, Henry, *To Engineer Is Human: The Role of Failure in Successful Design* (New York: Vintage, 1992).

22. Pfeffer, Jeffrey "Too Much Management Can Block Innovation, *Stanford GSB News* (September, 2003). http://www.gsb.stanford.edu/news/research/ob_toomuchmgmt.shtml

23. Foster, Joseph A., Peter N. Golder, and Gerard J. Tellis, "Predicting Takeoff for Whirlpool's New Personal Valet," *Marketing Science*, 23, no. 2 (Spring, 2004): 182–185; Golder and Tellis, "Will It Ever Fly?"

24. Spector, Robert, Amazon.com: *Get Big Fast* (New York: HarperCollins, 1997), 85.

25. Chandrasekaran and Tellis, "The Global Takeoff of New Products"; Tellis, Stremersch, and Yin, "The International Takeoff of New Products"; Golder and Tellis, "Will It Ever Fly?"

26. Sood, Ashish and Gerard J. Tellis, "Demystifying Disruptions: A New Model for Understanding and Predicting Disruptive Technologies," *Marketing Science*, 30, no. 2 (March-April, 2011): 339–354.

27. The numbers in this column should be viewed as suggestive rather than precise because the innovators had many other innovations during the time period.

28. For 2007 to 2010 only, as the increase after 2010 may be attributed to the iPad.

29. For 2007 to 2010 only, as the increase after 2010 may be attributed to the iPad.

30. All of this increase cannot be attributed just to LCD screens.

31. Fujita, Masahiro, "Culture of Innovation at Sony," presentation at the Advisory Board Meeting, USC Marshall Center for Global Innovation, May, 2012.

32. McGrath, "Falling Forward: Real Options Reasoning and Entrepreneurial Failure." *The Academy of Management Review*, 24, 1 (January 1999): 13–30.

33. Sood, Ashish and Gerard J. Tellis, "Do Innovations Really Pay Off? Total Stock Market Returns to Innovation," *Marketing Science*, 28, no. 3 (May/June, 2009): 442–456.

34. Lyons, Dan, "Prius Expands the Brand: 2012 Toyota Prius C," *Times Union* (March 6, 2012). Retrieved on July 20, 2012, from http://www.timesunion.com/news/article/Prius-Expands-the-Brand-2012-Toyota-Prius-c-3386045.php

35. Garrett, Jerry (2010), "Hybrid Superstar Shines Brighter," *The New York Times*, August 16, 2012.

36. "Toyota Prius Japan Top-Selling Car for Third Year," *Associated Press* (January 11, 2012). Retrieved July 20, 2012, from http://business.inquirer.net/39211/toyota-prius-japan-top-selling-car-for-third-year

37. Taylor, Alex, III. "The Birth of the Prius." *Fortune*, 153, no. 4 (March 6, 2006): 111.

38. Wald, Matthew L., "Next Wave of Electric Cars: Hybrids," *New York Times* (May 14, 1996): 1. Retrieved April 5, 2010, from http://www.nytimes.com/1996/05/14/science/next-wave-of-electric-cars-hybrids.html?pagewanted=all&src=pm

39. Taylor "The Birth of the Prius,"

40. Ibid.

41. Ibid.

42. "Why the Future Is Hybrid." *The Economist*, 373, no. 8404 (December 2, 2004): special section, 26–30.

43. Taylor, "The Birth of the Prius."

44. "Prius History." http://john1701a.com/prius/prius-history.htm

45. Taylor, "The Birth of the Prius."

46. Ibid.

47. Slywotzky, Adrian J. and John Drzik, "Countering the Biggest Risk of All," *Harvard Business Review, 83, no, 4 (April 2005): 78–88.*

48. Taylor, "The Birth of the Prius."

49. Fairley, Peter, "Hybrids' Rising Sun." *Technology Review*, 107, no. 3 (April 2004): 34.

50. Taylor, "The Birth of the Prius."

51. Ibid.

52. Thornton, Emily. "Japan's Hybrid Cars: Toyota and Rivals are Betting on Pollution Fighters. Will They Succeed?" *Business Week* (December 15, 1997): 26. http://www.businessweek.com/archives/1997/b3557013.arc .htm

53. Thornton, "Japan's Hybrid Cars."

54. Taylor, "The Birth of the Prius."

55. Ibid.

56. Welsh, Jonathan. "Weekend Journal: Hybrids Gear Up." *Wall Street Journal (Eastern Edition)* (June 18, 2004): W. 1

57. Thornton, Emily. "Japan's Hybrid Cars."

58. Taylor, "The Birth of the Prius."

59. Ritson, Mark, "U.S. Auto Brands Missed the Turning," *Marketing* (July 30, 2008): 25.

60. Ueno, Kiyori and Tetsuya Komatsu, "Toyota Prius Leaps to No. 1 in Japan on Incentives," Bloomberg.com (January 8, 2010). <http://www .bloomberg.com/apps/news?pid=20601209&sid=a1kPj_bJW8aI>

61. Maynard, Micheline. "Say 'Hybrid' and Many People Will Hear 'Prius.'" *The New York Times* (July 4, 2007). http://www.nytimes.com/ 2007/07/04/business/04hybrid.html

62. "Corporate Incentives for Hybrids and Alternative Cars." HybridCars.com (June 8, 2009). http://www.hybridcars.com/corporate-incentives.html.

63. Ibid.

64. Ibid.

65. Ueno and Komatsu. "Toyota Prius Leaps to No. 1 in Japan on Incentives."

66. New York State Truway Authority. "Green Pass Discount Plan." http://www.nysthruway.gov/ezpass/greentag.html; Ottman, Jacquelyn A., Edwin R. Stafford, and Cathy L. Hartman, "Avoiding Green Marketing Myopia," *Environment*, 48, no. 5 (June, 2006): 22.

67. "Toyota Prius Proves a Gas Guzzler in a Race with the BMW 520d." *The Sunday Times* (March 16, 2008).

68. Weernink, Wim Oude and Mark Rechtin, "Toyota Pushes for Prius Acceptance in Europe," *Automotive News*, 77, no. 6036 (May 5, 2003): 58.

69. Taylor, "The Birth of the Prius."

70. Kelley Blue Book. "2010 Best Resale Value Awards." http://www.kbb
    .com/car-awards/best-resale-value-awards/best-car-brand

71. Wikipedia. "Toyota Prius." Retrieved April 28, 2010, from http://en
    .wikipedia.org/wiki/Toyota_Prius_(XW20)#Awards

72. As of 10/14/2010.

73. Wingfield, Nick, "Amazon Reports Annual Net Profit for the First Time,"
    Wall Street Journal, 243, no. 19 (January 28, 2004): A3–A8.

74. Frey, Christine and John Cook, "How Amazon.com Survived, Thrived
    and Turned a Profit," *Seattle Post* (January 28, 2004). http://www.seattlepi
    .com/business/158315_amazon28.html

75. Frey and Cook, "How Amazon.com Survived, Thrived and Turned a
    Profit."

76. Tellis, Gerard J., and Peter N. Golder, *Will and Vision: How Latecomers
    Grow to Dominate Markets* (New York: McGraw-Hill, 2001).

77. Keefe, Collin, "Jeff Bezos: Founder and CEO, Amazon.com," *Dealerscope*
    (January, 2003): 76.

78. Spector, Amazon.com: *Get Big Fast*.

79. Ibid., 31.

80. Answers.com, "Jeff Bezos," (May 2003). Retrieved from http://www
    .answers.com/topic/jeff-bezos

81. Spector, Amazon.com: *Get Big Fast*.

82. The United States Patent and Trademark Office (USPTO) issued U.S.
    patent 5960411 for this technique to Amazon.com in September 1999:
    http://en.wikipedia.org/wiki/1-Click

83. Frey and Cook, "How Amazon.com Survived, Thrived and Turned a
    Profit."

84. Ibid.

85. Spector, Amazon.com: *Get Big Fast*.

86. Ibid., 165.

87. Ibid.

88. Bezos, Jeff, "1997 Letter to Shareholders," Amazon.com. http:
    //benhorowitz.files.wordpress.com/2010/05/amzn_shareholder-letter-
    20072.pdf

89. Frey and Cook, "How Amazon.com Survived, Thrived and Turned a
    Profit."

90. Schonfeld, Erick, "Facemash Returns as (What Else?) a Facebook App
    Called ULiken." *TechCrunch* (May 13, 2008). Retrieved May 25, 2010,
    from http://techcrunch.com/2008/05/13/facemash-returns-as-what-else-
    a-facebook-app-uliken/

91. Kaplan, Katharine A., "Facemash Creator Survives Ad Board." *The Har-
    vard Crimson* (Nov 19, 2003). Retrieved May 25, 2010, from http://www

.thecrimson.com/article/2003/11/19/facemash-creator-survives-ad-board-the/

92. McGirt, Ellen. "Hacker. Dropout. CEO." *Fast Company*. Boston: May 2007. Iss. 115.

93. Tabak, Alan J., "Hundreds Register for New Facebook Website: Facemash Creator Seeks New Reputation with Latest Online Project." *The Harvard Crimson* (Feb. 9, 2004). Retrieved May 25, 2010, from http://web.archive.org/web/20050403215543/www.thecrimson.com/article.aspx?ref=357292

94. McGirt, Ellen, "Hacker. Dropout. CEO," *Fast Company*, 115 (May 2007): 75.

95. Ibid.

96. Phillips, Sarah, "A Brief History of Facebook," *The Guardian* (July 25, 2007) http://www.guardian.co.uk/technology/2007/jul/25/media.newmedia

97. McGirt, "Hacker. Dropout. CEO."

98. Kirkpatrick, David, "Zuckerberg, the Temptation of Facebook's CEO," *Fortune* (May 6, 2010).

99. Kirkpatrick, "Zuckerberg, the Temptation of Facebook's CEO."

100. McGirt, "Hacker. Dropout. CEO."

101. Ibid.

102. Kirkpatrick, "Zuckerberg, the Temptation of Facebook's CEO."

103. McGirt, "Hacker. Dropout. CEO."

104. Kirkpatrick, "Zuckerberg, the Temptation of Facebook's CEO."

105. Ibid.

106. McGirt, "Hacker. Dropout. CEO."

107. Cutler, Kim-Mai, "Mark Zuckerberg on How to Build Hacker Culture Inside a Company." VentureBeat.com (October 24, 2009). Retrieved July 20, 2012, from http://venturebeat.com/2009/10/24/live-blogging-mark-zuckerbergs-talk-at-startup-school/

108. McGirt, Ellen. "Hacker. Dropout. CEO."; McGirt, Ellen, "Most Innovative Companies 2010: #1 Facebook," *Fast Company* (Feb. 17, 2010). http://www.fastcompany.com/mic/2010/profile/facebook

109. McGirt, "Most Innovative Companies 2010: #1 Facebook."

110. Facebook, "Company Timeline." Retrieved May 15, 2010, from http://newsroom.fb.com/content/default.aspx?NewsAreaId=20

111. Ibid.

112. Ibid.

113. McGirt, "Hacker. Dropout. CEO."

114. Facebook, "Company Timeline."

115. McGirt, "Hacker. Dropout. CEO."

116. McCarthy, Caroline, "Facebook's Zuckerberg: 'We Really Messed This One Up,'" *CNET News*, News Blog (September 8, 2006). http://news .cnet.com/8301–10784_3–6113700–7.html

117. McGirt, "Hacker. Dropout. CEO."

118. Cutler, "Mark Zuckerberg on How to Build Hacker Culture Inside a Company."

119. This episode is heavily based on David Kirkpatrick's *The Facebook Effect*. (New York: Simon & Schuster, 2010).

120. Kirkpatrick, "Zuckerberg, the Temptation of Facebook's CEO."

121. Hansell, Saul. "Yahoo Woos a Social Networking Site." *The New York Times* (September 22, 2006): 1.

122. McGirt, "Hacker. Dropout. CEO."

123. Kirkpatrick, David. "Zuckerberg, the Temptation of Facebook's CEO."

124. Kirkpatrick, "Zuckerberg, the Temptation of Facebook's CEO."

125. Ibid.

126. McGirt, "Hacker. Dropout. CEO."

127. Kirkpatrick, "Zuckerberg, the Temptation of Facebook's CEO."

128. McGirt, "Most Innovative Companies 2010: #1 Facebook."

129. McGirt, "Hacker. Dropout. CEO."

130. Ibid.

131. Hansell, "Yahoo Woos a Social Networking Site."

132. Kirkpatrick, *The Facebook Effect*

133. Kirkpatrick, "Zuckerberg, the Temptation of Facebook's CEO."

134. Kirkpatrick, *The Facebook Effect*.

135. Kirkpatrick, "Zuckerberg, the Temptation of Facebook's CEO."

136. McGirt, "Most Innovative Companies 2010: #1 Facebook."

137. McGirt, Ellen, "Facebook Is." *Fast Company*, 120 (November 2007): 84.

138. Ibid.

139. Ibid.

140. Cutler, "Mark Zuckerberg on How to Build Hacker Culture Inside a Company."

141. CBS News, "Facebook 'Cash Flow Positive,' Signs Show." (September 16, 2009). Retrieved May 25, 2010, from http://www.cbc.ca/technology/ story/2009/09/16/tech-facebook-300-million-users.html

142. Shiels, Maggie, "Facebook's Bid to Rule the Web as It Goes Social." *BBC News* (April 22, 2010). Retrieved April 22, 2010, http://news.bbc .co.uk/2/hi/technology/8590306.stm; Pepitone, Julianne, "Facebook Traffic Tops Google for a Week." *CNN* Money.com, (March 16, 2010). Retrieved May 25, 2010, http://money.cnn.com/2010/03/16/ technology/facebook_most_visited/index.htm.

143. Sigafoos, Robert A. *Absolutely, Positively Overnight!* (Memphis, TN: St. Luke's Press, 1983), 62.

144. Sigafoos, *Absolutely, Positively Overnight!*, 34.

145. McGirt, "Most Innovative Companies 2010: #1 Facebook."

146. Cutler, "Mark Zuckerberg on How to Build Hacker Culture Inside a Company."

Chapter 4

1. In-hyuk, Hwang, "Samsung Chairman Lee Kun-hee Calls for Greater Innovation," *Maeil Business Newspaper* (January 2, 2012).

2. Oliver, Christian, "Fast Follower Leads the Way," *Financial Times* (March 20, 2012).

3. Sood, Ashish and Gerard J. Tellis, "Technological Evolution and Radical Innovations," *Journal of Marketing*, 69, no. 3 (July, 2005): 152–168.

4. Yadav, Manjit S., Jaideep C. Prabhu, and Rajesh K. Chandy, "Managing the Future: CEO Attention and Innovation Outcomes," *Journal of Marketing*, 71 (October, 2007): 84–101.

5. Govindarajan, Vijay and Chris Trimble, "The CEO's Role in Business Model Reinvention," *Harvard Business Review*, 89, no. 1/2 (January-February, 2011): 108–114.

6. The author is grateful to Professor Rajesh Chandy for suggesting the relevance and theory of the availability and commitment biases.

7. Gilovich, Thomas R., Vallone Robert, and Amos Tversky, "The Hot-Hand in Basketball: On the Misperception of Random Sequences," *Cognitive Psychology*, 17 (1985): 295–314.

8. DeBondt, Werner, "What Do Economists Know About the Stock Market?" *Journal of Portfolio Management*, 17, no. 2 (1991): 84–91; Hendricks, Daryll, Jayendu Patel, and Richard Zeckhauser, "Hot-Hands in Mutual Funds: Short-Run Persistence of Performance, 1974–88," *Journal of Finance*, 48, no. 1 (1993): 93–130; Dhar, Ravi and Alok Kumar, "A Non-Random Walk Down the Main Street: Impact of Price Trends on Trading Decisions of Individual Investors," unpublished working paper, 2001.

9. Sood, Ashish, Gareth James, and Gerard J. Tellis, "The Functional Regression: A New Model for Predicting the Market Penetration of New Products," *Marketing Science*, 28, no. 1 (2009): 36–51.

10. Chandrasekaran, Deepa and Gerard J. Tellis, "The Global Takeoff of New Products: Culture, Wealth, or Vanishing Differences," *Marketing Science*, 27, no. 5 (September-October, 2008): 844–860; Tellis, Gerard J., Stefan Stremersch, and Eden Yin, "The International Takeoff of New Products: Economics, Culture and Country Innovativeness," *Marketing Science*, 22, no. 2 (Spring, 2003): 161–187. Golder, Peter N., and Gerard J. Tellis,

"Will It Ever Fly? Modeling the Takeoff of New Consumer Durables," *Marketing Science*, 16, no. 3 (1997): 256–270.

11. Really, it is the opposite phenomenon—"a cold-hand"—though we use the same term for the bias.

12. For example see Tversky, A. & D. Kahneman, "Judgments Under Uncertainty: Heuristics and Biases," *Science*, 185 (1974): 1124–1131.

13. *Ichthyology: Sharks, at the Florida Museum of Natural History*. Retrieved July 23, 2012, from http://www.flmnh.ufl.edu/fish/sharks/attacks/relarisksand.htm

14. Plous, Scott, *The Psychology of Judgment and Decision Making* (Columbus, OH: McGraw-Hill, 1993), 121.

15. Christensen, Clayton M., *The Innovator's Dilemma: When New Technologies Cause Great Firms to Fail* (Boston: Harvard Business School Press, 1997).

16. Kuhn, Thomas, *The Structure of Scientific Revolutions* (Chicago: University of Chicago Press, 1962).

17. Moorman, Christine and Anne S. Miner, "The Impact of Organizational Memory on New Product Performance and Creativity," *Journal of Marketing Research*, 34 (February 1997): 91–106.

18. Leonardi, Paul M., "Innovation Blindness: Culture, Frames, and Cross-Boundary Problem Construction in the Development of New Technology Concepts." *Organization Science*, 22, no. 3 (March-April, 2011): 347–367.

19. Ibid., 363.

20. Schanfeld, Erick and Chris Morrison, "Business 2.0.," *Money*, 8 no. 8 (September 2007), 56–64. Retrieved October 13, 2011, from http://money.cnn.com/magazines/business2/business2_archive/2006/10/01/8387096/

21. Public Broadcasting Service, "Traveling Through Time," pbs.org. Retrieved October 13, 2011, from http://www.pbs.org/wgbh/nova/time/through2.html

22. Strohmeyer, Robert, "The 7 Worst Tech Predictions of All Time," *PCWorld* (December 31, 2008).

23. Schofield, Jack. "Ken Olsen Obituary," *The Guardian* (February 9, 2011). Retrieved October 13, 2011, from http://www.guardian.co.uk/technology/2011/feb/09/ken-olsen-obituary

24. Libbenga, Jan, "BlackBerry Boss Blows Raspberries at iPhone," *The Register* (November, 8, 2007). Retrieved July 11, 2012, from http://www.theregister.co.uk/2007/11/08/why_iphone_is_no_threat_to_blackberry/

25. Staw, Barry M., "Knee-Deep in the Big Muddy: A Study of Escalating Commitment to a Chosen Course of Action," *Organization Behavior and Human Performance*, 16, no. 1 (June 1976): 27–44.

26. Schwartz, Barry, "The Sunk-Cost Fallacy: Bush Falls Victim to a Bad New Argument for the Iraq War," Slate.com (September 9, 2005). http://www

.slate.com/articles/news_and_politics/hey_wait_a_minute/2005/09/the_sunkcost_fallacy.html

27. Brockner, Joel and Jeffrey Rubin, *Entrapment in Escalating Conflicts: A Social Psychological Analysis* (New York: Springer-Verlag, 1985).

28. Foster, Richard, *Innovation: The Attacker's Advantage* (New York: Summit Books, 1986).

29. Ibid.

30. Chandrasekaran and Tellis, "The Global Takeoff of New Products."

31. "Definition of: VisiCalc," PCMAG.com. Retrieved from http://www.pcmag.com/encyclopedia_term/0,2542,t=VisiCalc&i=53977,00.asp

32. Bryant, Martin, "20 Years Ago Today, the World Wide Web Opened to the Public," *Insider* (August 6, 2011).

33. Yoffie, David B. and Michael Slind, "Apple Inc.," HBS No. 9-708-480 (Boston: Harvard Business School Publishing, 2008): 1–32.

34. Golder and Tellis, "Will It Ever Fly?"

35. Tellis, Gerard J., and Peter N. Golder, *Will and Vision: How Latecomers Grow to Dominate Markets* (New York: McGraw Hill, 2001).

35a. Sood, Ashish, Gareth James, Gerard J. Tellis, and Ji Zhu, "Predicting the Path of Technological Evolution," *Marketing Science*, 2013 forthcoming.

36. Sood, Ashish, Gareth James, Gerard J. Tellis, and Ji Zhu, "Predicting the Path of Technological Evolution," *Marketing Science*, 2012 forthcoming; Sood, Ashish, and Gerard J. Tellis, "Demystifying Disruptions: A New Model for Understanding and Predicting Disruptive Technologies," *Marketing Science*, 30, no. 2 (March-April, 2011): 339–354.

37. Tellis, Gerard J., and Ashish Sood, "A New Framework for choosing the Right Technology," *PDMA Visions*, October 2010, Vol. XXXIV, No. 3.

38. Tellis, Gerard J. and Ashish Sood, "A New Framework for Choosing the Right Technology," *PDMA Visions*, 34, No. 3 18–23 (October 2010).

39. Sood and Tellis, "Demystifying Disruptions."

40. Christensen, *The Innovator's Dilemma*.

41. Isaacson, Walter, *Steve Jobs* (Kindle ed.) (New York: Simon & Schuster, 2011), 567.

42. Hoffman, Donna L., Praveen Kopalle, and Thomas Novak, "The Right Consumers for Better Concepts: Identifying Consumers High in Emergent Nature to Develop New Product Concepts," *Journal of Marketing Research*, 47 (October 2010): 854–865.

43. Von Hippel, E., "Lead Users: A Source of Novel Product Concepts," *Management Science* 32, no. 7 (1986): 791–806; Luthje, C. and Herstatt,

C., "The Lead User Method: An Outline of Empirical Findings and Issues for Future Research," *R&D Management*, 34, no. 5 (2004): 553–568.

44. Tirunillai, Seshadri and Gerard J. Tellis, "Does Chatter Really Matter? The Impact of Online Consumer Generated Content on a Firm's Financial Performance," *Marketing Science*, 31, no. 2 (April 2011): 198–215.

45. Tirunillai, Seshadri and Gerard J. Tellis, "Extracting Dimensions of Satisfaction from Online Chatter," working paper, the USC Marshall School of Business, 2012.

46. Luthje, "The Lead User Method".

Chapter 5

1. Gerstner, Lou, *Who Says Elephants Can't Dance?* (New York: Harper-Collins, 2002), 187.

2. O'Connor, Gina Colarelli and Christopher M. McDermott, "The Human Side of Radical Innovation," *Journal of Engineering Technology Management*, 21 (2004): 11–30.

3. Pfeffer, Jeffrey, "Too Much Management Can Block Innovation," *Stanford GSB News* (September 2003). http://www.gsb.stanford.edu/news/research/ob_toomuchmgmt.shtml

4. Shah Raj, in a panel discussion, Conference on Innovating in a Global Environment, USC Marshall School of Business, March 2011.

5. Amabile, Teresa M., Philips, Goldfarb, and Shereen C. Brackfield, "Social Influences on Creativity; Evaluation, Coaction, and Surveillance," *Creativity Research Journal*, 3 (1990): 6–21; Amabile, Teresa M., "Effects of External Evaluation on Artistic Creativity," *Journal of Personality and Social Psychology*," 37 (1979): 221–233.

6. Deci, Edward L., and Richard M. Ryan, *Intrinsic Motivation and Self-determination in Human Behavior* (New York: Plenum, 1985).

7. Manso, Gustavo, "Motivating Innovation," draft paper, MIT Sloan Business School, February 28, 2009.

8. St. Peter, Anthony, *The Greatest Quotation of All Time*, Xlibris Corporation, 2010, p. 102.

9. Jobs, Steve, "You've Got to Find What You Love," Graduating Address at Stanford University. Palo Alto, California, June 12, 2005.

10. "The United States of Entrepreneurs," *The Economist* (March 12, 2009). http://www.economist.com/node/13216037

11. Jobs, Steve, "Person of the Week," interview with Diane Sawyer, ABC News (January 29, 1981). http://abcnews.go.com/WN/abcs-world-news-diane-sawyer-person-week-steve/story?id=9699563&page=1

12. Rediff Interview, "Innovation Best Comes from People Who Know Nothing About the Topic," *Rediff India Abroad* (2006). http://www.rediff .com/money/2006/aug/07kodak.htm

13. Senor, Dan and Saul Singer, *Start-Up Nation*, (New York: Twelve, 2009), 20.

14. Ibid., 32.

15. Senor and Singer, *Start-Up Nation*.

16. Gompers, Paul, Anna Kovner, Josh Lerner, and David S. Scharfstein, "Skill Versus Luck in Entrepreneurship and Venture Capital: Evidence from Serial Entrepreneurs," working paper 12592, National Bureau of Economic Research, 2006.

17. Wulf, Julie and Josh Lerner, "Innovation Incentives: Evidence from Corporate R&D," Social Science Research Network, Working Paper Series, w11944, 2006; Makri, Marianna, Peter J. Lane, and Luis Gomez-Mejia, "CEO Incentives, Innovation, and Performance in Technology-Intensive Firms: A Reconciliation of Outcome and Behavior-Based Incentive Schemes," *Strategic Management Journal*, 27 no. 11 (2006): 1057–1080.

18. Gneezy, Uri and Aldo Rustichini, "A Fine Is a Price," *Journal of Legal Studies*, 29, no. 1 (January 2000): 1–17.

19. Levitt, Steven D. and Stephen J. Dubner, *Freakanomics* (New York: Morrow, 2005).

20. Frey, Bruno S. and Felix Oberholzer-Gee, "The Cost of Price Incentives: An Empirical Analysis of Motivation Crowding-Out," *American Economic Review*, 87, no. 4 (1997): 746–755, Brafman, Ori and Rom Brafman, *Sway: The Irresistible Pull of Irrational Behavior* (New York: Broadway Business, 2009), 132–135, 141–143.

21. Ariely, Dan, *Predictably Irrational* (New York: HarperCollins, 2008), 86.

22. Jacob, Brian A. and Steven D. Levitt, "Rotten Apples: An Investigation of the Prevalence and Predictors of Teacher Cheating," *Quarterly Journal of Economics*, 118, no. 3 (2003): 843–877; Jacob, Brian A. and Steven D. Levitt, "Catching Cheating Teachers: The Results of an Unusual Experiments in Implementing Theory," *Brookings-Wharton Papers on Urban Affairs* (Washington, DC: Brookings Institution Press, 2003), 185–209.

23. Ariely, *Predictably Irrational*.

24. Gerstner, *Who Says Elephants Can't Dance?*

25. Ibid.

26. Ibid., 186.

27. Ibid.

28. Dullfo, Anne, "FT Global 500," *Financial Times* (2009). http://media .ft.com/cms/8289770e-4c79–11de-a6c5–00144feabdc0.pdf

29. Schmidt, Eric, "Google: Benefits." http://www.google.com/support/jobs/bin/static.py?page=benefits.html

30. Lashinsky, Adam, "Google Is No. 1: Search and Enjoy," *Fortune*, 155, no. 1 (January 10, 2007). http://money.cnn.com/magazines/fortune/fortune_archive/2007/01/22/toc.html

31. Vascellaro, Jessica E., "Google Searches for Ways to Keep Big Ideas at Home," *Wall Street Journal*, Technology, 253, no. 141 (June 18, 2009): B1–B5.

32. Lashinsky, "Google Is No. 1."

33. Ibid.

34. Ibid.

35. Olsen, Stefanie, "From the Googleplex to the Wine Bar," *CNET News*, (January 23, 2008). http://news.cnet.com/From-the-Googleplex-to-the-wine-bar/2100–1030_3–6227204.html

36. Zenger, Todd R. and Sergio G. Lazzarini, "Compensating for Innovation: Do Small Firms Offer High-Powered Incentives That Lure Talent and Motivate Effort?" *Managerial & Decision Economics*, 25, no. 6/7 (2004): 331.

37. Goo, Sara Kehaulani, "Building a 'Googley' Workforce," *Washington Post* (October 21, 2006).

38. Dickerson, Chad, "The Google Way," InfoWorld, February 20, 2004.

39. Olsen, Stefanie, "Google vs. Yahoo: Clash of Cultures," *CNET News* (June 21, 2005). http://news.cnet.com/Google-vs.-Yahoo-Clash-of-cultures/2100–1024_3–5752928.html

40. Lashinsky, "Google Is No. 1."

41. Google, "Google Gets the Message, Launches Gmail," Press Center, Google website, http://www.google.com/press/pressrel/gmail.html

42. Google, "Google Gets the Message."

43. Google, "Google Gets the Message."

44. Katdare, Kaustubh, "Interview with Paul Buchheit—Creator of Gmail, AdSense & FriendFeed," *CrazyEngineers*, March 1, 2009. Retrieved on July 20, 2012, from http://www.crazyengineers.com/mr-paul-buchheit-creator-of-gmail-adsense-friendfeed/

45. Ibid.

46. Ibid.

47. Mayer, Marissa, "Innovation, Imagination, Creativity—Google VP of Search Products Tells Story of Gmail," (October 26, 2007). http://idrather bewriting.com/2007/10/26/innovation-imagination-creativity-google-vp-of-search-products-talks-to-iinovate-podcasters/

48. Ibid.

49. Ibid.

50. Ibid.; Casnocha, B., "Success on the Side," *The American* (April 24, 2009).

51. Lashinsky, "Google Is No. 1."
52. Ibid.
53. Vascellaro, "Google Searches for Ways to Keep Big Ideas at Home."
54. Ibid.
55. "100 Best Employers to Work With," *Fortune* (February 2, 2009).
56. Amabile, Teresa M., "Motivational Synergy: Toward New Conceptualizations of Intrinsic and Extrinsic Motivation in the Workplace," *Human Resource Management Review*, 3, no. 3 (1993): 185–201.
57. Crowley, Stephen, "At G.M., Innovation Sacrificed to Profits," *The New York Times* (December 5, 2008). http://www.nytimes.com/2008/12/06/business/06motors.html?pagewanted=all
58. Ibid.
59. Taylor, Alex, III, "The Great Electric Car Race," *Fortune*, 164, no. 5 (April 14, 2009): 33.
60. Sony Pictures, "Who Killed the Electric Car?" (2006).
61. Levin, Doron and John Helyar, "'Already Bankrupt' GM Won't Be Rescued by U.S. Loan," *Bloomberg* (December 12, 2008). http://www.bloomberg.com/apps/news?pid=newsarchive&sid=abLGhi7QEIt8
62. Ibid.
63. Taylor, "The Great Electric Car Race."
64. Ibid.
65. Naughton, Keith and Allan Sloan, "Comin' Through!" *Newsweek Web Exclusive*, 2007. http://www.thedailybeast.com/newsweek/2007/03/11/comin-through.html
66. Stewart, Bennett, "GM's Second Great Crisis," *HBR NOW*, blogs.harvardbusiness.org, (May 29, 2009). www.blogs.hbr.org/hbr/hbr-now/2009/05/gms-second-great-crisis.html
67. Ibid.
68. Welch, David, Dan Beucke, Kathleen Kerwin, Michael Arndt, Brian Hindo, Emily Thornton, David Kiley, and Ian Rowley. "Why GM's Plan Won't Work," *Newsweek* (May 9, 2005): 84–93.
69. Ibid.
70. Ibid.
71. McCullagh, Declan, "Big Three Bailout? Not So Fast," CBS, (CNET), (November 12, 2008). http://www.cbsnews.com/2100–503363_162–4595068.html
72. Zenger, Todd R. and Sergio G. Lazzarini, "Compensating for Innovation," *Managerial & Decision Economics*, 25, no. 6/7 (September-November, 2004), 329–345.
73. Welch et al., "Why GM's Plan Won't Work."
74. "Why General Motors Failed," *Examiner,* April 17, 2009.

75. Wright, Patrick J. and John Z. DeLorean, *On a Clear Day You Can See General Motors: John Z. DeLorean's Look Inside the Automotive Giant* (Portland, OR: Wright Enterprises, 1979).

76. Rajagopalan, Nandini, "Strategic Orientations, Incentive Plan Adoptions, and Firm Performance: Evidence from Electric Utility Firms," *Strategic Management Journal*, 18, no. 10 (1997): 761–785.

77. Ibid.

78. Makri, Marianna, Peter J. Lane, and Luis R. Gomez-Mejia, "CEO Incentives, Innovation, and Performance in Technology-Intensive Firms: A Reconciliation of Outcome and Behavior-Based Incentive Schemes," *Strategic Management Journal*, 27, no. 11 (2006): 1057–1080.

79. "Who We Are," 3M Company. http://solutions.3m.com/wps/portal/3M/en_US/3M-Company/Information/AboutUs/WhoWeAre/

80. Mitsch, Ronald A., "Three Roads to Innovation," *Journal of Business Strategy*, 11, no. 5 (1990): 18–21.

81. Maiello, Michael, "Koulopolous on Innovation," Business Visionaries, *Forbes* (June 2, 2009).

82. "A Century of Innovation, The 3M Story," 3M Company. (2002), 15–16. http://multimedia.3m.com/mws/mediawebserver?77777XxamfIVO&Wwo_Pw5_W7HYxTHfxajYv7HYv7H777777—

83. Ibid.

84. Ibid.

85. Ibid.

86. Maiello, "Koulopolous on Innovation."

87. Ibid.

88. "A Century of Innovation, The 3M Story," 38, 40.

89. Ibid.

90. Ibid.

91. Ibid.

92. "A Century of Innovation, The 3M Story," 40.

93. Ibid.

94. "A Century of Innovation, The 3M Story," 38.

95. Ibid.

96. Ibid.

97. Ibid.

98. "3M—Where Innovation Rules," Editorial, *R&D Magazine*. http://www.rdmag.com/default.aspx?rid=362

99. Ibid.

100. Ibid.

101. Ibid.

102. "Virtual Worlds, Real Leaders: Online Games Put the Future of Business Leadership on Display," *A Global Innovation Outlook 2.0 Report*,

International Business Machines Corporation, 2007. http://www.seriosity .com/downloads/GIO_PDF_web.pdf

103. Ibid.
104. Ibid.
105. Ibid.
106. Garcia, Armando, "How Failure Breeds Success," *Business Week*, 3992 (July 10, 2006): 42–52.
107. Ibid.
108. Ibid.

Chapter 6

1. *Index of Silicon Valley*, Silicon Valley Community Foundation (2012). http://www.jointventure.org/images/stories/pdf/2012index.pdf
2. "Silicon Valley, London, NYC," *TechCrunch* (2012). Retrieved April 11, 2012, from http://techcrunch.com/2012/04/10/startup-genome-compares -top-startup-hubs/
3. Hamel, Gary, "Bringing Silicon Valley Inside," *Harvard Business Review* (September-October, 1997): 71–84.
4. Valikangas, Liisa and Gary Hamel (2001), "Internal Markets: Emerging Governance Structures for Innovation," paper presented at the Strategic Management Society, 21st Annual International Conference, San Francisco, 2001.
5. Vascellaro, Jessica E., "Google Searches for Ways to Keep Big Ideas at Home," *Wall Street Journal*, Technology, 253, no. 141 (June 18, 2009): B1–B5.
6. Hamel, "Bringing Silicon Valley Inside."
7. Libbenga, Jan, "BlackBerry Boss Blows Raspberries at iPhone," *The Register* (November, 8, 2007).
8. Reguly, Eric, "Failing in Face of Apple's Next Big Thing," *The Globe and Mail* (January 28, 2012).
9. Chandy, Rajesh and Gerard J. Tellis, "Organizing For Radical Product Innovation," *Journal of Marketing Research*, 35 (November 1998): 474–487.
10. Halal, William E., Ali Geranmayeh, and John Pourdehnad, *Internal Markets: Bringing the Power of Free Enterprise Inside Your Organization* (New York: Wiley, 1993); Valikangas and Hamel, "Internal Markets."
11. Birkinshaw, Julian, "Strategies for Managing Internal Competition," *California Management Review*, 44 (Fall 2001): 21–38.
12. Valikangas and Hamel, "Internal Markets."
13. Hamel, "Bringing Silicon Valley Inside."
14. Terwiesch, Christian, and Karl T. Ulrich, *Innovation Tournaments* (Boston: Harvard Business School Press, 2010). http://www.Innovation Tournaments.com

15. Howe, Jeff, "The Rise of Crowdsourcing," *Wired* (2006). http://www.wired .com/wired/archive/14.06/crowds.html

16. Hamel, "Bringing Silicon Valley Inside," 9.

17. Ibid.

18. Rosen, Evan, "The Hidden Cost of Internal Competition," *Bloomberg Business Week* (November 10, 2009). http://www.businessweek.com/managing/ content/nov2009/ca2009113_427287.htm; Heffernan, Margaret, "Dog Eat Dog," FastCompany.com (July 8, 2008). http://www.fastcompany .com/resources/talent/heffernan/072804.html

19. Gatto, Bob, "Culture of Innovation at Nestle," Advisory Board Meeting, USC Marshall School of Business, May 15, 2012.

20. National Collegiate Athletic Association.

21. Wingfield, Nick, "The Man Behind Android's Rise," *Wall Street Journal* (August 17, 2011): B1–B2.

22. Prahalad, C. K. and Gary Hamel, "The Core Competence of the Corporation," *Harvard Business Review* (May-June, 1990): 79–91.

23. Ouderkirk, Andrew J., "Culture of Innovation at 3M," Advisory Board Meeting, USC Marshall Center for Global Innovation, May, 2011.

24. Goparaju, Subu, "Culture of Innovation at Infosys," Advisory Board Meeting, USC Marshall Center for Global Innovation, May, 2012.

25. Rubera, Gaia and Gerard J. Tellis, "Spinoffs Versus Buyouts," working paper, USC Marshall School of Business, 2012.

Chapter 7

1. Kirkpatrick, David and Tyler Maronney, "The Second Coming of Apple Through a Magical Fusion of Man," Fortune (November 9, 1998).

2. Herper, Matthew, "The Luckiest Guy in the Drug Business." *Forbes* (May 1, 2008). http://www.forbes.com/2008/05/01/pfizer-esperion-pharmacuticals-biz-healthcare-cx_mh_0501pfizer.html

3. Pluskowski, Boris, "The 4 Laws of Enduring Innovation Success," *Complete Innovator* (July 4, 2010). http://completeinnovator.com/2010/04/07/the-4-laws-to-enduring-innovation-success/

4. Wiseman, Richard, "The Luck Factor," *Skeptical Inquirer*, 27, no. 3 (May-June, 2003): 1–5.

5. Ibid., 1

6. Tellis, Gerard J. and Peter N. Golder, *Will and Vision: How Latecomers Grow to Dominate Markets (New York*: McGraw-Hill, 2001); Tellis, Gerard J. and Golder, Peter N., "First to Market, First to Fail? The Real Causes of Enduring Market Leadership," *Sloan Management Review*, 37, no. 2 (1996): 65–75; Golder, Peter N. and Gerard J. Tellis, "Pioneering Advantage:

Marketing Logic or Marketing Legend," *Journal of Marketing Research, 30, no. 2* (1993): 158–170.

7. Wiseman, "The Luck Factor."

8. Markham, Stephen K. and Abbie Griffin, "The Breakfast of Champions," *Journal of Product Innovation Management*, 15 (1998): 436–454.

9. Ouderkirk, Andy, "Culture of Innovation at 3M," Presentation at the Advisory Board Meeting, USC Marshall Center for Global Innovation, May, 2012.

10. Friedrich, Richard, "Culture of Innovation at HP," Presentation at the Advisory Board Meeting, USC Marshall Center for Global Innovation, May, 2012.

11. O'Connor, Gina Colarelli, and Christopher M. McDermott, "The Human Side of Radical Innovation," *Journal of Engineering Technology Management*, 21 (2004): 11–30.

12. Holly, Krisztina "Z," "Accelerating the Impact of Universities in a Shifting Innovation Landscape," Conference on Innovating in a Global Environment, USC Marshall School of Business, March 17, 2011.

13. Shugan, Steven M., and Debanjan Mitra, "Metrics—When and Why Non-Averaging Statistics Work," *Management Science*, 55 (January 2009): 4–15.

14. Backer, Alex, Panel discussion, "Conference on Innovating in a Global Environment," USC Marshall School of Business, 2011.

15. Snell, Jason, "Steve Jobs on the Mac's 20th Anniversary," Macworld.com (February 2, 2004). http://www.macworld.com/article/1029181/the macturns20jobs.html

16. Levy, Steven, "Google Goes Globe-Trotting," *Newsweek* (November 12, 2007): 62–64.

17. Levy, Steven, *In the Plex: How Google Thinks, Works, and Shapes Our Lives* (New York: Simon & Schuster, 2011).

18. Levy, "Google Goes Globe-Trotting."

19. Ibid.

20. Ibid.

21. Ibid.

22. Ibid.

23. Ibid.

24. Stuart, Candace, "The Medicine Man," *DBusiness* (November 2008). http://www.dbusiness.com/DBusiness/November-2008/The-Medicine-Man/

25. Ibid.

26. Ibid.

27. Ibid.

28. Herper, "The Luckiest Guy in the Drug Business."

29. Newton, Roger, "Newton.mov: Can Science Be a Business?" *YouTube video.* Lafayette University, April 21, 2011, http://www.youtube.com/watch?v=302sjUypVw8&lr=1&feature=mhum

30. Ibid.

31. LaMattina, John, "The Story of Statins," *Chemical and Engineering News* (June 8, 2009). http://pubs.acs.org/cen/books/87/8723books.html

32. Stuart, "The Medicine Man."

33. Libby, Peter, "Review of Triumph of the Heart," *The Journal of Clinical Investigation*, 120, no. 1 (Jan 4, 2010).

34. Newton, Roger. "Dr. Roger Newton—Co-Discoverer of Lipitor," YouTube video. Retrieved April 10, 2012, from http://www.youtube.com/watch?v=GG_GoaAUdN8

35. Herper, "The Luckiest Guy in the Drug Business."

36. Newton, "Dr. Roger Newton—Co-Discoverer of Lipitor."

37. Ibid.

38. Herper, Mathew, "The Luckiest Guy in the Drug Business."

39. Bomey, Nathan, "Roger Newton's Esperion Therapeutics Launches First Clinical Trial." http://www.annarbor.com/business-review/esperion-therapeutics-launches-first-clinical-trial/

40. Ibid.

41. Ibid.

42. Diamond, Patricia F., "What Will Succeed Lipitor as the Next Blockbuster Cholesterol-Lowering Drug?" *GEN News* (January 11, 2011). http://www.genengnews.com/insight-and-intelligenceand153/what-will-succeed-lipitor-as-the-next-blockbuster-cholesterol-lowering-drug/77899355/

43. Newton, "Newton.mov: Can Science Be a Business?"

44. Tata Motors, Press Release, February 5, 2007.

45. Noronha, Christabelle, "The Making of the Nano," The South Asian.com (April-June, 2008). Retrieved July 23, 2012, from http://www.the-south-asian.com/April-June2008/Ratan_Tata_interview_Nano.htm

46. Foster, Peter and Pallavi Malhotra, "Ultimate Economy Drive: The £1,300 Car," *The Telegraph* (January 10, 2008). Retrieved on July 7, 2012, from http://www.telegraph.co.uk/news/worldnews/1575181/Ultimate-economy-drive-the-1300-car.html

47. Noronha, Christabelle, "The Making of the Nano," *The South Asian.com* (April–June, 2008).

48. Welch, David and Nandini Lakshman, "My Other Car Is a Tata," *Business-Week, 4066 (*January 3, 2008): 33–34.

49. Kripalani, Manjeet, "Inside the Nano Factory," *Business Week* (May 9, 2008): 16. http://www.businessweek.com/stories/2008–05–09/inside-the-tata-nano-factorybusinessweek-business-news-stock-market-and-financial-advice.

50. Ibid.

51. Noronha, Christabelle, "The Making of the Nano"

52. Ibid.

53. Tellis, Gerard J, "A Lesson for Detroit: Tata Nano," *San Francisco Chronicle*, March 31, 2009. The subsequent analysis was first published in this source.

54. Kripalani, Manjeet, "Tata Unveils World's Cheapest Car," *Business Week* (January 10, 2008).

55. Jon Rubinstein may also have played a role in championing the iPod. See Isaacson, Walter (2011), *Steve Jobs*. New York: Simon & Schuster, 2011.

56. Kahney, Leander, "Inside Look at Birth of the iPod."

57. Isaacson, Walter, *Steve Jobs* (Kindle ed.) (New York: Simon & Schuster, 2011).

58. Levy, Stephen, "The Perfect Thing" *Wired* (November 2006). http://www.wired.com/wired/archive/14.11/ipod.html

59. Sherman, Erik, "Inside Apple iPod Design Triumph," *Electronics Design Chain* (Summer, 2002).

60. Kahney, Leander, "Inside Look at Birth of the iPod."

61. Ibid.

62. Ibid.

63. Ibid.

64. Ibid.

65. Ibid.

66. Wingfield, Nick, "Hide the Button: Steve Jobs Has His Finger on It," *Wall Street Journal* (July 5, 2007): A1.

67. Walker, Rob, "The Guts of a New Machine," *The New York Times Magazine* (November 30, 2003).

68. Isaacson, Walter, *Steve Jobs*.

69. This case draws heavily from Nayak, P. Ranganath and John M. Ketteringham, *Breakthroughs: How Leadership and Drive Create Commercial Innovations That Sweep the World* (San Diego, CA: Pfeiffer, 1994).

70. Bellis, Mary, "The History of the Sony Walkman." http://inventors.about.com/od/wstartinventions/a/Walkman.htm

71. Nayak and Ketteringham, *Breakthroughs*, 119.

72. Ibid., p 124.

73. Wozniak, Steve, Interview on "Good Morning America," ABC News, on the death of Steve Jobs, October 6, 2011.

Chapter 8

1. Sood, Ashish and Gerard J. Tellis, "Demystifying Disruptions: A New Model for Understanding and Predicting Disruptive Technologies," *Marketing Science*, 30, no. 2 (March-April, 2011): 339–354; Tellis, Gerard J., Jaideep Prabhu, and Rajesh Chandy, "Innovation of Firms Across Nations: The Pre-Eminence of Internal Firm Culture," *Journal of Marketing*, 73, no. 1 (January 2009): 3–23; Sood, Ashish, and Gerard J. Tellis, "Technological Evolution and Radical Innovations," *Journal of Marketing*, 69, no. 3 (July 2005): 152–168; Chandy, Rajesh and Gerard J. Tellis, "The Incumbent's Curse? Incumbency, Size and Radical Product Innovation," *Journal of Marketing*, 64, no. 3 (July 2000): 1–17; Chandy, Rajesh and Gerard J. Tellis, "Organizing For Radical Product Innovation," *Journal of Marketing Research*, 35 (November 1998): 474–487; Sood, Ashish, and Gerard J. Tellis, "Do Innovations Really Pay Off? Total Stock Market Returns to Innovation," *Marketing Science*, 28, no. 3 (May-June, 2009): 442–456.
2. Mizik, Natalie, "The Theory and Practice of Myopic Management," *Journal of Marketing Research*, 47 (August, 2010): 594–611.
3. Sood and Tellis, "Do Innovations Really Pay Off?"
4. Schumpeter, Joseph, *Capitalism, Socialism and Democracy*, (New York: Harper, 1975). Originally published 1942.
5. Chandy and Tellis, "The Incumbent's Curse?"
6. The term *skunk works* was originally used to describe Lockheed Martin's Advanced Development Programs, which was responsible for a number of famous aircraft designs, such as the U-2. The term is used for a division or business unit that is given great autonomy to work on a secret project away from meddling by the established bureaucracy.
7. Christensen, Clayton M., *The Innovator's Dilemma: When New Technologies Cause Great Firms to Fail* (Boston: Harvard Business School Press, 1997).
8. Ibid., 24.
9. Sood and Tellis, "Demystifying Disruptions."
10. We do so to compare our results with Christensen who claimed that all his disruptive technologies are initially inferior in performance to the dominant technology on the primary dimension of performance.
11. Foster, Richard, *Innovation: The Attacker's Advantage* (New York: Summit Books, 1986).
12. Ibid., 34.
13. Ibid., 21.
14. Sood and Tellis, "Technological Evolution and Radical Innovations"; Sood, Ashish, and Gerard J. Tellis, "The S-Curve of Technological Innovation: Strategic Law or Self-Fulfilling Prophesy?" Marketing Science Institute working paper, no 04–116, 2004.
15. Ibid.

16. Gorski, Phillip, *The Disciplinary Revolution: Calvinism and the Rise of the State in Modern Europe* (Chicago: University of Chicago Press, 2003); DeLong, J. Bradford, "Productivity Growth, Convergence, and Welfare: Comment," *American Economic Review*, 78, no. 5 (1988): 1138–1154.

17. Weber, Max, *The Protestant Ethic and the Spirit of Capitalism*, (New York: Penguin Books, 2002). Originally published 1904.

18. Landes, David S., *The Wealth and Poverty of Nations: Why Some Are So Rich and Some So Poor* (New York: Norton, 1998).

19. Parker, Philip M., *Physioeconomic* (Cambridge, MA: MIT Press, 2000).

20. Diamond, Jared, *Guns, Germs and Steel: The Fates of Human Society* (New York: Norton, 1999).

21. Gutterman, Alan S. and Bentley J. Anderson, *Intellectual Property in Global Markets* Cambridge, MA: Kluwer Academic, 1997); Webster, Andrew, and Kathryn Packer, *Innovation and the Intellectual Property System* (Cambridge, MA: Kluwer Law International, 1996).

22. Landes, *The Wealth and Poverty of Nations*.

23. Freeman, Christopher, "Formal Scientific and Technical Institutions in the National System of Innovation," in Lundvall, Bengt-Ake (Ed.) *National Systems of Innovation* (London: Pinter Publishers, 1992), 169–187; Daniels, P., "Research & Development, Human Capital and Trade Performance in Technology-Intensive Manufactures: A Cross-country Analysis," *Research Policy*, 22, no. 3 (1993): 207–241.

24. Prahalad, C. K., *Fortune at the Bottom of the Pyramid*, (Upper Saddle River, NJ: Pearson, 2005); Meredith, Robyn, *The Elephant and the Dragon* (New York: Norton, 2007); Radjou, Navi, Jaideep Prabhu, and Simone Ahuja, *Jugaad Innovation* (San Francisco: Jossey-Bass, 2012).

25. PriceWaterhouseCoopers (2011) study. http://www.pwc.com/gx/en/world-2050/index.jhtml

26. Friedman, Thomas L., *The World Is Flat: A Brief History of the 20th Century* (New York: Farrar, Straus and Giroux, 2005).

27. Menzies, Gavin, *1421: The Year That China Discovered America* (New York: HarperCollins, 2002).

28. Meredith, *The Elephant and the Dragon*.

29. Hawksworth, John, "The World in 2050," PriceWaterhouseCoopers (2006). http://www.pwc.com/gx/en/world-2050/pdf/world2050emerging economies.pdf

30. Tellis, Prabhu, and Chandy, "Innovation of Firms Across Nations."

31. An example of a positively valenced item is: "We have no difficulty in introducing products that are radically different from existing products in the industry." An example of a negatively valenced item is: "Our firm rarely introduces products that are radically different from existing products in the industry."

32. See Chapter 1.

BIBLIOGRAPHY

"3M—Where Innovation Rules." Editorial, *R&D Magazine*.
    http://www.rdmag.com/default.aspx?rid=362

"100 Best Employers to Work With." *Fortune* (February 2, 2009): 159.

"A Century of Innovation, the 3M Story." 3M Company (2002).

Adams, Russell B., Jr. *King C. Gillette, The Man and His Wonderful Shaving Device*. Boston: Little, Brown, 1978.

Amabile, Teresa M. "Effects of External Evaluation on Artistic Creativity." *Journal of Personality and Social Psychology*, 37 (1979): 221–233.

Amabile, Teresa M. "Motivational Synergy: Toward New Conceptualizations of Intrinsic and Extrinsic Motivation in the Workplace." *Human Resource Management Review*, 3, no. 3 (1993): 185–201.

Amabile, Teresa M., Phyllis, Goldfarb, and Shereen C. Brackfield. "Social Influences on Creativity; Evaluation, Coaction, and Surveillance." *Creativity Research Journal*, 3 (1990): 6–21.

Answers.com. "Jeff Bezos." (2003.) Retrieved from http://www.answers.com/topic/jeff-bezos.

Ariely, Dan. *Predictably Irrational*. New York: HarperCollins, 2008.

Ariely, Dan. *The Upside of Irrationality*. New York: HarperCollins, 2010.

Backer, Alex. Paniel discussion. Conference on Innovating in a Global Environment, USC Marshall School of Business, 2011.

Barczak, Gloria, Abbie Griffin, and Kenneth B. Kahn. "Perspective: Trends and Drivers of Success in NPD Practices: Results of the 2003 PDMA Best Practices Study." *Journal of Product Innovation Management*, 26 (2009): 2–23.

Baumgartner, Jeffrey. "Prospect Theory, Risk and Innovation." *Innovation Tools* (June 10, 2009). http://www.innovationtools.com/Articles/EnterpriseDetails.asp?a=440

Bellis, Mary. "The History of the Sony Walkman." http://inventors.about.com/od/wstartinventions/a/Walkman.htm

Bezos, Jeff. "1997 Letter to Shareholders." Amazon.com (1997). http://benhorowitz.files.wordpress.com/2010/05/amzn_shareholder-letter-20072.pdf

Birkinshaw, Julian. "Strategies for Managing Internal Competition." *California Management Review*, 44 (Fall 2001): 21–38.

"Blade-snatching." *Newsweek* (November 22, 1962): 89–90.

Bomey, Nathan. "Roger Newton's Esperion Therapeutics Launches First Clinical Trial." http://www.annarbor.com/business-review/esperion-therapeutics-launches-first-clinical-trial/

Borah, Abhishek, and Gerard J. Tellis. "To Make or Not to Make: Stock Market Returns to Make Versus Buy Innovations." Working Paper, USC Marshall School of Business, 2012.

Brafman, Ori, and Rom Brafman. *Sway: The Irresistible Pull of Irrational Behavior*. New York: Broadway Business, 2009.

Brockner, Joel, and Jeffrey Rubin. *Entrapment in Escalating Conflicts: A Social Psychological Analysis*. New York: Springer-Verlag, 1985.

Brumley, Cal. "Stainless-Steel Razor Blades Could Be Shavers' Boon, Makers' Problem." *Wall Street Journal* (December 25, 1962): 7.

Bryant, Martin. "20 Years Ago Today, the World Wide Web Opened to the Public." *Insider* (Aug. 6, 2011). http://thenextweb.com/insider/2011/08/06/20-years-ago-today-the-world-wide-web-opened-to-the-public/

Carley, William M. "Battle of the Blades." *Wall Street Journal* (September 26, 1969): 38.

Casnocha, B. "Success on the Side." *The American* (April 24, 2009). http://www.american.com/archive/2009/april-2009/Success-on-the-Side/

CBS News. "Facebook 'Cash Flow Positive,' Signs Show." Retrieved May 25, 2010, from http://www.cbc.ca/technology/story/2009/09/16/tech-facebook-300-million-users.html,

Chakravarty, Subrata N. "We Had to Change the Playing Field." *Forbes*, 147, no. 3 (February 4, 1991): 82–86.

Chandrasekaran, Deepa, and Gerard J. Tellis. "The Global Takeoff of New Products: Culture, Wealth, or Vanishing Differences." *Marketing Science*, 27, no. 5 (September-October, 2008): 844–860.

Chandy, Rajesh, and Gerard J. Tellis. "Organizing For Radical Product Innovation." *Journal of Marketing Research*, 35 (November 1998): 474–487.

Chandy, Rajesh, and Gerard J. Tellis. "The Incumbent's Curse? Incumbency, Size and Radical Product Innovation." *Journal of Marketing*, 64, no. 3 (July 2000): 1–17.

"Cheek by Trowel." *Business Week* (December 22, 1962): 81–82.

Christensen, Clayton M. *The Innovator's Dilemma: When New Technologies Cause Great Firms to Fail*. Boston: Harvard Business School Press, 1997.

"The Coming Close Shave At Gillette." *Forbes* (December 15, 1976): 29.

"Corporate Incentives for Hybrids and Alternative Cars." *HybridCars.com* (June 8, 2009). http://www.hybridcars.com/corporate-incentives.html

Crawford, C. Merle. "Marketing Research and the New Product Failure Rate." *Journal of Marketing*, 41, no. 2 (1977): 51–61.

Crowley, Stephen. "At G.M., Innovation Sacrificed to Profits." *The New York Times* (December 5, 2008).

Cutler, Kim-Mai. "Mark Zuckerberg on How to Build Hacker Culture Inside a Company." *VentureBeat.com* (2009). Retrieved July 11, 2012, from http://venturebeat.com/2009/10/24/live-blogging-mark-zuckerbergs-talk-at-startup-school/

Dagmar, King. "Risk Taking Good for Business, CEO Says." *USC News* (August 2008). Retrieved July 20, 2012, from http://www.usc.edu/uscnews/stories/12050.html

Daniels, P. "Research & Development, Human Capital and Trade Performance in Technology-Intensive Manufactures: A Cross-country Analysis." *Research Policy*, 22, no. 3 (1993): 207–241.

DeBondt, Werner. "What Do Economists Know About the Stock Market?" *Journal of Portfolio Management*, 17, no. 2 (1991): 84–91.

Deci Edward L., and Richard M. Ryan. *Intrinsic Motivation and Self-Determination in Human Behavior*. New York: Plenum, 1985.

"Definition of: VisiCalc." *PCMAG.com*. Retrieved from http://www.pcmag.com/encyclopedia_term/0,2542,t=VisiCalc&i=53977,00.asp

DeLong, J. Bradford. "Productivity Growth, Convergence, and Welfare: Comment." *American Economic Review*, 78, no. 5 (1988): 1138–1154.

Denrell, Jerker, and James G. March. "Adaptation as Information Restriction: The Hot Stove Effect." *Organization Science*, 12, no. 5 (2001): 523–538.

Deutschman, A. "The Managing Wisdom of High-Tech Superstars." *Fortune*, 130, 8 (October 17, 1994): 197–206.

Dhar, Ravi, and Alok Kumar. "A Non-Random Walk Down the Main Street: Impact of Price Trends on Trading Decisions of Individual Investors." Unpublished working paper, 2001.

Diamond, Jared. *Guns, Germs and Steel: The Fates of Human Society*. New York: Norton, 1999.

Diamond, Patricia F. "What Will Succeed Lipitor as the Next Blockbuster Cholesterol-Lowering Drug?" *GEN News* (January 11, 2011). http://www.genengnews.com/insight-and-intelligenceand153/what-will-succeed-lipitor-as-the-next-blockbuster-cholesterol-lowering-drug/77899355/

Dvorak, Phred. "Bad Luck Swamped Successes During Stringer's Sony Tenure." *Wall Street Journal* (February 2, 2012): A10.

Ewen, Edward T. "Revolution on the Razor's Edge." *New York Times Magazine* (October 6, 1963): 58.

Facebook. "Company Timeline." Retrieved May 15, 2010, from http://newsroom.fb.com/content/default.aspx?NewsAreaId=20

Fairley, Peter. "Hybrids' Rising Sun." *Technology Review*, 107, no. 3 (2004): 34.

Fan, Shay. "The Slate: A History of Innovation." *The Next Bench Blog* (2010). http://h20435.www2.hp.com/t5/The-Next-Bench-Blog/The-Slate-A-History-of-Innovation/ba-p/52657

Dullfo, Anne. "FT Global 500." *Financial Times* (2009). http://media.ft.com/cms/8289770e-4c79–11de-a6c5–00144feabdc0.pdf

"Boston Blue Bladers." *Forbes* (November 15, 1952): 18–25.

Foster, Joseph A., Peter N. Golder, and Gerard J. Tellis. "Predicting Takeoff for Whirlpool's New Personal Valet." *Marketing Science*, 23, no. 2 (2004): 182–185.

Foster, Peter, and Pallavi Malhotra. "Ultimate Economy Drive: The £1,300 Car." *The Telegraph*. (January 10, 2008).

Foster, Richard. *Innovation: The Attacker's Advantage*. New York: Summit Books, 1986.

Freeman, Christopher. "Formal Scientific and Technical Institutions in the National System of Innovation." In Lundvall, Bengt-Ake (Ed.), *National Systems of Innovation*. London: Pinter, 1992, 169–187.

Frey, Bruno S., and Felix Oberholzer-Gee. "The Cost of Price Incentives: An Empirical Analysis of Motivation Crowding-Out." *American Economic Review*, 87, no. 4 (1997): 746–755.

Frey, Christine, and John Cook. "How Amazon.com Survived, Thrived and Turned a Profit." *Seattle Post* (January 28, 2004). http://www.seattlepi.com/business/158315_amazon28.html

Friedman, Thomas L. *The World Is Flat: A Brief History of the 20th Century.* New York: Farrar, Straus and Giroux, 2005.

Friedrich, Richard. "Culture of Innovation at HP." Presentation at the Advisory Board Meeting, USC Marshall Center for Global Innovation, May, 2012.

Fujita Masahiro. "Culture of Innovation at Sony." presentation at the Advisory Board Meeting, USC Marshall Center for Global Innovation, May, 2012.

Garcia, Armando. "How Failure Breeds Success." *Business Week*, 3992 (July 10, 2006): 42–52.

Gatto, Bob. "Culture of Innovation at Nestle." Advisory Board Meeting, USC Marshall School of Business, May 15, 2012.

Gerstner, Lou. *Who Says Elephants Can't Dance?* New York: HarperCollins, 2002.

Ghemawat, P. "Market Incumbency and Technological Inertia." *Marketing Science*, 10, no. 2 (1991): 161–171.

"Gillette Plans to Offer Stainless Steel Razor Blade in Few Months." *Wall Street Journal* (November 19, 1962): 7.

"Gillette to Spend $4,000,000 on Stainless Blade." *Advertising Age*, 4, (September 2, 1963): 46.

Gilovich, Thomas R., Vallone Robert, and Amos Tversky. "The Hot-Hand in Basketball: On the Misperception of Random Sequences." *Cognitive Psychology*, 17 (1985): 295–314.

Glazer, Emily. "Shaving's True Cost? It's All a Matter of Blade Life." *Wall Street Journal* (April 12, 2012): B8.

Gneezy, Uri, and Aldo Rustichini. "A Fine Is a Price." *Journal of Legal Studies*, 29, no. 1 (January 2000): 1–17.

Golder Peter N., and Gerard J. Tellis. "Pioneering Advantage: Marketing Logic or Marketing Legend." *Journal of Marketing Research*, 30, no. 2 (1993): 158–170.

Golder, Peter N., and Gerard J. Tellis. "Will It Ever Fly? Modeling the Take-off of New Consumer Durables." *Marketing Science*, 16, no. 3 (1997): 256–270.

Golder, Peter N., Julie Irwin, and Debanjan Mitra. "Do Economic Conditions Affect Long-Term Brand Leadership Persistence?" Presentation at the Conference of Theory and Practice of Marketing, Harvard Business School, May 5, 2012.

Gompers, Paul, Anna Kovner, Josh Lerner, and David S. Scharfstein. "Skill Versus Luck in Entrepreneurship and Venture Capital: Evidence from Serial Entrepreneurs." Working paper 12592, National Bureau of Economic Research, 2006.

Goo, Sara Kehaulani. "Building a 'Googley' Workforce." *Washington Post* (October 21, 2006).

Google. "Google Gets the Message, Launches Gmail." Press Center, Google website. http://www.google.com/press/pressrel/gmail.html

Goparaju, Subu. "Culture of Innovation at Infosys." Advisory Board Meeting, USC Marshall Center for Global Innovation. May, 2012.

Gorski, Phillip. *The Disciplinary Revolution: Calvinism and the Rise of the State in Modern Europe*. Chicago: University of Chicago Press, 2003.

Govindarajan, Vijay, and Chris Trimble. "The CEO's Role in Business Model Reinvention." *Harvard Business Review*, 89, no. 1/2 (January-February, 2011): 108–114.

Guth, Robert A. "Microsoft's Bid to Beat Google Builds on a History of Misses." *Wall Street Journal* (January 16, 2009): A1, A6.

Gutterman, Alan S., and Bentley J. Anderson. *Intellectual Property in Global Markets*. Cambridge, MA: Kluwer, 1997.

Guzzardi, Walter, Jr. "Gillette Faces the Stainless-Steel Dragon." *Fortune* (July 1963): 159.

Halal, William E., Ali Geranmayeh, and John Pourdehnad. *Internal Markets: Bringing the Power of Free Enterprise Inside Your Organization*. New York: Wiley, 1993.

Hamel, Gary. "Bringing Silicon Valley Inside." *Harvard Business Review*, September-October, 1997): 71–84.

Hansell, Saul. "Yahoo Woos a Social Networking Site." *The New York Times* (September 22, 2006): 1.

Hawksworth, John. "The World in 2050." PriceWaterhouseCoopers. (2006). http://www.pwc.com/gx/en/world-2050/index.jhtml

Heffernan, Margaret. "Dog Eat Dog." FastCompany.com (July 8, 2008). http://www.fastcompany.com/resources/talent/heffernan/072804.html

Hendricks, Daryll, Jayendu Patel, and Richard Zeckhauser. "Hot-Hands in Mutual Funds: Short-Run Persistence of Performance, 1974–88." *Journal of Finance*, 48, no. 1 (1993): 93–130

Herper, Matthew. "The Luckiest Guy in the Drug Business." *Forbes* (May 1, 2008). Forbes.com. http://www.forbes.com/2008/05/01/pfizer-esperion-pharmacuticals-biz-healthcare-cx_mh_0501pfizer.html

Hill, Andrew. "The Architecture of a Company Being Built from Within." *Financial Times* (April 14, 2011).

Hoffman, Donna L., Praveen Kopalle, and Thomas Novak. "The Right Consumers for Better Concepts: Identifying Consumers High in Emergent Nature to Develop New Product Concepts." *Journal of Marketing Research*, 47 (October 2010): 854–865.

Holly, Krisztina "Z." "Accelerating the Impact of Universities in a Shifting Innovation Landscape." Conference on Innovating in a Global Environment, USC Marshall School of Business, March 17, 2011.

Howe, Jeff. "The Rise of Crowdsourcing." *Wired* (October 2006). Retrieved Oct.13th, 2011, from http://money.cnn.com/magazines/business2/business2_archive/2006/10/01/8387096/

"How Failure Breeds Success." *Business Week*, 3992 (July 10, 2006): 42–52.

"How Gillette Plans to Keep Its No. 1 Spot." *Printers Time*. (December 4, 1959): 65–66.

Ichthyology: Sharks, at the Florida Museum of Natural History. Retrieved July 23, 2012, from http://www.flmnh.ufl.edu/fish/sharks/attacks/relarisksand.htm

Index of Silicon Valley. Silicon Valley Community Foundation (2012). http://www.jointventure.org/images/stories/pdf/2012index.pdf

Ingrassia, Lawrence. "Gillette Holds Its Edge by Endlessly Searching for a Better Shave." *Wall Street Journal* (December 10, 1992): 1.

In-hyuk, Hwang. "Samsung Chairman Lee Kun-hee Calls for Greater Innovation. *Maeil Business Newspaper* (January 2, 2012).

Isaacson, Walter. *Steve Jobs (*Kindle ed.*).* New York: Simon & Schuster, 2011.

Jacob, Brian A., and Steven D. Levitt. "Catching Cheating Teachers: The Results of an Unusual Experiments in Implementing Theory." *Brookings-Wharton Papers on Urban Affairs*. Washington, DC: Brookings Institution Press, 2003, 185–209.

Jacob, Brian A., and Steven D. Levitt. "Rotten Apples: An Investigation of the Prevalence and Predictors of Teacher Cheating." *Quarterly Journal of Economics*, 118, no. 3 (2003): 843–877.

Jaruzelski, Barry, and John Loehr. "The Global Innovation 1000." *Strategy+Business*, Booz & Company, 65 (Winter 2010).

Jobs, Steve. "Person of the Week." Interview with ABC News, Jan 29, 1981. http://abcnews.go.com/WN/abcs-world-news-diane-sawyer-person-week-steve/story?id=9699563&page=1

Jobs, Steve. "You've Got to Find What You Love." Graduating Address at Stanford University. Palo Alto, California, June 12, 2005.

Jordan, Michael. "Failure." *Nike Air Commercial*, 1984. Retrieved July 17, 2012, from http://www.youtube.com/watch?v=m-EMOb3ATJ0

Kahneman, Daniel, and Amos Tversky. "Prospect Theory: An Analysis of Decision under Risk." *Econometrica*, 47, no. 2 (March, 1979): 263–292.

Kahney, Leander. "Inside Look at Birth of the iPod." *Wired News* (July 21, 2004).

Kamien, M. I., and N. L. Schwartz. *Market Structure and Innovation*. Cambridge, MA: Cambridge University Press, 1982.

Kaplan, Katharine A. "Facemash Creator Survives Ad Board." *The Harvard Crimson*, Nov 19, 2003. Retrieved May 25, 2010, from http://www.thecrimson.com/article/2003/11/19/facemash-creator-survives-ad-board-the/

Katdare, Kaustubh. "Interview with Paul Buchheit—Creator of Gmail, AdSense & FriendFeed." *CrazyEngineers*, March 1, 2009. http://www.crazyengineers.com/mr-paul-buchheit-creator-of-gmail-adsense-friendfeed/

Keefe, Collin. "Jeff Bezos: Founder and CEO, Amazon.com." *Dealerscope* (January 2003): 76.

"Keen Drama: A Razor Is Born." *Newsweek* (October 11, 1971): 78–82.

Kelley Blue Book. "2010 Best Resale Value Awards." http://www.kbb.com/car-awards/best-resale-value-awards/best-car-brand

Khanna, Tarun, Jaeyong Song, and Kyungmook Lee. "The Paradox of Samsung's Rise." *Harvard Business Review*, 89, no. 7/8 (July/August, 2011): 142–147.

Kirkpatrick, David. "Zuckerberg, the Temptation of Facebook's CEO." *Fortune* (May 6, 2010).

Kirkpatrick, David. *The Facebook Effect: The Inside Story of the Company That Is Connecting the World*. New York: Simon & Schuster, 2010.

Kirkpatrick, David, and Tyler Maronney. "The Second Coming of Apple Through a Magical Fusion of Man." *Fortune* (November 9, 1998).

Kosdrosky, Terry, and John D. Stoll. "GM Puts Electric-Car Testing on Fast Track to 2010." *Wall Street Journal* (April 4, 2008).

Kripalani, Manjeet. "Inside the Tata Nano Factory." *BusinessWeek Online*. (May 12, 2008): 16. http://www.businessweek.com/stories/2008–05–09/inside-the-tata-nano-factorybusinessweek-business-news-stock-market-and-financial-advice

Kripalani, Manjeet. "Tata Unveils World's Cheapest Car." *BusinessWeek* (January 10, 2008).

Kuhn, Thomas. *The Structure of Scientific Revolutions*. Chicago: University of Chicago Press, 1962.

Kunii, Irene M., Cliff Edwards, and Jay Greene. "Can Sony Regain the Magic?" *BusinessWeek Online* (March 11, 2002). http://www.businessweek.com/stories/2002–03–10/can-sony-regain-the-magic

LaMattina, John. "The Story of Statins." *Chemical and Engineering News* (June 8, 2009). http://pubs.acs.org/cen/books/87/8723books.html

Landes, David S. *The Wealth and Poverty of Nations: Why Some Are So Rich and Some So Poor*. New York: Norton, 1998.

"Larry Page and Eric Schmidt Hold Court at Google Zeitgeist." *TechCrunch* (2011). http://techcrunch.com/2011/09/27/page-schmidt-zeitgeist-video/

Lashinsky A. "Google is No. 1: Search and Enjoy." *Fortune Magazine*, 155 no. 1 (January 10, 2007).

Lee, John M. "Gillette Will Market Its New Product in Two Cities." *New York Times* (August 27, 1963): 41.

Leonardi, Paul M. "Innovation Blindness: Culture, Frames, and Cross-Boundary Problem Construction in the Development of New Technology Concepts." *Organization Science*, 22, no. 3 (2011): 347–367.

Levin, Doron, and John Helyar. "'Already Bankrupt' GM Won't Be Rescued by U.S. Loan." *Bloomberg*, December 12, 2008.

Levitt, Steven D., and Stephen J. Dubner. *Freakanomics*. New York: Morrow, 2005.

Levy, Stephen. "The Perfect Thing." *Wired* (November 2006). http://www.wired.com/wired/archive/14.11/ipod.html

Levy, Steven. "Google Goes Globe-Trotting." *Newsweek* (November 12, 2007): 62–64.

Levy, Steven. *In the Plex: How Google Thinks, Works, and Shapes Our Lives*. New York: Simon & Schuster, 2011.

Libbenga, Jan. "BlackBerry Boss Blows Raspberries at iPhone." *The Register* (November 8, 2007). Retrieved July 11, 2012, from http://www.theregister.co.uk/2007/11/08/why_iphone_is_no_threat_to_blackberry/

Libby, Peter. "Review of Triumph of the Heart." *The Journal of Clinical Investigation*, 120, no. 1 (January, 2010).

Lucas, Henry C., and Jie Mein Goh. "Disruptive Technology: How Kodak Missed the Digital Photography Revolution." *Journal of Strategic Information Systems*, 18 (2009), 46–55.

Luthje, C., and Herstatt, C. "The Lead User Method: An Outline of Empirical Findings and Issues for Future Research." *R&D Management*, 34 no. 5 (2004): 553–568.

Lutz, Bob. "Thank You, Citizens of Volt Nation." April 1, 2008. GM FastLane Blog.

Lyons, Dan. "Prius Expands the Brand: 2012 Toyota Prius C." *Times Union* (March 6, 2012).

Maiello, Michael. "Koulopolous on Innovation, Business Visionaries." *Forbes* (June 2, 2009).

297

Makri, Marianna, Peter J. Lane, and Luis R. Gomez-Mejia. "CEO Incentives, Innovation, and Performance in Technology-Intensive Firms: A Reconciliation of Outcome and Behavior-Based Incentive Schemes." *Strategic Management Journal*, 27, no. 11 (2006): 1057–1080.

Manso, Gustavo. "Motivating Innovation." Draft paper, MIT Sloan Business School, February 28, 2009.

March, J. G., and Z. Shapira. "Managerial Perspectives on Risk Taking." *Management Science*, 33 (1987): 1404–1418.

Markham, Stephen K., and Abbie Griffin. "The Breakfast of Champions." *Journal of Product Innovation Management*, 15 (1998): 436–454.

Mayer, Marissa. VP of Search Products and User Experience at Google, Featured Interview, a podcast by students of Stanford University's Business and Design Schools, Friday, August 31, 2007. http://iinnovate.blogspot.com/2007/08/marissa-mayer-vp-of-search-products-and.html

Mayer, Marissa. "Innovation, Imagination, Creativity—Google VP of Search Products Tells Story of Gmail." (October 26, 2007). http://www.idratherbewriting.com

Maynard, Micheline. "Say 'Hybrid' and Many People Will Hear 'Prius.'" *The New York Times* (July 4, 2007).

McCarthy, Caroline. "Facebook's Zuckerberg: 'We Really Messed This One Up.'" *CNET News*, News Blog (September 8, 2006). http://news.cnet.com/8301-10784_3-6113700-7.html

McCullagh, Declan. "Big Three Bailout? Not So Fast." CBS (CNET) November 12, 2008). http://www.cbsnews.com/2100-503363_162-4595068.html

McGirt, Ellen. "Hacker. Dropout. CEO." *Fast Company*, 115 (May 2007): 75.

McGirt, Ellen. "Facebook Is." *Fast Company*, 120 (November, 2007): 84.

McGirt, Ellen. "Most Innovative Companies 2010: #1 *Facebook*." *Fast Company* (February 17, 2010).

McGrath, Rita Gunther. "Falling Forward: Real Options Reasoning and Entrepreneurial Failure." *The Academy of Management Review*, 24, no. 1 (January 1999): 13–30.

McKibben, Gordon. *Cutting Edge: Gilette's Journey to Global Leadership*. Boston: Harvard Business School Press, 1998.

Menzies, Gavin. *1421: The Year That China Discovered America*. New York: HarperCollins, 2002.

Meredith, Robyn. *The Elephant and the Dragon*. New York: Norton, 2007.

Moorman, Christine and Anne S. Miner. "The Impact of Organizational Memory on New Product Performance and Creativity." *Journal of Marketing Research*, 34 (February, 1997): 91–106.

Mitsch, Ronald A. "Three Roads to Innovation." *Journal of Business Strategy*, 11, no. 5 (1990): 18–21.

Mizik, Natalie. "The Theory and Practice of Myopic Management." *Journal of Marketing Research*, 47 (August, 2010): 594–611.

Morgan, Gareth. *Creative Organization Theory*. Thousand Oaks, CA: Sage, 1989: 144.

Naughton, Keith, and Allan Sloan. "Comin' Through!" *Newsweek Web Exclusive* (2007). http://www.thedailybeast.com/newsweek/2007/03/11/comin-through.html

Nault, Barrie R., and Mark B. Vandenbosch. "Eating Your Own Lunch: Protection Through Preemption." *Organizational Science*, 7, no. 3 (1996): 342–358.

Nayak, P. Ranganath, and John M. Ketteringham. *Breakthroughs: How Leadership and Drive Create Commercial Innovations That Sweep the World*. San Diego, CA: Pfeiffer, 1994.

Newton, Roger. "Newton.mov: Can Science Be a Business?" YouTube video. Lafayette University, April 21, 2011. http://www.youtube.com/watch?v=302sjUypVw8&lr=1&feature=mhum

Newton, Roger. "Dr. Roger Newton—CoDiscoverer of Lipitor." YouTube video (2012). Retrieved April 10, 2012. http://www.youtube.com/watch?v=GG_GoaAUdN8

New York State Truway Authority. "Green Pass Discount Plan." http://www.nysthruway.gov/ezpass/greentag.html

Noronha, Christabelle. "The Making of the Nano." *The South Asian.com* (April-June 2008). Retrieved on July 23, 2012 from http://www.the-south-asian.com/April-June2008/Ratan_Tata_interview_Nano.htm

O'Connor, Gina Colarelli, and Christopher M. McDermott. "The Human Side of Radical Innovation." *Journal of Engineering Technology Management*, 21 (2004): 11–30.

Oliver, Christian. "Fast Follower Leads the Way." *Financial Times* (March 20, 2012).

Olsen, Stefanie. "Google vs. Yahoo: Clash of Cultures." *CNET* News (June 21, 2005). http://news.cnet.com/Google-vs.-Yahoo-Clash-of-cultures/2100-1024_3-5752928.html

Olsen, Stefanie. "From the Googleplex to the Wine Bar." *CNET News* (January 23, 2008). http://news.cnet.com/From-the-Googleplex-to-the-wine-bar/2100-1030_3-6227204.html

Ottman, Jacquelyn A., Edwin R. Stafford, Cathy L. Hartman. "Avoiding Green Marketing Myopia." *Environment*, 48, no. 5 (June 2006): 22.

Ouderkirk, Andrew. J. "Culture of Innovation at 3M." Presentation at the Advisory Board Meeting, USC Marshall Center for Global Innovation." May, 2012.

Parker, Philip M. *Physioeconomics*, Cambridge, MA: MIT Press, 2000.

Pepitone, Julianne. "Facebook Traffic Tops Google for a Week." CNN *Money.com* (March 16, 2010). Retrieved May 25, 2010. http://money.cnn.com/2010/03/16/technology/facebook_most_visited/index.htm.

Petroski, Henry. *To Engineer Is Human: The Role of Failure in Successful Design*. New York: Vintage, 1992.

Pfeffer, Jeffrey. "Too Much Management Can Block Innovation." *Stanford GSB News* (September, 2003). http://www.gsb.stanford.edu/news/research/ob_toomuchmgmt.shtml

Phillips, Sarah. "A Brief History of Facebook." *The Guardian* (July 25, 2007). http://www.guardian.co.uk/technology/2007/jul/25/media.newmedia

Plous, Scott. *The Psychology of Judgment and Decision Making*. Columbus, OH: McGraw-Hill, 1993.

Pluskowski, Boris. "The 4 Laws of Enduring Innovation Success." *Complete Innovator* (2012). Retrieved April 9, 2012, from http://complete innovator.com/2010/04/07/the-4-laws-to-enduring-innovation-success/

Prahalad, C. K. *Fortune at the Bottom of the Pyramid*. Upper Saddle River, NJ: Pearson, 2005.

Prahalad, C. K., and Gary Hamel. "The Core Competence of the Corporation." *Harvard Business Review* (May-June, 1990): 79–91

PriceWaterhouseCoopers study, 2011, http://www.pwc.com/gx/en/world-2050/index.jhtml

"Prius History." http://john1701a.com/prius/prius-history.htm

Public Broadcasting Service. "Traveling Through Time." pbs.org. Retrieved October 13, 2011, from http://www.pbs.org/wgbh/nova/time/through2.html

Radjou, Navi, Jaideep, Prabhu, and Simone Ahuja. *Jugaad Innovation*. San Francisco: Jossey-Bass, 2012.

Rajagopalan, Nandini. "Strategic Orientations, Incentive Plan Adoptions, and Firm Performance: Evidence From Electric Utility Firms." *Strategic Management Journal*, 18, no. 10 (1997): 761–785.

Rediff Interview. "Innovation Best Comes from People Who Know Nothing About the Topic." *Rediff India Abroad* (2006). http://www.rediff.com/money/2006/aug/07kodak.htm

Reguly, Eric. "Failing in Face of Apple's Next Big Thing." *The Globe and Mail* (January 28, 2012).

Reinganum, J. F. "On the Diffusion of New Technology: A Game Theoretic Approach." *Review of Economic Studies*, 153 (1981): 395–406.

Ritson, Mark. "U.S. Auto Brands Missed the Turning." *Marketing* (July 30, 2008): 25.

Rose, Frank. "The Civil War Inside Sony." *Wired Magazine* (February 11, 2003). http://www.wired.com/wired/archive/11.02/sony.html

Rosen, Evan. "The Hidden Cost of Internal Competition." *Bloomberg BusinessWeek* (Nov. 10, 2009). http://www.businessweek.com/managing/content/nov2009/ca2009113_427287.htm

Rubera, Gaia, and Gerard J. Tellis. "Spinoffs Versus Buyouts." Working paper, USC Marshall School of Business, 2012.

Schanfeld, Erick and Chris, Morrison. "Business 2.0." *Money* (September 2007): 8, no. 8.

Schmidt, Eric "Google: Benefits." http://www.google.com/support/jobs/bin/static.py?page=benefits.html.

Schmidt, Eric, and Hal Varian. "Google: Ten Golden Rules." *Newsweek* (December 2, 2005): p 44.

Schofield, Jack. "Ken Olsen Obituary." *The Guardian.* (February 9, 2011). http://www.guardian.co.uk/technology/2011/feb/09/ken-olsen-obituary

Schonfeld, Erick. "Facemash Returns as (What Else?) a Facebook App Called ULiken." *TechCrunch (*May 13, 2008). Retrieved May 25, 2010, from http://techcrunch.com/2008/05/13/facemash-returns-as-what-else-a-facebook-app-uliken/

Schumpeter, Joseph. *Capitalism, Socialism and Democracy*. New York: Harper, 1975. (Originally published 1942).

Schwartz, Barry. "The Sunk-Cost Fallacy: Bush Falls Victim to a Bad New Argument for the Iraq War." *Slate.com* (September 9, 2005). http://www.slate.com/articles/news_and_politics/hey_wait_a_minute/2005/09/the_sunkcost_fallacy.html

Senor, Dan, and Saul Singer. *Start-Up Nation*, New York: Twelve, 2009.

Sharer, Kevin. "Innovation at Amgen." Dean's Business Breakfast, at USC Marshall School of Business, February 8, 2005.

Sherman, Erik. "Inside Apple iPod Design Triumph." *Electronics Design Chain* (Summer 2002).

Sherr, Ian. Tablet War Is an Apple Rout." *Wall Street Journal* (August 12, 2011): B1–B2.

Shiels, Maggie. "Facebook's Bid to Rule the Web as It Goes Social." *BBC News*. (April 22, 2010). Retrieved April 22, 2010, http://news.bbc.co.uk/2/hi/technology/8590306.stm

Shugan, Steven M., and Debanjan Mitra. "Metrics—When and Why Non-Averaging Statistics Work." *Management Science*, 55 (January, 2009): 4–15.

Sigafoos, Robert A. *Absolutely, Positively Overnight!* Memphis, TN: St. Luke's Press, 1983.

"Silicon Valley, London, NYC." *TechCrunch* (2012). Retrieved April 11, 2012, from http://techcrunch.com/2012/04/10/startup-genome-compares-top-startup-hubs/

Slywotzky, Adrian J., and John Drzik. "Countering the Biggest Risk of All." *Harvard Business Review on Managing External Ris*k. Boston: Harvard Business Press, 2009.

Smith, Geoffrey, William C. Symonds, Peter Burrows, and Ellen Neuborne, Paul C. Judge. "Can George Fisher Fix Kodak?" *Business Week* (October 9, 1997): 116–126.

Smith, Kenneth S. "Razor Blade War Growing Hotter." *New York Times* December 2, 1962): 7.

Smith, Richard Austin. "Gillette Looks Sharp Again." *Fortune* (June 1952): 100.

Snell, Jason "Steve Jobs on the Mac's 20th Anniversary." *Macworld.com* (February 2, 2004).

Sony Pictures. "Who Killed the Electric Car" (2006).

Sood, Ashish, and Gerard J. Tellis. "The S-Curve of Technological Innovation: Strategic Law or Self-Fulfilling Prophesy?" Marketing Science Institute working paper, no 04–116, 2004.

Sood, Ashish, and Gerard J. Tellis. "Technological Evolution and Radical Innovations." *Journal of Marketing*, 69, no. 3 (July, 2005): 152–168.

Sood, Ashish, and Gerard J. Tellis. "Do Innovations Really Pay Off? Total Stock Market Returns to Innovation." *Marketing Science*, 28, no. 3 (2009): 442–456.

Sood, Ashish, and Gerard J. Tellis. "Demystifying Disruptions: A New Model for Understanding and Predicting Disruptive Technologies." *Marketing Science*, 30, no. 2 (2011): 339–354.

Sood, Ashish, James Gareth, and Gerard J. Tellis. "The Functional Regression: A New Model for Predicting the Market Penetration of New Products." *Marketing Science*, 28, no. 1 (2009): 36–51.

Sood, Ashish, James Gareth, Gerard J. Tellis, and Ji Zhu. "Predicting the Path of Technological Innovation: SAW Versus Moore, Bass, Gompertz, and Kryder." *Marketing Science*, forthcoming, 2012.

Spector, Robert. *Amazon.com: Get Big Fast*. New York: HarperCollins, 1997.

Staw, Barry M. "Knee-Deep in the Big Muddy: A Study of Escalating Commitment to a Chosen Course of Action." *Organization Behavior and Human Performance*, 16, no. 1 (June 1976): 27–44.

Stevens, Greg A., and James Burley. "3,000 Raw Ideas = 1 Commercialized Success!" *Research Technology Management*, 40, 3 (1997).

Stewart B. "GM's Second Great Crisis." *HBR NOW* (May 29, 2009). http://blogs.hbr.org/hbr/hbr-now/2009/05/gms-second-great-crisis.html

St. Peter, Anthony, *The Greatest Quotation of All Time*, Xlibris Corporation, 2010, p 102.

Strohmeyer, Robert. "The 7 Worst Tech Predictions of All Time." *PCWorld* (December 31, 2008).

Stuart, Candace. "The Medicine Man." *DBusiness.com*. (November 2008). http://www.dbusiness.com/DBusiness/November-2008/The-Medicine-Man/

Swasy, Alicia. *Changing Focus: Kodak and the Battle to Save a Great American Company*. New York: Random House, 1997.

Tabak, Alan J. "Hundreds Register for New Facebook Website: Facemash Creator Seeks New Reputation with Latest Online Project." *The Harvard Crimson* (Feb. 9, 2004). http://web.archive.org/web/20050403215543/www.thecrimson.com/article.aspx?ref=357292

Tata Motors. Press Release. February 5, 2007.

Taylor, Alex. "The Great Electric Car Race." *Fortune*, 164, no. 5 (April 14, 2009): 33.

Taylor, Alex III. "The Birth of the Prius." *Fortune*. 153, no. 4 (2006): 111.

Tellis, Gerard J., and Golder, Peter N. "First to Market, First to Fail? The Real Causes of Enduring Market Leadership." *Sloan Management Review*, 37, no. 2 (1996): 65–75.

Tellis, Gerard J., and Peter Golder. *Will and Vision: How Latecomers Grow to Dominate Markets*. New York: McGraw Hill, 2001.

Tellis, Gerard J., Jaideep Prabhu, and Rajesh Chandy. "Innovation of Firms Across Nations: The Pre-Eminence of Internal Firm Culture." *Journal of Marketing*, 73, no. 1 (2009): 3–23.

Tellis, Gerard J., and Ashish Sood. "A New Framework for Choosing the Right Technology." *PDMA Visions*, 34, no. 3 (October 2010). http://www.bus .emory.edu/individuals/asood/documents/visions201010-dl.pdf

Tellis, Gerard J., Stefan Stremersch, and Eden Yin. "The International Takeoff of New Products: Economics, Culture and Country Innovativeness." *Marketing Science*, 22, no. 2 (2003): 161–187.

Terwiesch, Christian, and Karl T. Ulrich. *Innovation Tournaments*. Boston: Harvard Business School Press, 2009.

Tezuka, H. "Success as the Cause of Failure." *Sloan Management Review*, 38, no. 2 (1997): 83–89.

"The United States of Entrepreneurs." *The Economist* (March 12, 2009).

Thornton, Emily. "Japan's Hybrid Cars: Toyota and Rivals Are Betting on Pollution Fighters. Will They Succeed?" *Business Week* (December 15, 1997): 26.

Timmerman, Luke. "Amgen CEO Kevin Sharer's Report Card." *Xconomy* (2011). http://www.xconomy.com/national/2011/12/19/amgen-ceo-kevin-sharers-report-card-c/

Tirunillai, Seshadri, and Gerard J. Tellis. "Does Chatter Really Matter? The Impact of Online Consumer Generated Content on a Firm's Financial Performance." *Marketing Science*, 31, no. 2 (April 2011): 198–215.

Tirunillai, Seshadri, and Gerard J. Tellis. "Extracting Dimensions of Satisfaction from Online Chatter." Working paper, the USC Marshall School of Business, 2012.

"Toyota Prius Japan Top-Selling Car for Third Year." *Associated Press* (January 11, 2012).

"Toyota Prius Proves a Gas Guzzler in a Race with the BMW 520d." *The Sunday Times* (March 16, 2008).

Troianovski, Anton, and Sven Grundberg, "Nokia's Bad Call on Smartphones." *Wall Street Journal* (July 18, 2012). Retrieved July 23, 2012, from http://online.wsj.com/article/SB1000142405270230438800457753100 2591315494.html

Tversky, A., & Kahneman, D. "Judgments Under Uncertainty: Heuristics and Biases." *Science*, 185 (1974): 1124–1131.

Twain, Mark. *Following the Equator: A Journey Around the World*. Hartford, CT: American Publishing, 1897.

Ueno, Kiyori, and Tetsuya Komatsu. "Toyota Prius Leaps to No. 1 in Japan on Incentives." *Bloomberg.com* (January 8, 2010). http://www.bloomberg.com/apps/news?pid=20601209&sid=a1kPj_bJW8aI

Ulman, Neil. "Gillette Chairman Takes a Long View in Program to Brighten Profit Picture." *Wall Street Journal* (June 28, 1977): 12.

Valikangas, Liisa, and Gary Hamel. "Internal Markets: Emerging Governance Structures for Innovation." Paper presented at the Strategic Management Society, 21st Annual International Conference, San Francisco, 2001.

Vascellaro, Jessica E. "Google Searches for Ways to Keep Big Ideas at Home." *Wall Street Journal*, Technology, 253, no. 141 (June 18, 2009): B1–B5.

"Virtual Worlds, Real Leaders: Online Games Put the Future Of Business Leadership On Display." *A Global Innovation Outlook 2.0 Report*, International Business Machines Corporation, 2007. http://www.seriosity.com/downloads/GIO_PDF_web.pdf

Von Hippel, E. "Lead Users: A Source of Novel Product Concepts." *Management Science*, 32, no. 7 (1986): 791–806.

Wald, Matthew L. "Next Wave of Electric Cars: Hybrids." *New York Times* (May 14,1996): 1.

Walker, Rob. "The Guts of a New Machine." *The New York Times Magazine* (November 30, 2003).

Watson, Thomas J. Jr. *A Business and Its Beliefs: The Ideas That Helped Build IBM*. New York: McGraw-Hill, 2003,

Weber, Max. *The Protestant Ethic and the Spirit of Capitalism*. New York: Penguin, 2002. (Originally published 1904).

Webster, Andrew, and Kathryn Packer. *Innovation and the Intellectual Property System*. Cambridge, MA: Kluwer Law International, 1996.

Weernink, Wim Oude, and Mark Rechtin. "Toyota Pushes for Prius Acceptance in Europe." *Automotive News*, 77, no. 6036 (2003): 58.

Welch, David, and Nandini Lakshman. "My Other Car Is a Tata." *BusinessWeek*, 4066 (January 3, 2008): 33–34.

Welsh, Jonathan. "Weekend Journal: Hybrids Gear Up." *Wall Street Journal (Eastern Edition)* (June 18, 2004): W. 1.

Welch, David, Dan Beucke, Kathleen Kerwin, Michael Arndt, Brian Hindo, Emily Thornton, David Kiley, and Ian Rowley. "Why GM's Plan Won't Work." *Newsweek* (May 9, 2005): 84–93.

"What Words in an Ad Can't Say." *Business Week* (May 14, 1960): 45–48.

"Who Wants a Stainless Reputation?" *Financial Times* (London). (September 5, 1963).

"Who We Are." 3M Company. http://solutions.3m.com/wps/portal/3M/
en_US/3M-Company/Information/AboutUs/WhoWeAre/

"Why the Future Is Hybrid." *The Economist*, 373, no. 8404 (December 2,
2004): 26–30.

Wikipedia. "HP Slate 500." Retrieved August 17, 2011, from http://en
.wikipedia.org/wiki/HP_Slate_500

Wikipedia. "Toyota Prius." Retrieved April 28, 2010, from http://en
.wikipedia.org/wiki/Toyota_Prius_(XW20)#Awards

Wingfield, Nick. "Amazon Reports Annual Net Profit for the First Time." *Wall
Street Journal*, 243, no. 19 (Jan. 28, 2004): A3–A8.

Wingfield, Nick. "Hide the Button: Steve Jobs Has His Finger on It." *Wall
Street Journal* (July 5, 2007): A1.

Wingfield, Nick. "The Man Behind Android's Rise." *Wall Street Journal*
(August 17, 2011): B1–B2.

Wiseman, Richard. "The Luck Factor." *Skeptical Inquirer*, 27, no. 3 (2003):
1–5.

Worthen, Ben. "HP Needed to Evolve, CEO Says." *Wall Street Journal* (August
23, 2011): B1–B2.

Wozniak, Steve. Interview on "Good Morning America", ABC News, October
6, 2011.

Wright, Patrick J., and DeLorean, John Z. *On a Clear Day You Can See General
Motors: John Z. DeLorean's Look Inside the Automotive Giant*. Portland,
OR: Wright Enterprises, 1979.

Wulf, Julie, and Josh Lerner. "Innovation Incentives: Evidence from Corporate R&D." Social Science Research Network, Working Paper Series,
w11944, 2006.

Yadav, Manjit S., Jaideep C. Prabhu, and Rajesh K. Chandy. "Managing the
Future: CEO Attention and Innovation Outcomes." *Journal of Marketing*, 71 (October, 2007): 84–101.

Yoffie, David B., and Michael Slind. "Apple Inc." HBS No. 9-708-480
(Boston: Harvard Business School Publishing, 2008): 1–32. http:
//www.wiso.uni-hamburg.de/fileadmin/sozialoekonomie/
bwl/publicmanagement/Blog/Apple_Case_Inc._2008.pdf

Zenger, Todd R., and Sergio G. Lazzarini. "Compensating for Innovation:
Do Small Firms Offer High-Powered Incentives That Lure Talent and
Motivate Effort?" *Managerial & Decision Economics*, 25, no. 6/7 (2004):
329–345.

ACKNOWLEDGMENTS

This book has benefitted from the input of many coauthors, students, research assistants, reviewers, and family members.

To begin with, I thank my coauthors who helped me develop these ideas, collect data, analyze data, write up articles, and get them published in top-notch journals. In the order in which they joined my research, these coauthors include Peter Golder, Rajesh Chandy, Eden Yin, Stefan Stremersch, Deepa Chandrasekaran, Ashish Sood, Jaideep Prabhu, Seshadri Tirunillai, Abhishek Borah, Gaia Rubera, and Stav Rosenzweig. At various times and at various stages of my career, they stimulated my curiosity, expanded my thinking, brought in new ideas, and educated me about the nuances of theories and methods.

Then I thank those assistants that helped in the research for this book: Pongkhi Bujorbarua, Carlos Hernandez-Mireles, Monisha Coelho, Victoria Xie, Abhishek Borah, Om Singh, Abhinav Astavans, and Jeanne Almeida. In particular, Pongkhi Bujorbarua was a tremendous help in all aspects of the research and someone I could call upon at odd hours of the day. Carlos Hernandez-Mireles served as a valuable sounding board in the last stages of the manuscript. Monisha Coelho, Victoria Xie, Om Singh, Abhinav Astavans, and Jeanne Almeida helped with writing some cases.

Acknowledgments

I thank the large number of executives from numerous corporations who gave me feedback in private discussion and public presentations. Their thoughts and comments helped to refine my thinking. A special thanks to members of the board of advisers of the USC Marshall Center for Global Innovation for their feedback on presentations of various parts of this book.

I thank Vijay Govindarajan for his strong endorsement of this book in his insightful forward. I am also grateful for the generous endorsements of the book by David Aaker, Warren Bennis, George Day, Philip Kotler, Jaideep Prabhu, and Jagdish Sheth.

I thank two reviewers of the book who helped a great deal in strengthening the argument, polishing the layout, and completing the references: Gina O'Connor and Dick Nolan. I am grateful for Warren Bennis's enthusiastic support of my ideas and including the book in his Leadership Series. I thank Kathe Sweeney of Jossey-Bass for accepting the manuscript for publication and her suggestions for the title.

All my family members have been very supportive of my research. I especially thank two of my children, Kethan Tellis and Sonia Tellis, for their feedback on specific chapters.

Above all, I thank my wife, Cheryl Tellis, who has been a loving and enthusiastic partner throughout my research career. On top of that, she generously proofread all chapters of the book, including doing so multiple times for some chapters. Whenever I needed to sound off some argument, phrase, or term, she was prompt and sharp in her response. Her constant companionship and support added greatly to the joy of this journey.

Gerard J. Tellis
Hacienda Heights, California
May 19, 2012

THE AUTHOR

Gerard J. Tellis, PhD, is professor of Marketing, Management, and Organization, Neely Chair of American Enterprise, and director of the Center for Global Innovation at the Marshall School of Business, the University of Southern California.

Dr. Tellis is an expert in innovation, new product growth, global market entry, advertising, and quality. He has published four books and over a hundred papers (http://www.gtellis.net) that have won over twenty awards, including the Frank M. Bass, William F. Odell, Harold D. Maynard (twice), and Paul D. Converse awards. Dr. Tellis has received three lifetime contribution awards for his work in marketing, marketing strategy, and pricing. He has been awarded three fellowships from the Institute for the Study of Business Markets, the INFORMS Society of Marketing Science, Sidney Sussex College, Cambridge University, United Kingdom. Tellis is a Distinguished Chair in Marketing Research, Erasmus University, Rotterdam and a Senior Research Associate at the Judge Business School, Cambridge University, United Kingdom. He is an associate editor of *Marketing Science* and *Journal of Marketing Research* and has been on the editorial review boards of the *Journal of Marketing Research, Journal of Marketing*, and *Marketing Science* for several years. He was a trustee of the Marketing Science Institute and a sales development manager for Johnson & Johnson.

Dr. Tellis has served as a an expert witness or consultant for the Security and Exchange Commission (SEC), Coca-Cola Company, Procter and Gamble, Whirlpool, and other corporations. He has made over a hundred presentations at business and academic conferences, including many keynote addresses.

His book *Will and Vision: How Latecomers Grow to Dominate Markets* (coauthored with Peter Golder; McGraw-Hill) was cited as one of the top ten books in business by the *Harvard Business Review* and was the winner of the American Marketing Association Berry Award for the best book in marketing over the last three years. His book *Effective Advertising: How, When, and Why Advertising Works* summarizes almost fifty years of research on advertising effectiveness. It was twice nominated for the AMA/Berry Award for best book in marketing.

INDEX